The Way We Work

The Way We Work

An Encyclopedia of Business Culture

Volume 1
A–L

Edited by Regina Fazio Maruca

GREENWOOD PRESS
Westport, Connecticut • London

Library of Congress Cataloging-in-Publication Data

The way we work : an encyclopedia of business culture / edited by Regina Fazio Maruca.
   p. cm.
   Includes bibliographical references and index.
   ISBN-13: 978-0-313-33886-1 ((set) : alk. paper)
   ISBN-13: 978-0-313-33887-8 ((vol. 1) : alk. paper)
   ISBN-13: 978-0-313-33888-5 ((vol. 2) : alk. paper)
  1. Corporate culture—United States. 2. Work environment—United States.
I. Maruca, Regina Fazio.
HD58.7.W3328   2008
658—dc22   2007040510

British Library Cataloguing in Publication Data is available.

Library of Congress Catalog Card Number: 2007040510
ISBN: 978-0-313-33886-1 (set)
     978-0-313-33887-8 (vol. 1)
     978-0-313-33888-5 (vol. 2)

First published in 2008

Greenwood Press, 88 Post Road West, Westport, CT 06881
An imprint of Greenwood Publishing Group, Inc.
www.greenwood.com

Printed in the United States of America

The paper used in this book complies with the
Permanent Paper Standard issued by the National
Information Standards Organization (Z39.48–1984).

10 9 8 7 6 5 4 3 2 1

Contents

Alphabetical List of Entries

Action Learning
Age Discrimination
American Association of Retired
  Persons (AARP)
American Federation of Labor and
  Congress of Industrial
  Organizations (AFL-CIO)
Americans with Disabilities Act
The Apprentice
The Art of War
Balanced Scorecard
Benchmarking
Best Practice
Blanchard, Ken
Blue Collar
Bonus
Bootstrapping
Boundaryless Organization
Brainstorming
Branding
Bricks and Clicks

Budget
Business-to-Business/Business-to-
  Consumer (B2B/B2C)
Cafeteria Benefit
Carnegie, Dale/*How to Win
  Friends and Influence People*
Casual Friday
Change Agent/Change
  Management
Code of Ethics
Competitive Advantage
Competitive Intelligence
Core Competencies
Corner Office
Corporate Social Responsibility
Crisis/Risk Management
Cubicle
Dilbert
Diversity
Dot.com/Dot.bomb
Downsizing

Entries by Subject

Preface

"Business Culture" isn't tangible. You can shape it; you can talk about its characteristics; you can describe how people who work in a certain office behave as a result of it; but business culture isn't something that can be physically grasped.

Accordingly, business culture is one of those "soft" yet incredibly powerful elements of business as a whole. The importance of business culture can perhaps be seen in the way it affects the individuals operating in that culture. A strong and positive business culture can foster growth in an organization and bring out the best in people. A weak culture, or a culture of intimidation, can cause initially productive employees to become disgruntled and unhappy to the point where they leave—it can also keep those who remain from forming the kinds of teams that win in the marketplace.

Culture can be the difference between a company where employees spend time together after work, and one where they all go their separate ways at 5 P.M. It can be the difference between a company where employees spend a great deal of time meeting secretively behind closed doors, and a company where they engage freely in a relatively tension-free atmosphere. Culture can be the difference between a company where employees compete against one another, and a company where employees share information and stand united, focused on external competition and on the customer rather than internal issues.

Importantly, culture can change on a dime. The culture of work is dynamic. A new chief executive officer (CEO) can change a company's culture pretty quickly. Similarly, a new manager can infuse a department with a particular culture. Employees at all levels shape the culture of their companies constantly by how they act, what they say to one another, and how they represent the company to customers.

When you step back and consider business culture as it applies to *all* companies—even if you set the boundaries loosely as "companies based in the United States" and then limit the scope to "office" work—you see that culture still evolves and changes, morphs and flows quickly at the big-picture level.

Knowing this, our goal in compiling *The Way We Work* was to offer our readers as many trends, definitions, and facts as possible within the covers of these two volumes in order to capture a colorful and varied freeze-frame look at office culture in the United States in the early years of the twenty-first century. It is our hope that the contents will resonate with the people who are hard at work in offices as of this writing, and help them better understand the forces and factors that influence their organizations. The set also offers a wealth of information that can serve as a useful resource and starting point for high school and college students who are entering the workforce and seek some guidance on what office work is like, and how it is evolving.

What You Will Find

Over 100 entries, ranging from American Association of Retired Persons (AARP) to white collar workers, and covering topics such as diversity, learning organizations, mission statements, the glass ceiling, generation X (Y, Z, etc.), and the war for talent, are included in this encyclopedia. The topics and terms have been selected because each of them, in some way, shapes the big picture of business culture as we know it.

It must be noted that one person's opinion of the kinds of things that shape business culture will naturally differ from someone else's. And opinions continue to change over time. In part, this transient nature of individual and general opinion is why a team of people including academic researchers, journalists, corporate coaches, and executives and employees from a wide range of companies came together to compile this book. In deciding what to include—and what not to include—the team engaged in often-vigorous debate over whether a certain term, or fact, or trend was really a "culture-shaper" and so belonged in these pages. The items selected for inclusion needed to have significant influence on business culture; they also had to have enduring impact. If you don't expect to see something, and it's included, that is because the team determined that the term or topic was in some way a significant influence on business culture. If you do expect to see something, and it's *not* here, that is most likely because some other term or topic beat it out in the final analysis. As a result, many formal and informal networks, associations, and the like are not called out in the A–Z listings; where possible, these have been included as reference sources.

In addition to the A–Z entries, you'll also find a set of short features titled "Why I Do This." These are personal narratives that tap into the motivations, pros, and cons of a host of individuals' career choices and in doing so move beyond office culture to include other kinds of work that enable and assist office culture. If you think you want to be a Web-marketing expert, there is a "Why I Do This" that offers a glimpse into what day-to-day life in this job is like. Are you more interested in working as a dental office manager? What about a career as a finance executive? Librarian? Or maybe a limo driver, enabling a host of executives, consultants, and the like to work in multiple locations with relative ease? Driving limos is not only about sitting in traffic; this job offers surprising upsides.

The "Why I Do This" essays do not represent every job available; what they offer, however, is an insider's perspective of the world of office work and its supporting services from a diverse group of people located across the United States. An outsider's view of what work in a given office is like can be vastly misleading; hearing directly from the employees is often an eye-opener.

The encyclopedia also contains several feature articles that speak to particular aspects of the culture of work. Some of these—including Rob Galford's essay on *Leadership Mindsets*, and Constantine von Hoffman's interview on *Blogs and Work*—were written for these volumes. Others, such as the articles reprinted from Knowledge@Wharton, an online resource offering business insights, analysis,and information from a variety of sources, have been included here because they offer particular insights into other cultural elements of office life, and because they bring dedicated research to bear on these issues.

The encyclopedia contains one key book chapter, reprinted from *Aligning the Stars* by Thomas Tierney and Jay Lorsch, and appearing here as an appendix. This piece provides an in-depth look at what culture means inside professional service firms. And a series of short pieces, appearing under the heading Signs of Changing Culture, reflect behaviors, happenings, trends, and other influences of culture as reported in major newspapers and magazines during the period when these volumes were being researched.

Finally, the bibliography represents a host of resources available for those who want to extend their research on business culture, or plumb the depths of one or another topic in particular.

Themes

Interestingly—though perhaps not surprisingly—across all of the elements in this work, several common themes emerge. Among them:

- An awareness of the social and environmental issues facing the world—poverty, inequality and global warming among them—and an increasing resolve to contribute to solutions.
- A continuing struggle over where the lines are and should be drawn with regard to the work/life balance. Can anyone who works in an office really "unplug" anymore? Should they?
- An awareness of the phenomenon of the "rise of the customer," or the increasing influence that consumers have on what companies make and market, and how responsive companies must be to consumers in order to succeed . . .
- A continuing and intensifying struggle to get the most out of human capital—people—in a competitive landscape where businesses increasingly compete in their ability to muster and channel talent.
- An ongoing effort to get Web-based business "right" including marketing, reach, and coordination with physical stores, so that companies don't compete against themselves in their online and physical worlds, and so that customers can expect to shop as easily whether they're on the computer or down town.

These themes and others are illuminated in related, cross-referenced entries in this work. They surface in the short, "Signs of Changing Culture" notes, and in the essays, interviews, and articles that flavor the encyclopedia throughout. They're also reflected in the "Why I Do This" narratives, to the extent that they have shaped people's expectations of the work they do, and the way in which they spend their days.

If You're Looking for a Job

One of the most interesting insights that surfaced during the process of putting together this encyclopedia is how different one job can be from another, even given the same necessary skills, and in many cases, the same job title. Culture is a prime differentiator. People with the "same" jobs at one company have profoundly different work experiences at another company, and sometimes, even when working for the same employer in different departments, or units, or functions.

This isn't really a surprising insight. But when you're faced with it, time and again, across the amount of information that gets considered for an encyclopedia, the range of different experiences, even given broad commonalities, is daunting.

The take-away from this insight is to search for the *culture* that fits an individual, not just one that works as a skills-match. There are any number of jobs out there that cause people to work in and around an office. But someone with financial skills can work for a zoo, or a bank, or a fire department, or an opera company, and have a profoundly different daily experience at work than their peers-in-skill work in other environments. Someone who works in human resources can be surrounded by lawyers, architects, consultants, cleaners, security guards, computer programmers, writers, designers, nurses, you name it. Again, while the job title may be the same, each alternative offers a different daily existence.

Extremes

While collecting and coordinating materials for this encyclopedia, we expected to find general themes. But many cultural "extremes" have also come to light. Job-seekers again take note. For example, consider the company whose top executive demands complete obedience from his employees—and also takes it upon himself to manage and support employees' personal lives, even offering marital and general life advice on a regular basis—the kind of company where employees call this senior leader in the middle of the night to discuss their personal lives. Or think about the insurance company that owns and stocks its own ponds, expects employees to spend time fishing, and allows them to keep what they catch. (This company also pays for a weight loss program; employees front some of the cost, but get their money back if they lose the weight they set out to lose. If not, the money goes to charity.)

These are merely samples of the individual cultures cultivated by certain companies. Scratch the surface of any company and you'll find unique cultural attributes. But scratch the surface of some, and you'll find "norms" that truly stand out.

Culture-Shaped Challenges

Our research also highlighted, time and again, the challenges and conflicts that make and break individuals, teams, and entire businesses, on any given workday. Battles rage over health care benefits, workplace standards, and equal employment opportunity. Tensions spiral out of control when directors and leadership teams clash over executive compensation, acquisitions, and divestitures. Bosses, peers, and direct reports face off over a market positions, pricing strategies, performance reviews, and the right way to make decisions. And all of these conflicts are framed and fueled by the culture at work in the organization at hand.

We hope that in these pages, you find resources that shed light on many different perspectives of "the way we work" and that the material herein informs your understanding of the forces shaping business culture, and opens new avenues of thought.

Wherever possible, we've included suggestions or links to additional information on any given topic for further research. We urge you to utilize these connections, and hope that you find them useful. Mostly, we hope you find what's in these pages interesting and provocative; we hope this encyclopedia encourages students and professionals alike to examine or re-examine their role or potential in the world of work as well as their contributions to business culture.

Acknowledgments

This work reflects the efforts of so many people—too many to name here. You know who you are. Your essays, your thoughts about business culture, your views about your own choice of jobs and careers, and your advice about sources and content are reflected on every page that follows. You have our profound and heartfelt gratitude.

We would like to recognize a few people explicitly, because of their unique and substantive contributions to this work:

Our thanks go to Nick Phillipson, who had the idea to do an encyclopedia of business culture designed primarily for students considering "office" work. His vision shaped the project from the early days; his thoughtful editing provided the guidelines for the encyclopedia's various elements.

Without Nick, the project would not have existed. Without Greenwood's Kristi Ward, it would not have been completed. Kristi stepped in at a crucial time to edit, to encourage, and literally to pull together and organize all of the many different editorial components that make up the whole. Her unflagging enthusiasm, her patience, and her expertise drove the project forward. She truly shouldered this encyclopedia and pushed it to completion.

Christine Marra's efforts were also utterly essential to the project's completion. Christine stepped in to edit the many alphabetical entries and other components of the encyclopedia. Her keen eye, efficient editing, and level-headed approach kept the project on track, and allowed us to picture what it would look like as a finished work, even when it was far from being finished.

Credit for the content in the A–Z entries goes largely to a team of skilled researchers, namely Marie M. Bell, Diane R. Walker, Catherine A. Cotins, and Rochelle Stewart. An encyclopedia requires researchers who are able to cast a wide net, assess a great deal of information, and select and present that which they believe really "captures" a definition succinctly and clearly. These folks were up to that task.

We would like to acknowledge, with deeply felt thanks, Sheryl Rowe's formidable editing and production skills, Bridget Austiguy-Preschel's production expertise, Megan Chalek's diligence and attention to detail, and the patience and skill of all of the other people who worked tirelessly behind the scenes at Greenwood to see this through.

Finally, our thanks as ever go to our families, for their patience, tolerance, encouragement and love.

Action Learning

You remember the old phrase "learn on the job," or "learn by doing." Well, action learning is a new, more advanced and aware way to learn by doing.

Essentially, action learning refers to a problem-solving technique where success means more than just solving the problem. Action learning calls for groups of people to work together on a real challenge and to concentrate at the same time on capturing the kinds of lessons they learn during the problem solving process. Put simply, it is an attempt to get groups of people to solve problems, and also to learn about the best way to approach problems and to work together. The idea is to learn more about the process of learning each time a problem is solved. People engaged in "action learning," ask: What did we learn as individuals from this process? In addition to solving the problem at hand, what lessons can we carry forward? Beyond the solution we found this time, what did we learn that can help our company at large?

Noel Tichy is a professor of organization and management at the University of Michigan and the former head of Crotonville, General Electric Co.'s leadership development organization. Tichy captured the importance of action learning with regard to leadership in an interview with *ComputerWorld*, published October 2, 2006. In that interview, he said: "It is up to the leaders of an organization to be the teachers. Only small minorities of leaders do this, but the ones who do are role models. And they don't teach Harvard Business School cases; they get their leaders to work on real projects as part of their development."

The following explanation and opinion of action learning is reprinted with permission from the February 18, 2004, edition of the George Washington University newspaper *By George!*

*Action Learning: A Powerful New Training Tool
for Developing Individuals, Teams and Organizations*

By Michael J. Marquardt, professor of human
resource development and international affairs

Action learning has suddenly emerged as a key training and problem-solving tool for companies as diverse as Nokia, United Technologies, Motorola, Marriott, General Motors, the US Department of Agriculture, Deutsche Bank, and British Airways. These and hundreds of companies around the world now employ action learning for strategic planning, for developing managers, for identifying competitive advantages, for reducing operating costs, for creating high-performing teams, and for becoming learning organizations.

What exactly is action learning? Simply described, action learning is a dynamic process that involves a small group of people solving real problems, while at the same time focusing on what they are learning and how their learning can benefit each group member, the group itself and the organization as a whole.

Perhaps action learning's most valuable capacity is its amazing, multiplying impact to equip individuals, especially leaders, to more effectively respond to change. Learning is what makes action learning strategic rather than tactical. Fresh thinking and new learning are needed if we are to avoid responding to today's problems with yesterday's solutions while tomorrow's challenges engulf us.

Components of an Action Learning Program

Developed by Professor Reg Revans in England in the middle of the twentieth century, action learning was slow to be understood and applied until Jack Welch began using it at General Electric. Over the past twenty years, various approaches to action learning have appeared, but the model that has gained wide-spread acceptance is the Marquardt Model, which incorporates the successful elements of both European and American forms of action learning. This model contains six interactive and interdependent components that build upon and reinforce one another:

1. **A problem (project, challenge, opportunity, issue, or task).**
   Action learning centers around a problem, project, challenge, issue, or task, the resolution of which is of high importance to an
   individual, team, and/or organization. The problem should be
   significant, urgent and be the responsibility of the team to solve.
   It should also provide an opportunity for the group to generate
   learning opportunities, to build knowledge, and to develop individual, team, and organizational skills. Groups may focus on a single problem of the organization or multiple problems introduced
   by individual group members.

2. **An action learning group or team.** The core entity in action
   learning is the action learning group (also called a set or team).
   Ideally, the group is composed of four-to-eight individuals who
   examine an organizational problem that has no easily identifiable
   solution. The group should have diversity of background and experience so as to acquire various perspectives and to encourage
   fresh viewpoints. Depending upon the action learning problem,
   groups may be volunteers or appointees, may be from various
   functions or departments, may include individuals from other organizations or professions, and may involve suppliers as well as
   customers.

3. **A process that emphasizes insightful questioning and reflec-
   tive listening.** Action learning emphasizes questions and reflection above statements and opinions. By focusing on the right
   questions rather than the right answers, action learning focuses on
   what one does not know as well as on what one does know. Action learning tackles problems through a process of first asking
   questions to clarify the exact nature of the problem, reflecting and
   identifying possible solutions, and only then taking action. The
   focus is on questions since great solutions are contained within
   the seeds of great questions. Questions build group dialogue and
   cohesiveness, generate innovative and systems thinking, and enhance learning results.

4. **Taking action on the problem.** Action learning requires that the
   group be able to take action on the problem it is working on.
   Members of the action learning group must have the power to
   take action themselves or be assured that their recommendations

will be implemented (barring any significant change in the environment or the group's obvious lack of essential information). If the group only makes recommendations, it loses its energy, creativity, and commitment. There is no real meaningful or practical learning until action is taken and reflected upon; for one is never sure an idea or plan will be effective until it has been implemented. Action enhances learning because it provides a basis and anchor for the critical dimension of reflection. The action of action learning begins with taking steps to reframe the problem and determining the goal, and only then determining strategies and taking action.

5. **A commitment to learning.** Solving an organizational problem provides immediate, short-term benefits to the company. The greater, longer-term, multiplier benefit, however, is the learning gained by each group member as well as the group as a whole and how those learnings are applied on a systems-wide basis throughout the organization. Thus, the learning that occurs in action learning has greater value strategically for the organization than the immediate tactical advantage of early problem correction. Accordingly, action learning places equal emphasis on the learning and development of individuals and the team as it does on the solving of problems; for the smarter the group becomes, the quicker and better will be the quality of its decision-making and action-taking.

6. **An action learning coach.** Coaching is necessary for the group to focus on the important (i.e., the learnings) as well as the urgent (resolving the problem). The action learning coach helps the team members reflect both on what they are learning and how they are solving problems. Through a series of questions, the coach enables group members to reflect on how they listen, how they may have reframed the problem, how they give each other feedback, how they are planning and working, and what assumptions may be shaping their beliefs and actions. The learning coach also helps the team focus on what they are achieving, what they are finding difficult, what processes they are employing and the implications of these processes. The coaching role may be rotated among members of the group or may be a person assigned to that role throughout the duration of the group's existence.

Action learning power is at its peak when all six of these components are in operation. In addition to these six components, the Marquardt Model of action learning has two ground rules: (1) statements can only be made in response to questions, and (2) the action learning coach has the power to intervene whenever he/she sees an opportunity for learning. Action learning, when systematically implemented, can effectively and efficiently solve problems with innovative and sustaining strategies, develop teams that continuously improve their capability to perform, and apply valuable knowledge at the individual, group, and community levels.

See also: Knowledge Management; Learning Organization; Training and Development

Note: Action Learning is used courtesy of Mike Marquardt. Michael J. Marquardt, professor of human resource development and international affairs, GSEHD, has written two books on action learning—*Action Learning in Action Transforming Problems and People for World-Class Organizational Learning* (Davies-Black Publishing, 1999) and *Optimizing the Power of Action Learning: Solving Problems and Building Leaders in Real Time* (Davies-Black Publishing, 2004).

Further Reading

Action Learning: How the World's Top Companies are Re-Creating Their Leaders and Themselves (Jossey Bass Business and Management Series) by David L. Dotlich and James L. Noel (Jossey-Bass, 1998).

Learning in Action: A Guide to Putting the Learning Organization to Work, by David A. Garvin, Harvard Business School Press, New edition (March 25, 2003).

Optimizing the Power of Action Learning: Solving Problems and Building Leaders in Real Time, by Michael J. Marquardt, Davies-Black Publishing (March 25, 2004).

www.humtech.com
www.12manage.com

Age Discrimination

Age discrimination means that someone has been unfairly treated in an employment situation because of his or her age. Usually, age discrimination implies that someone has been unfairly treated because they are older. Such discrimination is prohibited by a law called The Age Discrimination in Employment Act of 1967 (ADEA). Essentially, the law protects people who are forty years old, or older, from unfair treatment based on age. The law, ADEA, covers both people who are currently in jobs (employees) and also those who are applying for jobs. If, for example, someone is passed over for a job they apply for—even if they are clearly the most qualified for that job—in favor of a younger applicant, that person may have a claim according to the law.

According to the U.S. Equal Employment Opportunity Commission website, in November 2006, the law actually covers "any term, condition, or privilege of employment." That is, the ADEA applies to hiring, firing, pay, benefits, assignments, training, and layoffs. If a company must do a round of layoffs, for example, and only people who are older lose their jobs, those who are let go may have a claim. Or if only younger people are selected for a particular training session, the older people who were excluded may have a claim.

The law also protects people who come forward and let their employer or others know when they feel age discrimination is an issue. According to the website, it is unlawful "to retaliate against an individual for opposing employment practices that discriminate based on age or for filing an age discrimination charge, testifying, or participating in any way in an investigation, proceeding, or litigation under the ADEA."

The ADEA does not apply to all organizations, but it does apply to any company with twenty or more employees. It applies in local, state, and federal government employment situations, and also to labor organizations and employment agencies.

Following are some more specifics about how the law applies in different contexts, according to the website:

APPRENTICESHIP PROGRAMS

It is generally unlawful for apprenticeship programs, including joint labor-management apprenticeship programs, to discriminate on the basis of an individual's age. Age limitations in apprenticeship programs are valid only if they fall within certain specific exceptions under the ADEA or if the EEOC grants a specific exemption.

JOB NOTICES AND ADVERTISEMENTS

The ADEA makes it unlawful to include age preferences, limitations, or specifications in job notices or advertisements. As a narrow exception to that general rule, a job notice or advertisement may specify an age limit in the rare circumstances where age is shown to be a "bona fide occupational qualification" (BFOQ) reasonably necessary to the essence of the business.

PRE-EMPLOYMENT INQUIRIES

The ADEA does not specifically prohibit an employer from asking an applicant's age or date of birth. However, because such inquiries may deter older workers from applying for employment or may otherwise indicate possible intent to discriminate based on age, requests for age information will be closely scrutinized to make sure that the inquiry was made for a lawful purpose, rather than for a purpose prohibited by the ADEA.

BENEFITS

The Older Workers Benefit Protection Act of 1990 (OWBPA) amended the ADEA to specifically prohibit employers from denying benefits to older employees. An employer may reduce benefits based on age only if the cost of providing the reduced benefits to older workers is the same as the cost of providing benefits to younger workers.

WAIVERS OF ADEA RIGHTS

At an employer's request, an individual may agree to waive his/her rights or claims under the ADEA. However, the ADEA, as amended by OWBPA, sets out specific minimum standards that must be met in order for a waiver to be considered knowing and voluntary and, therefore, valid. Among other requirements, a valid ADEA waiver: (1) must be in writing and be understandable; (2) must specifically refer to ADEA rights or claims; (3) may not waive rights or claims that may arise in the future; (4) must be in exchange for valuable consideration; (5) must advise the individual in writing to consult an attorney before signing the waiver; and (6) must provide the individual at least twenty-one days to consider the agreement and at least seven days to revoke the agreement after signing it. In addition, if an employer requests an ADEA waiver in connection with an exit incentive program or other employment termination program, the minimum requirements for a valid waiver are more extensive. www.eeoc.gov

The issue of age discrimination is receiving increasing scrutiny as the "Baby Boomers" age. "Boomers" are people who were born between 1946 and 1964. According to AARP (www.aarp.org), "By 2014, nearly one-third of the total U.S. workforce (32 percent) will be age fifty or older, up from 27 percent in 2005."

In the March 2003 issue of the AARP Bulletin Online, Trish Nicholson wrote, "As more baby boomers move into their 50s, they are finding something new to protest: age discrimination in the workplace. And they aren't wasting any time. Fueled by charges from workers in their 40s and 50s, the number of age bias complaints filed with the U.S. Equal Employment Opportunity Commission (EEOC) jumped from 14,141 in 1999 to 19,921 in 2002, up 41 percent."

The article, entitled, "Boomers Discover Age Bias: Age Complaints Surge as Midlife Workers Find the Going Harder," quoted EEOC chairwoman Cari M. Dominiquez as saying, "Baby boomers believe they helped develop the core values of our society, which prohibit discrimination. "[They] see the [civil rights] laws that are on the books today as part of their own efforts." The article said that Dominiquez believes that "boomers" are very comfortable standing up for their rights.

Every year, AARP compiles a list entitled "Best Employers for Workers Over Fifty." According to the AARP website, the list "is an annual recognition program that acknowledges companies and organizations whose best practices and policies for addressing aging workforce issues are roadmaps for the workplaces of tomorrow."

The AARP list was first compiled in 2001, as the "Best Companies" for older workers. The organization changed the name in order to encourage nonprofit organizations to apply as well. The list is currently also open to government employers.

According to the AARP list, the top fifteen employers for older workers were: (1) Mercy Health System, www.mercyhealthsystem.org; (2) Lee Memorial Health System, www.leememorial.org; (3) Bon Secours Richmond Health System, www.bonsecours.com; (4) LRMC/TVRH, www.leesburgregional.org; (5) Yale–New Haven Hospital, www.ynhh.org; (6) Volkswagen of America, Inc., www.vw.com; (7) Massachusetts Institute of Technology, www.mit.edu; (8) Oakwood Healthcare System, Inc., www.oakwood.org; (9) First Horizon National Corporation, www.firsthorizon.com; (10) Hoffmann-LaRoche, Inc., www.rocheusa.com; (11) Centegra Health System, www.centegra.com; (12) Stanley Consultants, www.stanleyconsultants.com; (13) Scripps Health, www.scrippshealth.org; (14) Brevard Public Schools, www.brevard.k12.fl.us; (15) Beaumont Hospitals, www.Beaumonthospitals.com.

Other sources of information about older workers, and their rights, include The Society for Human Resource Management, in Alexandria, VA; The National Older Worker Career Center, in Arlington, VA (www.nowcc.org); the Center for Corporate Citizenship at Boston College, Chestnut Hill, MA; The American Society on Aging, San Francisco, CA; The National Center for Productive Aging, Rockville, MD; and The National Council on Aging (www.ncoa.org).

See also: American Association of Retired Persons (AARP); Diversity; Equal Employment Opportunity Commission; Glass Ceiling; Job Sharing; Lifetime Employment; Sexual Harassment; War for Talent

Further Reading

Age Discrimination in the American Workplace: Old at a Young Age, by Raymond F. Gregory, Rutgers University Press (March 2001).
Age Discrimination in Employment: Cross Cultural Comparison and Management Strategies, by Bahaudin Mujtaba and Frank Cavico, BookSurge Publishing (January 12, 2006).

American Association of Retired Persons (AARP)

American Association of Retired Persons (AARP) is an advocacy and support organization for people age fifty and above. According to its website, www.aarp.org, the organization is "the leading nonprofit, nonpartisan membership organization for people age fifty and over in the United States."

AARP has more than thirty-five million members. Its services include advocacy on legislative, consumer, and legal issues pertaining to people over fifty, and also a host of discount programs, opportunities to network, and connections to other groups offering support to those age fifty and above, whether or not they have retired from the workforce.

Originally, AARP was called the American Association of Retired Persons, but changed its name in 1999 to AARP, to reflect its growth and expanded mission. U.S. citizenship is not a requirement. Nor do members have to be retired; as of this writing, more than 44 percent of AARP members work either part time or full time.

The organization was founded in 1958 by a retired high school principal named Dr. Ethel Percy Andrus. Andrus had already founded the National Retired Teachers Association in 1947, to help other retired teachers get health insurance, and promote their well being. (As the AARP website says, "At that time, private health insurance was virtually unavailable to older Americans; in fact, it was not until 1965 that the government enacted Medicare, which provides health benefits to persons over age sixty-five." Andrus went on to add programs and services to the Teacher's Association, and eventually founded AARP to offer benefits and programs to all retired persons in the United States, not just teachers. The National Retired Teachers Association is now a division of AARP.

For a few years in the 1960s, AARP had offices in Switzerland, and offered services to retired people outside of the United States. Ultimately, though, the organization closed its international office, and today promotes connections to the worldwide community of retired people through networks and coalitions that extend outside of the United States.

AARP's founding principles, which it still adheres to, are:

- To promote independence, dignity, and purpose for older persons
- To enhance the quality of life for older persons
- To encourage older people "To serve, not to be served"

And as of this writing, the organization has two affiliated groups. These are the AARP Foundation, and AARP Services, Inc. According to the website, "The AARP Foundation is AARP's affiliated charity. Its mission is to build a society in which everyone ages with dignity and purpose. The Foundation leads positive social change to help people fifty and older, especially the most vulnerable, by delivering information, education and direct service to communities and families."

Specific AARP Foundation programs include:

- A work training program for low-income persons age fifty-five and over.
- Free tax preparation and counseling for older Americans.
- Improvement to legal hotlines through technical assistance and training.
- Training and assistance for aging advocates in elder law and advocacy.

- Support for housing counselors in their work with older homeown-
  ers seeking reverse mortgages.

In addition, the Foundation supports AARP Foundation Litigation, a national group that focuses on major litigation benefiting older Americans.

The site says that AARP Services, Inc. (ASI), is "a wholly owned subsid-
iary of AARP. ASI manages a range of products and services made available
to AARP members, provides marketing services to AARP and its member
service providers, and manages the organization's website. ASI is also responsible for developing new products and services that reflect the changing needs and interests of AARP members."

ASI manages programs that address long-term health care issues and
offer or facilitate supplements to Medicare; automobile, home and life insurance; discounts on prescription drugs, eye-health services, and eyewear
products. The website says that "ASI also oversees discounts on hotels and
motels, auto rental, airlines, cruise lines, vacation packages, entertainment
products and consumer goods." AARP members receive several publications, including the bimonthly AARP magazine, and the AARP Bulletin,
published eleven times a year. Additionally, AARP publishes a quarterly
Spanish-English newspaper called *Segunda Juventud*, targeting the over-
fifty Hispanic community.

AARP can be reached by phone at 1-888-687-2277, or by mail at 601
E Street NW, Washington, D.C., 20049.

See also: Age Discrimination; Lifetime Employment

Further Reading

The AARP: America's Most Powerful Lobby and the Clash of Generations, by
   Charles R. Morris, Crown; 1st edition (June 18, 1996).
Trust Betrayed: Inside the AARP, by Dale Van Atta, Regnery Pub (February
   1998).

American Federation of Labor and Congress of Industrial Organizations (AFL-CIO)

The American Federation of Labor and Congress of Industrial Organizations (AFL-CIO) is a voluntary federation of fifty-three national and international labor unions. According to its website, www.aflcio.org,

Today's unions represent nearly nine million working women and men of every race and ethnicity and from every walk of life. We are teachers and truck drivers, musicians and miners, firefighters and farm workers, bakers and bottlers, engineers and editors, pilots and public employees, doctors and nurses, painters and laborers—and more. The AFL-CIO was created in 1955 by the merger of the American Federation of Labor and the Congress of Industrial Organizations. In 1995, the biennial convention elected President John J. Sweeney, Secretary-Treasurer Richard Trumka, and Executive Vice President Linda Chavez-Thompson. They have been re-elected three times since then, most recently in 2005 for four-year terms.

The organization's mission, according to the website, reads as follows:

The mission of the AFL-CIO is to improve the lives of working families—to bring economic justice to the workplace and social justice to our nation. To accomplish this mission we will *build* and *change* the American labor movement.

We will build a broad movement of American workers by organizing workers into unions. We will recruit and train the next generation of organizers, mass the resources needed to organize and create the strategies to win organizing campaigns and union contracts. We will create a broad understanding of the need to organize among our members, our leadership and among unorganized workers. We will lead the labor movement in these efforts.

We will build a strong political voice for workers in our nation. We will fight for an agenda for working families at all levels of government. We will empower state federations. We will build a broad progressive coalition that speaks out for social and economic justice. We will create a political force within the labor movement that will empower workers and speak forcefully on the public issues that affect our lives.

We will change our unions to provide a new voice to workers in a changing economy. We will speak for working people in the global economy, in the industries in which we are employed, in the firms where we work, and on the job every day. We will transform the role of the union from an organization that focuses on a member's contract to one that gives workers a say in all the decisions that affect our working lives—from capital investments, to the quality of our products and services, to how we organize our work.

We will change our labor movement by creating a new voice for workers in our communities. We will make the voices of working families heard across our nation and in our neighborhoods. We will create vibrant community labor councils that reach out to workers at the local level. We will strengthen the ties of labor to our allies. We will speak out in effective and creative ways on behalf of all working Americans.

The AFL-CIO is governed by a quadrennial convention at which all federation members are represented by elected delegates of the participating unions. At these conventions, the organization's broad goals and policies are determined. Elections are also held every four years for AFL-CIO officers. In addition to being a union organizer/protector, the AFL-CIO is also a resource for information and data on jobs, labor relations, union membership, and union news.

The AFL-CIO has a history of great political clout, but according to a *Washington Post* article ("AFL-CIO Looks for United Front on Election Day" by Dan Baiz and Michael A. Fletcher, Sunday, September 3, 2006, page AO4), "There have been concerns among Democrats that last year's split within the AFL-CIO could diminish the effectiveness of what long has been considered an integral element of the party's Election Day effort." Elsewhere in that same article, however, Karen Ackerman, AFL-CIO political director said, "If we meet our goals, we will contribute more than 1.2 million more votes for our endorsed candidates than we were able to in 2002."

See also: Equal Employment Opportunity Commission (EEOC)

Further Reading

The Black Worker: From the Founding of the CIO to the AFL-CIO Merger, 1936–1955, by Ronald L. Lewis, Temple University Press (June 1983).

Not Your Father's Union Movement: Inside the AFL-CIO, edited by Jo-Ann Mort, Verso; Paperback edition (November 1998).

Americans with Disabilities Act

Reduced to its essentials, the Americans with Disabilities Act (ADA) is a law that protects the rights of people with disabilities, and calls for them to be treated fairly. Just as the law prohibits anyone from discriminating against someone because of their age (*see* **Age Discrimination**), so to does the law protect those with disabilities.

The ADA's roots appear to be traceable to the 1960s, also known as the Civil Rights Era, according to the website www.dbtac.vcu.edu. (This website is a Disability and Technical Assistance Center, which offers a wealth of information on the ADA and also provides links to local assistance centers.) In 1963, Martin Luther King, Jr. delivered his famous "I have a Dream" speech, which laid out his vision of a "just and inclusive society." In 1964, the first major civil rights statute was enacted: the "Civil Rights Act of 1964." In 1965, the Voting Rights Act was enacted. And in 1968, the Fair Housing Act was passed.

All of these events marked major steps in terms of fairness, but none of them covered people with disabilities. However, they did trigger the movement towards including people with disabilities under laws that called for fairness.

From the 1970s through 1990, additional acts and amendments were passed to gain more rights for disabled people in different venues. According to the website, however, "Disability would not be linked to the mainstream of civil rights law which flowed from the Civil Rights Act of 1964 until Section 504 of the Rehabilitation Act of 1973 was enacted."

In 1986, according to the website, the "National Council on Disability issued, 'Toward Independence,' recommending that a comprehensive law requiring equal opportunity for individuals with disabilities be enacted." And in 1990 that law—the Americans with Disabilities Act—was passed.

The U.S. Department of Labor provides a full-text copy of the act on its website. Essentially, the first sections of the act set the context of the law. For example, it says that some 43,000,000 Americans have disabilities and that the number will increase as the population of the United States ages. The act also says that historically, people with disabilities have often been isolated from those without disabilities, and that such discrimination is still a social problem despite progress on some fronts.

The ADA focuses in on discrimination against disabled people in "such critical areas as employment, housing, public accommodations, education, transportation, communication, recreation, institutionalization, health services, voting, and access to public services." It goes on to say that people with disabilities "have often had no legal recourse to redress such discrimination."

The ADA confirms that people with disabilities have suffered due to such discrimination and lack of legal recourse, that such discrimination is not fair, and that the purpose of the act is to ensure that such discrimination does not continue, and that people with disabilities should have "the opportunity to compete on an equal basis and to pursue those opportunities for which our free society is justifiably famous." It also notes that discrimination against people with disabilities costs the United States "billions of dollars in unnecessary expenses resulting from dependency and nonproductivity."

Here is how the ADA lays out its purpose and goals:

(b) Purpose.—It is the purpose of this Act—
   (1) to provide a clear and comprehensive national mandate for the elimination of discrimination against individuals with disabilities;
   (2) to provide clear, strong, consistent, enforceable standards addressing discrimination against individuals with disabilities;
   (3) to ensure that the Federal Government plays a central role in enforcing the standards established in this Act on behalf of individuals with disabilities; and
   (4) to invoke the sweep of congressional authority, including the power to enforce the fourteenth amendment and to regulate commerce, in order to address the major areas of discrimination faced day-to-day by people with disabilities.

Another good source of information about the Americans with Disabilities Act (ADA) is the Job Accommodation Network (JAN; www.jan .wvu.edu/links/adasummary.htm). The Job Accommodation Network is a service of the Office of Disability Employment Policy (ODEP) of the U.S. Department of Labor. According to the JAN website, the network's mission

is to facilitate the employment and retention of workers with disabilities by providing employers, employment providers, people with disabilities, their family members and other interested parties with information on job accommodations, self-employment and small business opportunities and related subjects. JAN's efforts are in support of the employment, including self-employment and small business ownership, of people with disabilities. JAN represent the most comprehensive resource for job accommodations available, JAN's work has greatly enhanced the job opportunities of people with disabilities by providing information on job accommodations since 1984. In 1991, JAN expanded to provide information on the Americans with Disabilities Act. JAN consultants have obtained at least one Master's degree in their specialized fields, ranging from rehabilitation counseling to education and engineering. The development of the JAN system has been achieved through the collaborative efforts of the U.S. DOL Office of Disability Employment Policy, the International Center for Disability Information at West Virginia University, and private industry throughout North America.

The JAN website provides an overview of the ADA, again with a disclaimer stating that its information is "a brief overview which cannot possibly set forth everything about the ADA and which, for purposes of brevity or as part of an effort to state legal concepts simply and in plain English, may describe the law in a manner which is not necessarily precise and/or accurate in every respect."

According to the JAN site, the ADA "is a wide-ranging legislation intended to make American Society more accessible to people with disabilities." The JAN website goes on to say that the act, "is divided into five titles":

1. Employment (Title I) Business must provide reasonable accommodations to protect the rights of individuals with disabilities in all aspects of employment. Possible changes may include restructuring jobs, altering the layout of workstations, or modifying equipment. Employment aspects may include the application process, hiring, wages, benefits, and all other aspects of employment. Medical examinations are highly regulated.

2. Public Services (Title II) Public services, which include state and local government instrumentalities, the National Railroad Passenger Corporation, and other commuter authorities, cannot deny services to people with disabilities, participation in programs or activities which are available to people without disabilities. In addition, public transportation systems, such as public transit buses, must be accessible to individuals with disabilities.

3. Public Accommodations (Title III) All new construction and modifications must be accessible to individuals with disabilities. For existing facilities, barriers to services must be removed if readily achievable. Public accommodations include facilities such as restaurants, hotels, grocery stores, retail stores, etc., as well as privately owned transportation systems.

4. Telecommunications (Title IV) Telecommunications companies offering telephone service to the general public must have telephone relay service to individuals who use telecommunication devices for the deaf (TTYs) or similar devices.

5. Miscellaneous (Title V) Includes a provision prohibiting either (a) coercing or threatening or (b) retaliating against the disabled or those attempting to aid people with disabilities in asserting their rights under the ADA.

The ADA's protection applies primarily, but not exclusively, to "disabled" individuals. An individual is "disabled" if he or she meets at least one of the following tests:

1. He or she has a physical or mental impairment that substantially limits one or more of his/her major life activities;
2. He or she has a record of such an impairment; or
3. He or she is regarded as having such an impairment.

Other individuals who are protected in certain circumstances include 1) those, such as parents, who have an association with an individual known to have a disability, and 2) those who are coerced or subjected to retaliation for assisting people with disabilities in asserting their rights under the ADA.

While the employment provisions of the ADA apply to employers of fifteen employees or more, its public accommodations provisions apply to all sizes of business, regardless of number of employees. State and local governments are covered regardless of size.

The www.ada.gov website is a primary source of information for the ADA. This website provides, among other things, current information about the ADA, information on design standards, technical assistance, new or proposed regulations, and links to other resources.

The ADA "home page" also provides a "Myths and Facts" page, at www.ada.gov/pubs/mythfct.txt. The text on that page, as of November 2006, was as follows:

Myths and Facts about the Americans with Disabilities Act

MYTH: ADA suits are flooding the courts.

FACT: The ADA has resulted in a surprisingly small number of lawsuits—only about 650 nationwide in five years. That's tiny compared to the six million businesses, 666,000 public and private employers, and 80,000 units of state and local government that must comply.

MYTH: The ADA is rigid and requires businesses to spend lots of money to make their existing facilities accessible.

FACT: The ADA is based on common sense. It recognizes that altering existing structures is more costly than making new construction accessible. The law only requires that public accommodations (e.g., stores, banks, hotels, and restaurants) remove architectural barriers in existing facilities when it is "readily achievable," i.e., it can be done "without much difficulty or expense." Inexpensive, easy steps to take include ramping one step; installing a bathroom grab bar; lowering a paper towel dispenser; rearranging furniture; installing offset hinges to widen a doorway; or painting new lines to create an accessible parking space.

MYTH: The government thinks everything is readily achievable.

FACT: Not true. Often it may not be readily achievable to remove a barrier—especially in older structures. Let's say a small business is located above ground. Installing an elevator would not, most likely, be readily achievable—and there may not be enough room to build a ramp—or the business may not be profitable enough to build a ramp. In these circumstances, the ADA would allow a business to simply provide curbside service to persons with disabilities.

MYTH: The ADA requires businesses to remove barriers overnight.

FACT: Businesses are only required to do what is readily achievable at that time. A small business may find that installing a ramp is not readily achievable this year, but if profits improve it will be readily achievable next year. Businesses are encouraged to evaluate their facilities and develop a long-term plan for barrier removal that is commensurate with their resources.

MYTH: Restaurants must provide menus in Braille.

FACT: Not true. Waiters can read the menu to blind customers.

MYTH: The ADA requires extensive renovation of all state and local government buildings to make them accessible.

FACT: The ADA requires all government programs, not all government buildings, to be accessible. "Program accessibility" is a very flexible requirement and does not require a local government to do anything that would result in an undue financial or administrative burden. Local governments have been subject to this requirement for many years under the Rehabilitation Act of 1973. Not every building, nor each part of every building needs to be accessible. Structural modifications are required only when there is no alternative available for providing program access. Let's say a town library has an inaccessible second floor. No elevator is needed if it provides "program accessibility" for persons using wheelchairs by having staff retrieve books.

MYTH: Sign language interpreters are required everywhere.

FACT: The ADA only requires that effective communication not exclude people with disabilities—which in many situations means providing written materials or exchanging notes. The law does not require any measure that would cause an undue financial or administrative burden.

MYTH: The ADA forces business and government to spend lots of money hiring unqualified people.

FACT: No unqualified job applicant or employee with a disability can claim employment discrimination under the ADA. Employees must meet all the requirements of the job and perform the essential functions of the job with or without reasonable accommodation. No accommodation must be provided if it would result in an undue hardship on the employer.

MYTH: Accommodating workers with disabilities costs too much.

FACT: Reasonable accommodation is usually far less expensive than many people think. In most cases, an appropriate reasonable accommodation can be made without difficulty and at little or no cost. A recent study commissioned by Sears indicates that of the 436 reasonable accommodations provided by the company between 1978 and 1992, 69 percent cost nothing, 28 percent cost less than $1,000, and only 3 percent cost more than $1,000.

MYTH: The government is no help when it comes to paying for accessibility.

FACT: Not so. Federal tax incentives are available to help meet the cost of ADA compliance.

MYTH: Businesses must pay large fines when they violate the ADA.

FACT: Courts may levy civil penalties only in cases brought by the Justice Department, not private litigants. The Department only seeks such penalties when the violation is substantial and the business has shown bad faith in failing to comply. Bad faith can take many forms, including hostile acts against people with disabilities, a long-term failure even to inquire into what the ADA requires, or sustained resistance to voluntary compliance. The Department also considers a business' size and resources in determining whether civil penalties are appropriate. Civil penalties may not be assessed in cases against state or local governments or employers.

MYTH: The Justice Department sues first and asks questions later.

FACT: The primary goal of the Department's enforcement program is to increase voluntary compliance through technical assistance and negotiation. Under existing rules, the Department may not file a lawsuit unless it has first tried to settle the dispute through negotiations—which is why most every complaint settles.

MYTH: The Justice Department never files suits.

FACT: The Department has been party to twenty suits under the ADA. Although it tries extensively to promote voluntary compliance, the Department will take legal action when entities continue to resist complying with the law.

MYTH: Many ADA cases involve frivolous issues.

FACT: The Justice Department's enforcement of the ADA has been fair and rooted in common sense. The overwhelming majority of the complaints received by the Justice Department have merit. Our focus is on fundamental issues related to access to goods and services that are basic to people's lives. We have avoided pursuing fringe and frivolous issues and will continue to do so.

MYTH: Everyone claims to be covered under the ADA.

FACT: The definition of "individual with a disability" is fraught with conditions and must be applied on a case-by-case basis.

MYTH: The ADA protects people who are overweight.

FACT: Just being overweight is not enough. Modifications in policies only must be made if they are reasonable and do not fundamentally alter the nature of the program or service provided. The Department has received only a handful of complaints about obesity.

MYTH: The ADA is being misused by people with "bad backs" and "emotional problems."

FACT: Trivial complaints do not make it through the system. And many claims filed by individuals with such conditions are not trivial. There are people with severe depression or people with a history of alcoholism who are judged by their employers, not on the basis of their abilities, but rather upon stereotypes and fears that employers associate with their conditions.

See also: Equal Employment Opportunity Commission (EEOC)

Further Reading

Understanding the Americans with Disabilities Act, Second Edition (Paperback), by William D. Goren, American Bar Association (May 25, 2007).

Voices from the Edge, Narratives about the Americans with Disabilities Act (Paperback), edited by Ruth O'Brien. Foreword by Rogers M. Smith. Oxford University Press (December 18, 2003).

The Apprentice

Reality TV shows have been all the rage in recent years, and the subject matter has ranged from finding a husband, to racing around the world, to handling the politics and dangers of living with a group of strangers in a remote locale, and even to the boardroom. No, not even the world of management has escaped the attention of reality show TV and paying tribute to the reality craze is *The Apprentice*.

Some may wonder what could be more frightening than being left on a desert island with total strangers. *The Apprentice* seems to pose an even more daunting option—a high-stakes interview for the job of a lifetime. While TV viewers watch, the interviewees defend their actions and sweat under the eye of billionaire real estate mogul Donald Trump who decides whether to keep them in the interview process for another week (until the next show) or whether to end their career hopes with his trademark phrase: "You're Fired!"

Put simply, *The Apprentice* is a hit TV reality show on NBC, starring Donald Trump as the boss. According to the TV Guide website, the show's premise is: "A kind of 'Survivor' in pinstripes." *Apprentice* "contestants" compete in teams in a variety of business challenges, each vying for the winning title of apprentice, and a guaranteed real job in the Trump empire. At the end of each episode, "the Donald," as Trump is known, says "You're fired," to one of the contestants on the losing team; leaving one less person in the game.

Essentially, this show brings the job interview process to a very public and competitive forum, with a few "made for TV" twists, such as having the contestants live together in New York City while the "game" is on. Taglines for the show have included: "What if you could have it all?" "It's nothing personal . . . it's just business," and "The Ultimate Job Interview."

A summary of the 2004 season of the show, credited to NBC and posted on the website www.imdb.com, called *The Apprentice* a fifteen-episode, unscripted drama that included sixteen job candidates who would "endure rigorous tasks each week while living together in a hip Manhattan loft apartment." In one subsequent season, the locale was shifted to California, where the winners of each week's "task" lived in luxury in a mansion, while the losers "camped out" in tents on the property.

The Apprentice premiered on January 8, 2004; its success has given rise

---

Why I Do This: Online Editor

Marie Gendron

I am an editor for Herald Interactive, a web-based media company owned by the *Boston Herald* newspaper. My job is to generate strong editorial content to drive job seekers to Jobfind.com, which is a regional job search site. Working with a dozen freelance writers, I assign and edit career-related stories, columns and other features. I then format those stories—and any associated artwork—for the web and FTP them to the site.

This job was a natural transition from my former position as a business reporter for the *Boston Herald*. My typical day entails editing stories, posting them to the web, checking in with freelancers by phone or e-mail, creating story budgets and deadline schedules for upcoming issues, and filing the paperwork needed to get everyone paid. Since my job is web-based, the hours are incredibly flexible. I work about half my hours at home. I think the key skills to succeeding in my job are organization, creativity, and flexibility.

---

to several knock-off shows, including an apprentice series starring Martha Stewart, and a UK version of the contest.

There are many websites devoted to *The Apprentice*. Among them are www.theapprenticerules.com and www.theapprenticeblog.com. The NBC website has the show's "home page." And the website www.imdb.com, source of the summary above, also posts reviews. The site, www.tv.com, is also a good source of information and links pertaining to the show.

See also: War for Talent; Water Cooler; White Collar

Further Reading

Trump: The Art of the Deal, by Donald. J. Trump and Tony Schwartz, Ballantine Books (December 28, 2004).

The Art of War

The Art of War, written by Sun Tzu, is a classic book of military strategy. Written sometime between the fifth and eighth centuries B.C., and commonly known as "the oldest military treatise in the world," *The Art of War* remains a top seller to this day. It has been translated many times from the original Chinese into many other languages and published in a variety of forms.

Though intended as a guide for the military, Sun Tzu's lessons in strategy have been liberally referenced and applied in the world of management. One book devoted to that task is *The Art of War for Managers: 50 Strategic Rules,* by Sun Tzu and Gerald A. Michaelson. Written by Michaelson, this book, published in 2001 by Adams Media, draws on the words of Sun Tzu to create guidelines for success in the corporate world.

Other similar books stick to the military premise, albeit knowing that readers will draw their own connections between Sun Tzu's intent and their own contexts.

Reviews of these texts vary as the treatments vary, but Lionel Giles's translation, published in 1910, seems to be the classic work, consistently well regarded.

The website, http://www.chinapage.com/sunzi-e.html, contains the basic text of *The Art of War,* as translated by Lionel Giles, M.A., in 1910. Here's a taste of the book, from that site:

All warfare is based on deception.

Hence, when able to attack, we must seem unable; when using our forces, we must seem inactive; when we are near, we must make the enemy believe we are far away; when far away, we must make him believe we are near.

Hold out baits to entice the enemy. Feign disorder, and crush him.

If he is secure at all points, be prepared for him. If he is in superior strength, evade him. If your opponent is of choleric temper, seek to irritate him. Pretend to be weak, that he may grow arrogant.

If he is taking his ease, give him no rest. If his forces are united, separate them.

Attack him where he is unprepared, appear where you are not expected.

Brian Bruya, reviewing a paperback edition of *The Art of War* (translated by Thomas Cleary, published in November 2002 by Dover Publications) on Amazon.com, called it "the Swiss army knife of military theory." The question does arise of how relevant this book really is in the context of today's business world. The answer depends on whom you ask. To some, the principles laid out in the book are highly relevant. As the Amazon book description for another Michaelson book (*Sun Tzu Strategies for Winning the Marketing War: 12 Essential Principles for Winning the War for Customers* (McGraw-Hill, October 2003) says, "Millions of business warriors have been inspired by lessons from one of the world's greatest strategists, Sun Tzu."

See also: Competitive Advantage

Further Reading

Understanding Sun Tzu on the Art of War, by Robert Cantrell, Center For Advantage (July 15, 2004).

Balanced Scorecard

The balanced scorecard is a management system and tool that enables organizations to clarify their vision and strategy and translate them into actions. As its name suggests, the scorecard allows managers to measure and assess performance on a variety of fronts that are important to the success of a business. Developed in the early 1990s by Drs. Robert Kaplan (Harvard Business School) and David Norton (president of Renaissance Solutions), the balanced scorecard allows managers to recognize some of their organization's weaknesses; it can also help managers identify areas where a particular management approach has not been effective.

With the scorecard in place, managers have a common set of measures to assess over time, and can work to strengthen corporate performance. The idea is to ensure that both relevant financial and nonfinancial inputs inform decision-making. As *Publisher's Weekly* noted in its Amazon.com description of Kaplan and Norton's original book on the topic: "Purely financial evaluations of performance . . . no longer suffice in a world where intangible assets, relationships and capabilities increasingly determine the prospects for success."

According to SkyMark.com, an article by Kaplan and Norton entitled "The Balanced Scorecard—Measures that Drive Performance" that was published in the *Harvard Business Review* in 1992 sparked interest in the method, and led to the authors' business bestseller, *The Balanced Scorecard: Translating Strategy into Action*, published in 1996. Kaplan and Norton describe the innovation of the balanced scorecard on the Balance Scorecard Institute's website (www.balancedscorecard.org):

The balanced scorecard retains financial measures. But financial measures tell the story of past events, an adequate story for industrial age companies for which investments in long-term capabilities and customer relationships were not critical for success. These financial measures are inadequate, however, for guiding and evaluating the journey that information age companies must make to create future value through investment in customers, suppliers, employees, processes, technology, and innovation.

According to an article entitled "How to use the Balanced Scorecard," which was published in the May 15, 2002, issue of *CIO Magazine*, a fully implemented Scorecard cascades from the top levels of a company all the way down. In the same article, Norton tells *CIO Magazine* that it is ideal to implement the Balanced Scorecard throughout the enterprise because that framework helps foster alignment between business and IT.

Linda Bankston, CIO of DuPont Engineering Polymers, a $2.5 billion division of DuPont Chemicals in Wilmington, Delaware, was quoted in the same article, saying that when a company uses the scorecard, "the conversation is around strategy and impact, rather than just whether you can or can't do something" (http://www.cio.com/archive/051502/scorecard .html).

Library Journal (located on Amazon.com) summed up the scorecard approach this way:

Kaplan (accounting, Harvard) and Norton, president of Renaissance Solutions Inc., created the "balanced scorecard" to assist businesses in moving from ideas to action, achieving long-term goals, and obtaining feedback about strategy. The balanced scorecard consists of four sections: clarifying and translating vision and strategy; communicating and linking strategic objectives and measures; planning, setting targets, and aligning strategic initiatives; and enhancing strategic feedback and learning.

See also: Six Sigma; Total Quality Management (TQM)

Further Reading

Balanced Scorecard Step-by-Step: Maximizing Performance and Maintaining Results, by Paul R. Niven, Wiley; Second edition (September 1, 2006).
The Balanced Scorecard: Translating Strategy into Action, by Robert S. Kaplan and David P. Norton, Harvard Business School Press (September 1996).

Benchmarking

When a company's leaders and managers are trying to improve a practice, a process, or performance overall, they require a way of measuring if they are setting reasonable expectations. A company must have a way to determine whether it is truly doing the best that it can, on any given performance front.

One way for a company to measuring improvement or evaluating expectations is to "benchmark" their performance against another company that is known as the leader in whatever area is chosen. Benchmarking, in short, means comparing an aspect of your own personal or corporate performance against the same aspect of another organization's performance. Generally, companies try to identify the "best in class" to benchmark against, and then they strive to meet or exceed those top-level standards.

"Benchmarking is the process of determining who is the very best, who sets the standard, and what that standard is. In baseball, you could argue that seven consecutive World Series Championships made the New York Yankees the benchmark," says F. John Reh, a management professional with broad experience and an Internet Management Consultant, in an article posted on About.com (2007 About, Inc., A part of The New York Times Company). Reh goes on to say that benchmarking is usually part of a larger effort, usually a Process Re-engineering or Quality Improvement initiative. Reh also says benchmarking is important so that a business can compare itself against the standard.

All companies benchmark their work to some degree. Even a very small business, seeking to build a customer base, will often compare—albeit informally—its performance with similar competitor's offerings. But larger organizations often approach benchmarking in a very formal and analytical way. The benefits of such analysis are great; when a company identifies a suitable benchmark, managers can better assess their own performance in the context of their own companies. They can also set more accurate and reasonable goals for progress.

Benchmarking does not and should not necessarily be conducted within the confines of a business type or even one particular geography. A great deal can be learned, for example, from comparing front-line service to customers across different types of businesses in the same general field (fast-food coffee shops and high-end restaurants, for instance) and across different industries (front-line service at a library, versus, say, a busy doctor's

---

Why I Do This: Editor-in-Chief, MarketWatch

David Callaway

Running an online news team is like sprinting up a hill all day long. Because we cover financial markets around the world, breaking news never stops for us. From the moment I wake up at 4:30 A.M. in San Francisco (West Coast hours are brutal when you follow the markets) to the time I sign off around 10 P.M., there is always something breaking and some work to be done.

I do it because I'm a news junkie and love the thrill of being on top of all the major stories of the day. We have more than 100 reporters in bureaus in the United States, London, and Hong Kong so somebody is always on deadline. The type of person I hire is also somebody that thrives on action and likes to tell a story using the Internet, video, audio graphics, or any other way.

While the job is busy, the rewards are amazing and almost instantaneous. The stories we do are read all over the world, and I never cease to be amazed when somebody writes in from Thailand, South Africa, or Brazil to comment on a news story we did out of Chicago or Los Angeles. In my twenty years as a journalist, this is the most exciting job I've ever held.

---

practice). Much can also be learned by comparing or benchmarking against levels and standards of service across geographies. Benchmarking, at its best, provides inspiration for creativity, and motivation that is guided by measurable progress.

Benchnet.com describes benchmarking as a tool to help you improve your business process. But the site also cautions that too often, companies seek to benchmark their work in too narrow a way. Benchnet.com notes,

> One of the biggest mistakes people make when beginning their benchmarking endeavor is that they only look to benchmark someone within their own industry. Although this doesn't hurt, you probably already know enough about your industry to know what works and what doesn't. Worse yet, some people think they must benchmark their competitor. What if the competition is worse than your company? Seems like a pretty big waste of time and energy. Instead how about benchmarking a company that is well known for being a good model? Sometimes referred to as Best Practices, Exemplary Practices, Business Excellence. (2007 Benchmarking Exchange, http://www.benchnet.com/wib.htm)

Some companies choose to identify benchmarking targets by themselves, and construct and conduct their own internal systems for benchmarking. But there are many consulting firms ready and willing to engage in benchmarking work as well.

Ann Evans, director of Benchmarking PLUS (Benchmarking PLUS 1999), an organization that provides benchmarking solutions, says there are plenty of opportunities for benchmarking to go wrong. She advises her readers to avoid the following ten benchmarking mistakes: confusing benchmarking with participating in a survey, thinking there are pre-existing "benchmarks" to be found, forgetting about service delivery and customer satisfaction, creating a benchmarking process that is too large to be manageable, confusing benchmarking with research, misalignment, picking a topic that is too intangible and difficult to measure, not establishing a baseline, not researching benchmarking partners thoroughly, and not having a code of ethics and contract agreed with partners.

Benchmarking can be fraught with potential problems, ranging from simple misunderstandings to serious legal problems, according to isixsigma .com. The website's recommendations—which are attributed to a code-of-conduct produced by the Benchmarking Clearinghouse—include:

> Don't enter into discussions or act in any way that could be construed as illegal, either for you or your partner. Potential illegal activities include, for example, such simple actions as discussing costs or prices, if that discussion could lead to allegations of price fixing or market rigging.
>
> Don't ask questions of your benchmarking partner that you are not willing to answer yourself to the same level of detail.
>
> Benchmarking's golden rule: treat your partner and their information the way you'd like them to treat you and yours.

See also: Best Practice; Performance Management/Performance Measurement

Further Reading

Benchmarking for Nonprofits: How To Measure, Manage, and Improve Performance, by Jason Saul, Amherst H. Wilder Foundation (October 30, 2004).
Benchmarking: The Search for Industry Best Practices That Lead to Superior Performance, by Robert C. Camp, Productivity Press (August 30, 2006).

Best Practice

A best practice is a process or procedure that consistently produces superior results. Best practice is also a management idea which says that there is a technique, method, process, activity, incentive, or reward that is more effective at delivering a particular outcome than any other technique, method, or process. When one firm in an industry establishes a best practice, its competitors seek to diffuse that advantage by adopting a similar or better practice themselves.

When a company is known for a best practice process or system, other companies often seek to "benchmark" against it (*see* **Benchmarking**). When a company aspires to achieve a best practice process or system, it is trying to be the standard by which other organizations measure their own performance.

The *Glossary of Project Management* defines best practice as a superior method or innovative practice that contributes to the improved performance of an organization, usually recognized as "best" by other peer organizations. "It implies accumulating and applying knowledge about what is working and not working in different situations and contexts, including lessons learned and the continuing process of learning, feedback, reflection and analysis (what works, how and why)."

The term, best practice, is in widespread use throughout the world of business; it's also part of the common language in education, government, and a host of other fields.

For example, Teresa L. Kramer, Ph.D. and William N. Glazer, M.D., write on psychiatryonline.org that the best-practices movement in medicine has much to offer practitioners who hope to demonstrate their value in a commodity-driven market. In their article, they review and explore the current status of the best-practices movement in general medicine and psychiatry.

> The ability to identify and implement best practices in industry has differentiated the successful organization from the unsuccessful organization. Because longevity and financial viability are determined by the quality of customer services and products, there has been a significant increase in comparative techniques that recognize the best and worst performers in the commercial world . . . In recent years, the best-practices movement has filtered into general medicine and to some extent mental health care, perhaps in the part because of pres-

sure from employers—payers—who have witnessed the value of this process. (Kramer and Glazer; Psychiatric Services, www.psychiatryon-line.org, 52:157–159, February 2001).

See also: Benchmarking; Performance Management/Performance Measurement

Further Reading

www.bestpracticedatabase.com
www.bestpractice.org

Blanchard, Ken

Ken Blanchard is known in the business world for his influence on how the role of the leader in an organization has evolved in the 1980s and 1990s. Blanchard is the owner and chief spiritual officer of the Ken Blanchard Companies, a management training and consulting firm that he and his wife, Dr. Majorie Blanchard, founded in 1979 in San Diego, California. He is also a visiting lecturer at his alma mater, Cornell University, where he is a trustee emeritus of the Board of Trustees.

According to Ninth House, a company that helps organizations develop current and future leaders, Blanchard is a prominent, gregarious, sought-after author, speaker, and business consultant known around the world simply as Ken.

Blanchard is also cofounder of *The Center for FaithWalk Leadership*, which is dedicated to helping leaders walk their talk in the marketplace, while honoring their own integrity and spirituality. He is well known for his contribution to the Blanchard and Hersey Model of situational leadership theory (with Paul Hersey). The Situational Leadership Method holds that managers must use different leadership styles depending on the situation. The model allows you to analyze the needs of the situation you're dealing with, and then adopt the most appropriate leadership style.

According to the Chimaera Consulting Limited website, this model is popular because: "It's simple to understand, and it works in most environments for most people. The model doesn't just apply to people in leadership or management positions: we all lead others at work and at home."

The consulting firm's site goes on to note that Blanchard and Hersey characterize leadership style in terms of the amount of direction and of support that the leader gives to his or her followers. For example, leaders can "direct" by defining employee's roles and the type of work they need to do. In a "directing" style, leaders make the decisions and generally communicate only from the top down. When a leader is a "coach," on the other hand, he or she will look for some feedback from employees to inform his or her decisions. When leaders take on a "supporting" role, they may delegate many decisions, facilitating the decision-making process.

Blanchard is also well known for the concept he created with Spencer Johnson: *The One-Minute Manager*. His book on the topic, and all of the ancillary literature that has followed (creating a *One Minute Manager Library*) has sold millions of copies and has also been widely translated. The concept explains and explores three simple techniques: One-minute goal setting, one-minute praising, and one-minute reprimands. Blanchard and Johnson tout the concept as resulting in more effective leadership.

See also: Corner Office; Executive Coach; Management by Objectives; Performance Management/Performance Measurement

Further Reading

Leading at a Higher Level: Blanchard on Leadership and Creating High Performing Organizations, by Ken Blanchard, FT Press (October 2006).
The One Minute Manager Meets the Monkey, by Ken Blanchard, William Morrow (1989).
www.kenblanchard.com

Blue Collar

Blue Collar is an adjective that describes those who work for hourly wages, especially manual or industrial laborers. A blue-collar worker is a working-class employee who performs manual or technical labor, such as in a factory or in technical maintenance trades such as plumbing or electronics, in contrast to a white-collar worker, who does non-manual work generally at a desk.

The term is derived from the history of blue-collar worker's uniform dress code. Typically, industrial and manual workers wore clothing that can be soiled or scrapped. The characteristic uniform has been and still is a light or navy blue shirt. Blue is also a popular color for coveralls. Blue is contrasted with the white dress shirt that has long been associated with

---

Why I Do This: Contractor
Barry Keene

When I got out of the army, I was looking for work, and I started working for a relative in the construction business. We started out doing excavation, things like that. I found that I liked working outside, and I liked seeing the "finished products" when a job was complete.

After a few years, though, I got out of contracting, and started working for a delivery company because it seemed as if it would be less stressful getting a steady paycheck. As it turned out, the paycheck end of things was less stressful, but other parts of the job turned out to be more stressful. I found that I had enjoyed being my own boss; I didn't enjoy having my schedule—and all aspects of my job, really—controlled by someone else.

Once you became a manager, at that job, you were often working 24/7.

So eventually I left that job (after fourteen years!) and opened my own construction company. We do mostly houses, additions, renovations. We've done a small spattering of commercial work. It's a small company; at our biggest, we've had three full-time employees.

I like it this way, though. I can subcontract larger jobs, and still have control over my time and life.

You might like this kind of job if you enjoy being outside, if you like working with your hands and seeing a finished product when you're done, and if you don't need someone else pushing you to get going. (You have to be a self-starter.)

You do have to deal with a lot of different types of people. You have a new "boss" (that is, client) on every job. So there's that; sometimes the clients aren't always agreeable. But 95 percent of the people you work with are easy to work with.

---

office workers. (The white dress shirt, for its part, is not nearly as universally equated with office work as it once was. Although some professions, including financial services, still maintain a more formal "white collar" style, many people who work in offices no longer adhere to that custom and dress in far more casual clothing.)

For many who fall under the category, there is great pride associated with being a blue collar worker—blue collar workers are seen as hard-working people who helped make the United States the country it is today. With very few exceptions, being a blue-collar worker is without stigma and increasingly well paid.

Despite the need, however, there is an increasing shortage of blue-collar workers. As more of the work done in the United States is office-based, and companies increasingly offer services and compete on "knowledge"

Why I Do This: Plumber
Cliff Irving

I am a master plumber, and I have my own business. If you're going to be a plumber, you can either be a journeyman, or a master. Journeymen cannot hire help; you can be in business for yourself, but you can't have anyone working for you. When you're a master plumber, you can hire employees, so the opportunity to create a bigger business (with more headaches and stress!) is there if you want it.

You need certification to be a plumber. Currently, it takes three years of apprenticeship and 300 hours of schooling to get certified as a journeyman by the state. To be a master plumber, you need an additional one year of apprenticeship, and 100 hours of school.

You can be an apprentice all your life, if that's what you want to do. Being an apprentice simply means that you are a working for a plumber.

I didn't set out to be a plumber; I wanted, originally, to be a carpenter. But when I went to vocational school, my grades were not the best, and so the teachers and guidance counselors put me in classes other than the ones I had picked for myself. One of those classes was plumbing and heating, and I loved it. My grades went up immediately; my father told me that plumbing was a good trade; and so I stuck with it. I graduated in 1976, and I've been a plumber ever since.

You might like this kind of work if you enjoy working with your hands and you have patience. You also have to enjoy being able to think ahead, and see in your mind what the finished product is going to look like. You might also like this kind of work if you enjoy helping people—almost all of the time, you're doing something that helps someone directly, and they're appreciative.

If you're going to make money at this kind of work, you have to be organized, and you have to have something of a head for business. It's hard, sometimes, when you're doing a job for a friend, or an elderly person, to charge them the fees that you should. And sometimes, you just don't. But if you need to make the business work, you have to have a certain discipline.

I'm in business for myself. That means that sometimes I have more work than I can handle. A lot of the work is emergency work; you have to be responsive, so you can't plan your days out as you might hope to. On the other hand, last year, I took six months off and walked the Appalachian Trail with my son. One of the benefits of working for yourself is that you can take that kind of time off without worrying about losing your job! There is a lot of flexibility, when you work for yourself. I didn't miss any of my kids' plays, or sports games; I was able to go to all of them. And that's huge.

(and outsource manufacturing jobs), there has been less interest among young people in pursuing blue-collar work.

According to a November 23, 2004, *Boston Globe* article titled "Looking for Mr. Goodwrench: Blue-collar jobs abound, but skilled workers are hard to find" by Kimberly Blanton, just 4 percent of high school graduates pursue careers in technical fields, whether auto or boat mechanic, plumber, heating and air-conditioning technician, or factory worker. In the article, Blanton reported that: "Mechanically minded young people are instead pushed by parents and guidance counselors to attend college or are pulled by the high-technology industry into a cutting-edge field."

Joe Lamacchia, a Newton, Massachusetts-based landscaping entrepreneur, was quoted in the article as saying, "If they don't go to college and don't work in a cubicle," they think "they're not going to make it." Lamacchia's website, www.bluecollarandproudofit.com promotes employment in the trades. Young adults ill-suited to working in an office environment at a desk, Lamacchia said, pass up opportunities to make good money in challenging blue-collar jobs.

The *Globe* article goes on to cite the National Center on Education and the Economy, a Washington, D.C.-based organization that studies worker training, as reporting that at least one million U.S. jobs, most of which do not require a four-year degree, went unfilled in 2004 because employers could not find workers with the necessary skills.

See also: White Collar.

Further Reading

"Blue-Collar Work Helps City See Green," an editorial published Wednesday, August 29, 2007 in the *Seattle Times*, www.seattletimes.nwsource.com.

"Blue-Collar Work Buoyed by Boom in the Economy" by John Rather, published March 29, 1998 in the *New York Times*, www.nytimes.com.

Limbo: Blue-Collar Roots, White-Collar Dreams, by Alfred Lubrano, Wiley (2003).

"Reactions to Blue-Collar Work: A Comparison of Women and Men" by Karyn A. Loscocco, State University of New York, Albany, published 1990 in *Work and Occupations*, Vol. 17, No. 2, by SAGE Publications: wox.sagepub.com/cgi/content/abstract/17/2/152.

Work and Occupations, Vol. 17, No. 2, 152–177 (1990).

www.bluecollarandproudofit.com

Bonus

Bonuses are something an employer gives to an employee, generally on an annual basis, above and beyond the employee's agreed-upon compensation. A bonus is usually cash, but can also take the form of stock, gifts such as a turkey or a ham during the holidays, a gift certificate to a local store or restaurant or, on a larger scale, a trip.

Bonuses have been the "norm" in the world of work for a long time. Recall Charles Dickens' famous *Christmas Story*, in which the ever-stingy Ebenezer Scrooge (after much angst) finally finds his heart and bestows a wonderful holiday bonus of food and goods on long-suffering employee Bob Cratchitt and his family, including the small, frail son, Tiny Tim. As it was at that time, bonuses were outright gifts, given annually by employers as a way of saying "thank you" for a year's worth of effort. But increasingly, it seems that companies are shying away from such annual gift-giving, and instead, tying employee bonuses directly to performance.

According to an article entitled "The Vanishing Holiday Bonus," by Marilyn Gardner, published in the *Christian Science Monitor* on November 27, 2006, increasing numbers of companies are choosing not to bestow regular annual "holiday" bonuses.

Brian Drum, president of Drum Associates in New York, was quoted in that article, saying, "Thirty-five years ago, when I first dealt with a lot of companies that used to pay the so-called Christmas bonus, it was a gift. Today, as companies are becoming larger and consolidated, they are giving because it's performance-related."

Now, the article said, bonuses are increasingly linked to corporate performance. The article said that bonuses rose an estimated 10–15 percent in 2006 over 2005. "For top-tier bankers," the article said, bonuses "can swell to $20 million or more."

An article published on November 16, 2005, found on the website www.management-issues.com, concurs. This article, entitled "Performance-related pay replacing the annual bonus" says that variable pay programs (performance-based bonuses) are now offered by almost eight out of every ten employers. The article cited a global survey by the HR services firm, Hewitt Associates, to report that holiday bonuses are not as "traditional" as they once were.

According to *Fortune* magazine's list of the Best Companies to Work For in 2007, salaried employees at the David Weekley Homes company receive the biggest average annual cash bonuses. The average annual cash bonus there is $59,104. Employees at Paychex received the second biggest average annual cash bonuses, reporting in at $53,955.

See also: Executive Compensation; Performance Management/Performance Measurement

Further Reading

"Employee Incentive Systems: Why, and When, They are So Hard to Change," published May 31, 2006 in Knowledge@Wharton, http://knowledge.wharton.upenn.edu.
"Incentives Can Be Bad for Business," by Alfie Kohn, *Inc.* magazine (January 1998).
Performance Management: Key Strategies and Practical Guidelines, by Michael Armstrong, Kogan Page; 3rd Edition (March 2006).
"Why Incentive Plans Cannot Work," by Alfie Kohn, *Harvard Business Review* (September–October 1993).

Bootstrapping

There is an old phrase that says, "He raised himself up by his own bootstraps." Generally spoken with praise and respect, this phrase means that an individual is self-made. That is, the individual had little means but, based solely on his or her own will and determination, escaped poverty and excelled despite adversity and achieved success.

The same definition remains true for the term as it is used in the business world. According to BestforBusiness.com, bootstrapping means starting a new business without start-up capital and/or running that business on minimum expenditure. Another website, 1000Ventures.com, notes that bootstrapping "is characterized by high reliance on any internally generated retained earnings, credit cards, second mortgages, and customer advances."

That website, 1000Ventures.com, goes on to note that bootstrapping is the most likely source of initial equity for more than 90 percent of technology firms. It also noted that in the United States, venture capitalists often will not fund small start-up organizations "(seeking less than $5 million), regardless of the quality of the venture, because of their very specific investment criteria and high costs of due diligence, negotiating, and monitoring. Bootstrapping offers many advantages for entrepreneurs and is probably the best method to get an entrepreneurial firm operating and well positioned to seek equity capital from outside investors at a later time" (1000Ventures.com).

Bootstrapping can allow a company to put a toe in the market and assess demand without having an obligation to an outside funder. However, boostrapping can also mean taking on a great deal of personal risk.

The National Federation of Independent Business provides tips for bootstrapping your new business. The essentials include: having expertise in your field; taking on debt with great care; working out of your home to keep expenses down until cash flow warrants leasing an office; accepting that your customers will determine your schedule; always striving to be better than your competition in quality of service and customer care; and allowing yourself time for rest and rejuvenation.

Networking can also be a help to would-be bootstrappers. The local chamber of commerce, or local and national trade associations, can provide connections with more experienced and/or retired business owners who might be able to offer sound advice.

According to an article titled "Bootstrapping Your Startup" by David Worrell published in the October 2002 issue on Entrepreneur.com, "99.9 percent of business owners will struggle alone, pulling themselves up by their bootstraps."

The article also noted, however, that it's not necessary to "struggle alone" when you're bootstrapping. And it is possible to balance the risk of starting a business in this manner by doing careful research, and also possibly maintaining another job while the new business is in its infancy. As Worrell wrote, "At the concept stage, a business is like an egg that has not yet hatched—and the incubation process can be expensive. Doing research, making phone calls and buying supplies can eat through thousands of dollars before the business is really even born. Many entrepreneurs limit their risk and expense by keeping their day job and letting the idea percolate during evenings and weekends."

Worrell also wrote that some entrepreneurs take advantage of some of the resources of an established business. Bootstrapping in this sense resembles being "incubated" by a larger or more established business, while the new venture finds its footing. Contacts at another job, or at a previous job, can prove invaluable to the businessperson at the helm of a start-up. Sometimes the established business will provide space. Sometimes, the leader of the established business will provide use of equipment during "down time."

Would-be entrepreneurs beware, though: these activities should be known and condoned by the leaders of the established organization. And, as Worrell noted, "Not all employers will so generously support the moonlighting activities of employees. But keeping a steady income during the planning phases of a business is the best start to bootstrapping any new venture" (David Worrell, Entrepreneur.com).

See also: Entrepreneur; Networking; Skunkworks

Further Reading

"The Art of Bootstrapping" blog post by Guy Kawasaki, January 26, 2006, http://blog.guykawasaki.com.

Bootstrap: Lessons Learned Building a Successful Company from Scratch, by Kenneth L. Hess, S-Curve Press (September 2001).

The Boostrapper's Bible, by Seth Godin, Upstart Publishing Co. (1998).

"Bootstrapping Your Startup: No, You Don't Need Investors to Start Your Dream Business. Here's How to Make It Happen with Your Own Money," by David Worrell, *Entrepreneurs Start-Ups* magazine, October 2002, www.entrepreneur.com, or http://www.entrepreneur.com/money/financing/selffinancing/article55776.html.

"The Economy's Down and Investors are Wary: It's a Good Time to Launch Your Company," published January 17, 2001 in Knowledge@Wharton, http://knowledge.wharton.upenn.edu.

Boundaryless Organization

A "boundaryless organization" is one in which information and knowledge flows easily from department to department, and across multiple levels of management, resulting in a work environment where synergy is the norm. The term "boundaryless" should not, then, be taken literally. It does not imply an organization without form, or an organization that does business internationally; rather, the term refers to the way in which information flows through communication channels within a company.

The concept of Boundarylessness was developed at General Electric (GE) in the late 1980s and early 1990s, and it is one of the cultural elements General Electric credits for its phenomenal success over the last fifteen years. Proponents of boundarylessness believe traditional boundaries between layers of management (vertical boundaries) and divisions between functional areas (horizontal boundaries) have stifled the flow of information and ideas among employees. A boundaryless culture seeks to overcome the limitations imposed by these and other internal corporate divisions" (Sam Falk, *Organizational Evolution in a "Boundaryless" Organization*, submitted to the Alfred P. Sloan School of Management at the Massachusetts Institute of Technology, May 11, 2001).

Falk notes that Ron Ashkenas, Dave Ulrich, Todd Jick, and Steve Kerr are the primary authors writing about boundaryless organizations, in large part because they worked closely with General Electric as GE aspired to become a boundaryless organization. Their book on the topic, *The Boundaryless Organization*, was published by Jossey-Bass in October 1998.

Falk writes: "According to proponents of boundarylessness, for most of the twentieth century, size, role clarity, specialization, and control were among the crucial dimensions against which companies measured themselves to become successful . . . Boundaryless organization literature treats as true the notion that in the late 1980s and 1990s, the world's competitive landscape changed, and new dimensions defined corporate success or failure" (Sam Falk, *Organizational Evolution in a 'Boundaryless' Organization*, submitted to the Alfred P. Sloan School of Management at the Massachusetts Institute of Technology).

Jack Welch, chairman and CEO of General Electric between 1981 and 2001, believed that GE would be much more effective if the cultural, geographical and organizational barriers that separated the employees become more permeable, writes Allen Brown of The Open Group in his article "The Boundaryless Organization," which was published in December 2003 on financial-i.com. As Brown noted, Welch "put the emphasis on the boundaries' ability to enable business, rather than get in its way." Brown went on to say that "in the next era of the information age, we will expect to have information at our fingertips, all integrated to suit our specific needs, instantly available, across geographies, time zones and organization structures."

See also: Bricks and Clicks; Business-to-Business/Business-to-Consumer (B2B/B2C); Competitive Advantage; Offshoring

Further Reading

The Boundaryless Organization: Breaking the Chains of Organization Structure, revised and updated, by Ron Ashkenas, Dave Ulrich, Todd Jick, and Steve Kerr, Jossey-Bass (January 2002).

The Effective Global Workforce, published by Mercer Management Consulting, May 2007, www.mercer.com.

Brainstorming

Brainstorming refers to an informal exchange of ideas, designed to surface—among other things—innovative solutions to existing corporate challenges, new product concepts, and better processes or systems.

Interestingly enough, this deliberately informal exchange can often follow a very formal structure. Many companies schedule brainstorming sessions, in which they explicitly gather employees from different levels and different areas in an organization to share knowledge and feed off of each others' perspectives.

Often, brainstorming sessions take place in front of a white board, with one or more participants jotting down notes or pictures in an attempt to capture ideas and frame them accurately for further discussion. Sometimes, brainstorming can take the form of an e-mail round-robin of sorts.

According to the jpb.com website, developed by the JPB group, brainstorming can be an effective way to generate lots of ideas on specific issues and then determine which idea—or ideas—is the best solution. The site says: "Brainstorming is most effective with groups of 8–12 people and should be performed in a relaxed environment. If participants feel free to relax and joke around, they'll stretch their minds further and therefore produce creative ideas."

It goes on to advise that: "Creativity exercises, relaxing exercises, or other fun activities before the session can help participants relax their minds so that they will be more creative during the brainstorming session."

According to *MindTools*, a career-skills publication, the exact beginnings of brainstorming are not recorded. The publication states, "While the fundamentals of brainstorming have been put to use throughout history, a name wasn't exactly put to the process until Alex Osborn, a 1940s advertising executive, decided that the conventional methods of overcoming obstacles and creating new ideas were too inhibitive and weren't conducive to real creativity."

Effectivemeetings.com says brainstorming should be used to generate ideas during meetings: "When scheduling the meeting, be sure to include a brief explanation of the problem and its history. This will help participants prepare mentally for the session and focus on the particular issue. The more specific and focused a session, the better the results will be." This website goes on to note that brainstorming sessions are most effective when they're kept to a maximum time of forty minutes. It also notes that brainstorming sessions can be even more effective when participants know that there will be a follow-up meeting.

Erich Joachimsthaler, in his book, *Hidden in Plain Sight* (Harvard Business School Press, 2007) notes that the kind of innovations that cause competitors to say, "Why didn't I think of that!?" often stem from immersing oneself in the world of the consumer. The best brainstorming, then, doesn't necessarily even occur among corporate colleagues. In fact, it can occur when a company's employees talk with customers; the customer may not even be aware that he or she is "brainstorming."

Of course, brainstorming is only as valuable as a company's ability to follow through and implement promising new ideas, processes, and systems. As Rob Galford and Ann Drapeau noted in their book, *The Trusted Leader* (Free Press, 2002), when a company's leaders encourage brainstorming and actively solicit new ideas, and then fail to follow through, the result can be a drop in productivity and morale.

See also: Innovation

Further Reading

"Great Ideas: Brainstorming Sessions Your Staff Won't Dread," published in *Canadian Business Online*, April 26, 2007, www.canadianbusiness.com.

Instant Creativity: Simple Techniques to Ignite Innovation & Problem Solving, by Brian Glegg and Paul Birch, Kogan Page, New Ed edition (February 2007).

The Leader's Guide to Lateral Thinking Skills: Unlocking the Creativity and Innovation in You and Your Team, by Paul Sloane, Kogan Page, Second Edition (November 2006).

Branding

Strictly defined, a brand is a trademark or a name that explicitly identifies a product or a manufacturer. Branding, then, means to mark to show ownership or to publicize using a brand name.

But the term "brand" has long since left that narrow definition behind, and now encompasses a host of different meanings, chief among them being the "promise" that a product or service makes to the customer.

Brands set expectations. When a customer selects one brand over another, he or she is often basing their decision on an expectation that the product or service they are purchasing will deliver on one or more characteristics. Some brands are known for being less expensive than others. Some are known for delivering premium quality, often at premium prices. Some promise reliability; some promise fun, excitement, or a certain association of style.

Allen Adamson, managing director of preeminent strategic brand and design consultancy Landon Associates, talked to Business Management magazine (Issue 181) about his book *BrandSimple*:

> Although the activities involved in getting an organization on board with a brand idea may seem like an expensive proposition, consider the idiom "penny-wise and pound-foolish." The effort may cost you money upfront, but you'll make up for it ten times over as you build and manage your brand. The true value of understanding the meaning of your brand and getting your employees gainfully engaged will become obvious when you compare that cost to the cost of making up for employees who have no idea how to deliver the brand promise. (http://www.busmanagement.com / pastissue / article.asp?art=268772 &issue=181)

A brand is a key differentiator. Even if a product or service is not necessarily unique (think of coffee or water), branding seeks to ensure that potential customers pick up on a feature or point that sets it apart from competitors' offerings. Marketing consultant and author Sam Hill discussed this idea in depth in his article "How to Brand Sand" (CITE). While a brand may once have been simply a recognizable logo, the logo now cannot stand alone; it must stand for some concept, theory, lifestyle, price, or experience.

See also: Competitive Advantage; One-to-One Marketing; Relationship Marketing

Signs of Changing Culture:
Nonprofit Brands: Don't Waste Their Power

This article was reprinted with permission from Valuenewsnetwork.com. It originally appeared in the February/March 2006 edition of *Value: Tomorrow's Markets, Enterprise & Investment* magazine.

Is there a sea-change currently underway, in 2006, with regards to the way in which nonprofit organizations operate? Is the nonprofit world being shaken up? Re-invented? Re-invigorated? Could be all of the above? Consider this one perspective, on the brand equity some nonprofits hold, and what they could/should do with it.

Value recently had the opportunity to talk with John A. Quelch of the Harvard Business School about the value of nonprofit brands. Quelch is senior associate dean and Lincoln Filene Professor of Business Administration at HBS. Broadly speaking, his research focuses on global marketing and branding in emerging as well as developed markets. Research projects currently in the works focus on understanding the brand power of global nongovernmental organizations and on formalizing marketing and customer metrics that boards of directors can use to help them assess their organizations.

Professor Quelch is the author, co-author, or editor of twenty books, including *The New Global Brands* (2005), *Global Marketing Management* (5th ed., 2005), *The Global Market* (2004), *Cases in Advertising and Promotion Management* (4th ed., 1996), and *The Marketing Challenge of Europe 1992* (2nd ed., 1991). He has published over fifty articles on marketing and public policy issues in leading managerial journals such as *Harvard Business Review*, *McKinsey Quarterly*, and *Sloan Management Review*.

VALUE: What is it that managers of nonprofits are missing about the value of their brands?

QUELCH: Several things—and they're all interwoven in terms of their implications for how nonprofits think about and use their brands going forward. First, it's important to understand that nongovernmental organizations, or NGOs, that operate on a global scale have some of the most trusted brands in the world. (Let's get the definition clear at the outset. By NGOs, I mean both nonprofit associations trying to provide social services on a global scale, and nonprofit organizations that attempt to achieve economic changes on a global scale by influencing governments and corporations.)

When surveys are conducted that ask people to indicate their level of trust in these NGO brands, versus, say, for-profit brands such as major soft drinks or fast-food franchises, the nonprofits come out way ahead. This makes them extremely valuable.

The problem is, many large nonprofits don't realize the veritable gold mine they have at their fingertips, in terms of brand equity. But most for-profit companies have figured it out, and so they're eager to engage with the not-for-profits in alliances and in co-marketing efforts and the like.

The for-profits are thirsting for connections with strong nonprofit brands. The nonprofits are in large part ignorant of just how much those connections are worth. If nonprofits don't get up to speed on the value of their brands, they're going to shortchange themselves (and that's putting it mildly) in terms of the amount of money and other concessions they can expect or demand from a for-profit in a partnership arrangement.

VALUE: How is it that global nonprofits have created such strong brands? You seem to be implying, at the same time, that they don't know a great deal about branding . . .

QUELCH: The people running not-for-profits often don't know a lot about the depths of marketing research and the nuances of segmenting customers. They don't have the time or the resources to pursue that knowledge. And so, in many cases, they've chosen one brand name and stuck with it everywhere in the world. And guess what? In the global economy, that is the optimal solution.

These organizations have very strong brand names that are readily identifiable all over the world. Consider, by contrast, a company that uses the same formula, or essentially the same product, all around the world, yet markets that offering under a different name in every country, or region, thus diluting the equity.

What's more, the global not-for-profit brand names are backed by, or driven by, missions that people perceive as very important. Their nonprofit status gives them a substantial "trust halo." And all of those factors sustain and build their brand power, even given that their level of accountability and transparency is generally very weak relative to what's required in for-profit companies.

VALUE: There have been some very smart PR efforts . . .

QUELCH: Of course, in many cases nonprofits have done an excellent job of public relations. Take Greenpeace, for example, which has done some very thoughtful and well-received publicity. But that's a public-relations effort. It shouldn't be confused with a full understanding of brand valuation.

VALUE: The lack of marketing knowledge has been a double-edged sword for nonprofits . . .

QUELCH: They don't fully appreciate the magnitude of the advantage that they have. And in not appreciating it, they don't or won't leverage it effectively.

VALUE: What would be an example of a nonprofit effectively leveraging the value of its brand?

QUELCH: The first example that comes to mind is the partnership between the World Wildlife Federation and Lafarge (WWF), the Paris-based building-materials giant.

Now, Lafarge operates in some seventy-five countries, and it has a workforce of about 77,000 people, with, I believe, some 245,000 shareholders. And Lafarge and WWF have created a productive partnership, where WWF gets funding to support its research and communications, and Lafarge gets the benefit of the WWF brand affiliation. Now importantly, WWF also gets conservation, in the form of a performance agreement with Lafarge. The agreement includes certain milestones that Lafarge has committed to meeting and committed to being monitored on by an independent auditor.

That's a good example of a multipronged partnership, and I don't think it would be as equitable if WWF did not have a sense of the worth of its brand.

VALUE: That seems ideal. But there's a potential downside to nonprofit for-profit partnerships, of course.

QUELCH: Of course. And there are some NGOs that religiously continue to refuse all collaboration with the for-profit sector. Some believe that their core values and the perception of their integrity would be impugned if they were in collaboration with for-profits. Some fear the spillover effects if the for-profit partner were party to a scandal of any kind. Those are valid concerns.

VALUE: But then there are other NGOs, such as Habitat for Humanity or WWF, that see partnering with for-profits as a way to achieve scale in their work that they might not otherwise be able to do.

QUELCH: The NGOs that tend not to become involved with for-profit collaborations tend to be more advocacy-oriented. These are the NGOs that have strong positions in the marketplace of ideas. Amnesty International would be one, for example. But perhaps these organizations are being slightly too myopic. They're leaving on the table too much of an opportunity—the potential to scale up their activities in a significant way.

VALUE: Why is it important to understand the value of nonprofit brands now, as opposed to five years ago, or next year?

QUELCH: The root cause of the urgency to understand this issue now is the sea change in the way people perceive social and humanitarian challenges.

The size and scale of the challenges facing humanity are obviously very substantial. They're probably no more substantial than they have been, but today, with an increasingly global media, they are being understood and measured differently than they had been in the past.

Twenty years ago, you would hear about these problems in a very limited, contextual way. You'd hear "X number of people in a given country are suffering from this or that." You wouldn't hear about, say, the global HIV problem. You'd hear about it in slices.

Today, it's "normal" to hear about the global total number of people who suffer from a particular disease or are affected by a particular environmental danger. The problems are being articulated as global problems, and as a result, the magnitude of these problems is apparent. And the call is for global solutions.

VALUE: But the NGO marketplace, at the moment, is far too fragmented. The barriers to entry are very low. And as a result, there are a huge number of NGOs competing for resources and competing to deliver relief.

QUELCH: If this were the for-profit sector, there would be massive consolidation in order to extract scale efficiencies. But because it is not the for-profit sector, there are not obvious upsides to consolidations—say, in the form of stocks or options. Merger and acquisition activity in the nonprofit sector is motivated by the need for survival on the part of the acquired entity and the people employed by it, not a positive force for good.

Think about it, though. You can imagine that there are probably many organizations doing, say, malaria relief around the world. Imagine what you could do if you consolidated all of those efforts under one or a few organizations. Imagine the scale efficiencies, the caliber of management you could afford to hire, the management information systems that you could put in place to track the money, the control systems. At every level, consider the difference between a $10 billion corporation and a $500 million or $50 million corporation.

VALUE: Most of the biggest NGOs don't come close to that size.

QUELCH: Sure. Most of these big entities are still typically short of a billion dollars. And there on the for-profit side, you have Exxon Mobil tracking something like $400 billion.

But what people running NGOs have got to come to grips with is that for them to have an impact they do have to achieve scale. They don't need to hit $400 billion, clearly, but consider an order-of-magnitude difference of 200 to one.

And then consider that most dispassionate, objective observers would say that there's a better chance of me making a difference in the world by influencing Exxon Mobil than by worrying about working through a smaller organization, even if that organization's purpose is singularly oriented around a given mission. There's the penalty that fragmentation and independence and zero barriers to entry brings.

The NGO marketplace is extremely cluttered. And therefore—although it may sound crassly commercial to a lifetime not-forprofit executive—turning your brand into a mega brand is the way to break through the clutter.

VALUE: What would a practical action step be?

QUELCH: One step would be shifting the focus of the organization from the recipients of the service to the donors who fund the service. It's a radical concept, but think what could happen if NGOs viewed their donors as their customers and the recipients of their services as secondary.

Let me back up a bit. When you go into business, you face the reality of the marketplace. If customers do not value the additional brand or product, it's not going to be around that long. To use a very simplistic analogy, consider the number of ice cream flavors available or the number of shades of paint. Does the world need another variation on the theme? If not, it doesn't fly.

That marketplace reality doesn't come into play aggressively in the NGO arena. One reason is that a lot of these organizations limp along on relatively little money. They survive, but they don't thrive, and there are no shareholders to hold their feet to the fire. Another is that the "customer" in the nonprofit sector has never really been defined correctly.

VALUE: In the for-profit world, if I buy the ice cream or the paint, I'm going to consume it or use it (or at least know if it was received satisfactorily).

QUELCH: In the NGO world, it's harder to define the term "customer." The donors are not the recipients—so you have two very distinct customers. And of course most NGOs are set up to address the needs of recipients. But if you haven't got any money from donors, you aren't going to be able to deliver to recipients.

Consider another analogy: the television industry. Who is the customer of CBS? The customer is actually the advertiser, not the "end consumer."

People go into NGO work because they're motivated by the needs of recipients. But if we had a few more donor-motivated NGOs or donor-focused NGO leaders, think of the potential gains.

Of course the recipients would be there in the "customer mix," but if you were adding value to donors, you would automatically be taking into account the impact on recipients. The donor expects the organization to take care of the recipients. But the donor expects a host of other things—depending on who that donor is. Social standing, recognitions—there are all sorts of reasons people and organizations give beyond the obvious cause. If the organization marketed itself more to the donors, the potential upside is enormous. Recipients would, of course, benefit.

VALUE: You seem to want to make another point about NGOs surviving versus thriving.

QUELCH: Yes, and this is a digression because it's a comment directed at donors, but it's an important point. NGOs that merely survive tend to eat up a large proportion of the money that comes in to cover administrative expenses. That measure—how much money is used in administrative costs—is one of the standard benchmarks people use to determine which charity to give to.

But making the choice to donate based on an administrative cost rate can be a huge mistake. Better to consider—at least in equal proportions—the organization's approach to solving problems. A start-up organization might have a brilliant new idea, or new approach, but extremely high administrative costs because of its start-up status. It might be "surviving" because it needs the traction to take off, as opposed to "surviving" because it has little to offer.

Which, of course, opens up another avenue of inquiry for for-profit organizations considering the brand valuation of NGOs. Put the brand-valuation issue up against the value of the new idea or approach of a struggling "new" NGO with a relatively unknown brand . . .

Bricks and Clicks

Bricks and clicks is term used to describe a business strategy that integrates offline and online resources. It is also known as click-and-mortar or clicks and bricks. If your company has an online store, but your customers can return or exchange products at a physical location, that's one use of bricks and clicks. If your financial institution offers online banking in addition to live tellers at local branches, that's bricks and clicks as well.

Businesses that operate in the virtual world and the physical world simultaneously are not necessarily full participants in a bricks and clicks culture. If the distribution channels are not synchronized (or at least, if they do not appear seamless to customers), then bricks and clicks doesn't really apply. Many companies aspire to join the bricks and clicks culture. Increasingly, companies are learning to coordinate their efforts in both realms. But the process isn't easy—though it may be easier for new companies that open their businesses as bricks and clicks ventures from the get-go.

Anne Stuart, a former senior editor at *CIO Magazine*, writes in the March 15, 2000, issue in an article titled "Clicks & Bricks" that David S. Pottruck, president and co-CEO of San Francisco-based Charles Schwab & Co. coined the phrase. As the article notes,

Pottruck used the catchy phrase in a speech at an Internet conference in July 1999 as he described the discount brokerage's successful efforts to coordinate all its services so that customers can trade stock online, in person at its walk-in retail branches or by telephone, either using an automated touch-tone system or by talking to a call center representative. In his speech, Pottruck predicted that future business success will hinge not on pitting brick-and-mortar companies against online-only efforts, but in successfully integrating the two.

In her article, Stuart goes on to say that the term signals an important shift in the way in which business leaders approach strategy. The article described Sears' approach, where customers often use the company website to learn about products before visiting the physical store.

In the October 18, 2004, issue of U.S. News & World Report, an article titled "Bricks and clicks: New approaches blur the line between traditional classrooms and online learning," points out that many universities are integrating the bricks and clicks business model through online courses. "A further attraction of the bricks-and-clicks model is that it mitigates the need for more bricks."

As Joel Hartman, vice provost for information technologies and resources at the University of Central Florida, said in that article: "We estimate that we've avoided about $3.6 million in construction costs." The University of Central Florida integrates online instruction with classroom work, the article said, to get more mileage out of its space.

See also: Business-to-Business/Business-to-Consumer (B2B/B2C)

Further Reading

"Adding Bricks to Clicks: The Effects of Store Openings on Sales through Direct Channels," by Jill Avery, Mary Caravella, John Deighton, and Thomas Steenburgh, published February 2007 by *Harvard Business School Working Knowledge for Business Leaders*, http://hbswk.hbs.edu.

Bricks To Clicks: The Details of Retail, by Sucharita Mulpuru, Tamara Mendelsohn, and Carrie Johnson, April 5, 2007, http://blogs.forrester.com.

www.valuebasedmanagement.net/methods_bricks_clicks.html

**Signs of Changing Culture: Hobbies, Paid Work
Blend on Internet**

"*Virtual Piecework*: Trolling the Web for Free Labor,
Software Upstarts Are New Force" by Robert A. Guth

Noted in the *Wall Street Journal*, Monday, November 13, 2006, Page
1, Column 5

As more people "grow up" with the Internet as second-nature, it's
no surprise that web-based businesses are on the rise. Weaker ventures,
and fad businesses may flame out, but behind them will come another
wave, and some will have staying power. In this article, author Robert
A. Guth writes about Zimbra—an e-mail program that he notes may
threaten established giants in the industry. As Guth states, Zimbra's core
is made up of "a virtual army of software hobbyists who collaborate online to create free programs. Like bloggers and YouTube addicts, they
hang out on the Web at all hours, largely for no pay."

Guth goes on to say that start-up companies "are helping themselves
to this software, piecing it together like Lego blocks into new commercial products. Often, they post the products' underlying code on the
Web and tap more volunteers to help improve it. Then they sell the software online, saving the cost of a large sales force."

Zimbra Inc., the article noted, employed just fifty-five people at the
time the article was written. And co-founder Staish Dharmaraj runs the
place "from a tiny cubicle with a laptop."

Budget

A budget is a financial plan that seeks to establish the financial parameters
of a business. How much can the business invest in capital expenditures?
How much can it afford to pay in salaries? How much can investors expect
to receive in return? The answers to these questions all hinge on a company's budget—and on leaders' ability to create a viable budget for the
business.

According to the U.S. Small Business Administration's (SBA) website,
the three main elements of a budget are sales revenue, total costs, and

profit. "Sales are the cornerstone of a budget. It is crucial to estimate anticipated sales as accurately as possible. Base estimates on actual past sales figures. Once you target sales, you can calculate the related expenses necessary to achieve your goals." The website goes on to report,

> Total costs include fixed and variable costs. Estimating costs is complicated because you must identify which costs will change and by how much and which costs will remain unchanged. You also must consider inflation and rising prices when applicable. Variable costs are those that vary directly with sales. One example is the purchase cost of inventory. The more inventory you sell, the higher your purchasing costs; the less you sell, the lower your purchasing costs. . . . Fixed costs are those that do not change, regardless of the sales volume. Rent is considered a fixed cost. . . . Semi-variable such as salaries, wages, and telephone expenses, have both variable and fixed components. For budgeting purposes, you may need to break semi-variable costs into these two components. The fixed element represents the minimum cost of supplying a good or service. The variable element is that portion of the cost influenced by changes in activity.

As the SBA notes, a budget is only as good as the accuracy and relevance of the information used to create it.

Effective budgets are often not static. The ebbs and flows of demand in the marketplace can demand that a budget be adjusted. The better able a company is to adjust its budget to accommodate upswings or downswings in demand for a product or service, the more likely the company will be to excel in good times and survive in bad times.

An effective budget, then, is responsive. It also is set up to allow managers to identify, for example, the specific reason for a shortfall in profits. By contrast, it allows managers to pinpoint potential growth areas.

In that spirit, Business Link (http://www.businesslink.gov.uk) advises reviewing your budget regularly. According to the site, "This is particularly true if your business is growing and you are planning to move into new areas. Using up-to-date budgets enables you to be flexible, and lets you manage your cash flow and identify what needs to be achieved in the next budgeting period."

See also: Competitive Advantage; Scenario Planning

Further Reading

"Adding Time to Activity-Based Costing," a Q&A with Robert S. Kaplan by Sarah Jane Gilbert, April 11, 2007 by *Harvard Business School Working Knowledge for Business Leaders,* http://hbswk.hbs.edu.

"Breaking Free from Budgets: Exasperated by Budgets that Hamstring Creativity, a Growing Number of Companies are Tossing Off Financial Constraints— and Still Holding the Line on Spending," by Suzanne McGee, *Inc.* magazine, October 2003, www.inc.com.

"Gimme Some Money," by Hannah Clark, published in *Inc.Com* (September 17, 2007).

Business-to-Business/Business-to-Consumer (B2B/B2C)

As of this writing the year is 2007 and the Internet is far from new. Yet, as time goes on, more businesses are "discovering" web-based or facilitated distribution channels than ever before, and more individuals are finding new levels of efficiency and ease in purchasing goods and services online, from hotel reservations to airline tickets to clothes, electronics, sporting goods, financial services—you name it.

E-commerce refers to all online transactions. But under that umbrella are two sub-categories. The first, B2C, stands for "business-to-consumer" and essentially means businesses selling to non-commercial end users, or retailing, electronic-style. The second, B2B, stands for "business-to-business" and essentially means online transactions between two or more companies.

Business-to-business websites allow businesses to deal directly with their suppliers and distributors online, according to A-K Strategic Business Solutions (www.akstrategic.com). Business-to-consumer websites link customers to suppliers. Some of the major B2C websites include eBay, an online auction site, and ZDNet, a technology marketplace.

Amazon.com, another major B2C site, had roots in online book sales, but has expanded to offer a wide range of products and also facilitates purchases with other retailers. These businesses exist primarily on the Internet and offices and warehousing are born from the necessity of their Internet success.

According to an article in *CIO Magazine,* compiled by Susannah Patton, and published March 6, 2007, "B2C e-commerce went through some tough times, particularly after the technology-heavy NASDAQ crumbled in 2000. In the ensuing dotcom carnage, hundreds of e-commerce sites shut their virtual doors and some experts predicted years of struggle for online retail ventures. Since then, however, shoppers have continued to flock to the web in increasing numbers" (*CIO Magazine*, "The ABCs of E-commerce" http://www.cio.com).

A B2B site primarily deals with other businesses, not the general public. B2B sites are a portal to conduct business transactions that are usually more complex and have higher security needs. Business-to-business customers are other companies while B2C customers are individuals. The first B2B applications were for buying finished goods or commodities that are simple to describe and price, according to *CIO Magazine*.

As the *CIO* article put it, "B2B e-commerce can save or make your company money. Some ways companies have benefited from B2B e-commerce include: managing inventory more efficiently, adjusting more quickly to customer demand, getting products to market faster, cutting the cost of paperwork, reigning in rogue purchases and obtaining lower prices on some supplies."

In his blog, Internet Marketing B2B B2C ("Marketing Comparisons for the Twenty-First Century" published September 29, 2004), James A. Warholic writes that B2B requires a commitment of time and good customer service prior to ever making the first sale.

Warholic notes, "Most B2C customers are looking for the best price possible with a commitment of good customer service . . . When it comes to purchasing a consumer product, I do extensive research online to check the specifications on a product and price from online sources. If that product is displayed on a website from a company with also a brick and mortar outlet, I am most likely to buy it locally, even if the price is slightly higher. If not found locally then I would look for the best price online checking their return policy and customer service feedback information."

Warholic's comments raise another B2C issue, albeit indirectly. As of this writing, although many major retailers have created successful online sites, many others still struggle with website design, and the right alignment between their online and bricks-and-mortar venues. The distribution channels for each stream of business can differ in significant ways, and it can be difficult for a company to offer customers a seamless experience across those channels.

See also: Branding, Bricks and Clicks; One-to-One Marketing; Relationship Marketing

Further Reading

"Top Tech Execs: Keith Krach," by Lisa DiCarlo, *Forbes.com* (December 7, 2000), www.forbes.com.
www.ecommercetimes.com
www.managementhelp.org

Cafeteria Benefit

A cafeteria benefit is a particular employee benefit selected from a company plan offering a variety of choices to suit individual needs. Just as a cafeteria offers a variety of foods, allowing patrons to assemble meals that suit their own tastes, the term, "cafeteria benefits" or "cafeteria plans"—also known as Section 125 plans—describes a system that allows employees to select from a range of offerings to assemble the benefits package that they feel best suits their needs.

Put another way, according to Barron's Education Series, Inc., a cafeteria benefit plan is an arrangement under which employees may choose their own employee benefit structure. "For example, one employee may wish to emphasize health care and thus would select a more comprehensive health insurance plan for the allocation of premiums, while another employee may wish to emphasize retirement and thus allocate more of the premiums to the purchase of pension benefits."

Proponents of cafeteria benefits believe that the approach allows companies to offer their employees benefits that are more tailored to their needs. Another school of thought, however, holds that cafeteria benefits allow employers to pass along more of the cost of providing benefits to their workers.

In a 2001 article that ran in the *Journal of Accountancy,* John G. Simmons, writes that "Cafeteria plans under IRC section 125 and non-125 flexible benefit plans can help small employers provide necessary benefits in a way that helps mitigate rising costs."

A 2002 article on GovExec.com, a daily news service of *Government Executive* magazine discusses mixed feelings on cafeteria plans. In 2002, a House subcommittee chairman pushed the idea of cafeteria-style benefits for federal employees. But the proposal also drew concern from labor leaders. Dan Weldon, R-Fla., chairman of the House Government Reform Subcommittee on Civil Service, Census and Agency Organization, was quoted in the article as saying that the U.S. government has to compete for talented employees with companies that offer cafeteria plans. But the article also said that Derrick Thomas, national vice president of the American Federation of Government Employees' 2nd District, told the subcommittee that cafeteria plans "would make health care unaffordable for a large number of federal employees because they put responsibility for paying benefits onto the employee instead of where they belong, on the employer."

"Cafeteria plans are deceptive," Thomas was quoted as saying. "The plans force employees into 'either-or' decisions between benefits that should be provided universally."

According to Freedombenefits.org, though, cafeteria benefit plans are an effective way for a small business "to customize its benefits for maximum tax savings and appeal to employees."

Generally, very small businesses, or businesses without salaried employees, will not find cafeteria plans suitable. But for those that do, the range of benefits includes health insurance, medical savings accounts, education expenses, disability insurance, and life insurance. Employees who participate can often contribute toward aspects of the plan (such as child care) on a pre-tax basis.

See also: American Federation of Labor and Congress of Industrial Organizations (AFL-CIO)

Further Reading

www.entrepreneur.com/humanresources/compensationandbenefits
www.govexec.com

**Signs of Changing Culture:
Pension Plan Safety Net Has Holes**

In February 2007, Hewlett-Packard announced it would be phasing out its pension plan for new employees and replacing it with a 401(k).

As the *Wall Street Journal* reported in an article by Lee Gomes published Wednesday, March 14, 2007 (page B1), time was, large, established technology companies offered generous pensions and a host of other gifts to employees upon retirement. But, as the article says, even "the old-guard tech companies, the last bastions of traditional pensions, finally have joined their younger counterparts in the New Economy."

As the article says, "Many of today's retirees wonder whether their children or grandchildren will do as well as they did after their careers end." The article goes on to note, "while it's possible to do perfectly well with [a 401(k)], more often than not, that doesn't happen." The article says that according to Andrew Eschtruth, of the Center for Retirement Research at Boston College, "Figures from the Federal Reserve . . . show that the average 401(k) balance for heads of household between ages 55 and 64 is just $60,000, not nearly enough to retire on.

Carnegie, Dale/*How to Win Friends and Influence People*

Dale Carnegie's philosophy of presentation and his belief in the ability of individuals to improve their situations and positions in life and work influenced millions of people in the world of work. His book, *How to Win Friends and Influence People,* was first published in 1936, sold over thirty million copies and remains popular today. (He also wrote a biography of Abraham Lincoln, called *Lincoln the Unknown.*)

Carnegie developed a self-improvement program called The Dale Carnegie Course. According to the DaleCarnegie.com website, which features information on the training program, Dale Carnegie Training has "evolved from one man's belief in the power of self-improvement to a performance-based training company with offices worldwide."

In an obituary published in the *New York Times* on November 2, 1955, Carnegie is described as "one of the world's most phenomenal bestsellers." The obit said that Carnegie "was born in poverty on a Missouri farm, but found that a silver tongue could be more useful than a silver spoon in winning wealth and fame."

Carnegie turned that insight into a business and a wildly successful career teaching people the art of public speaking and the art of communicating effectively in the work environment.

According to the obit, a review of Carnegie's book, published in the *New York Times* on February 14, 1937, "said in effect that Mr. Carnegie's prescription for success was to smile and be friendly, not to argue or find fault and never to tell another person he was wrong."

See also: Training and Development

Further Reading

www.DaleCarnegie.com

Casual Friday

Casual Friday is an American and Canadian business custom where some offices celebrate a reprieve from the formal dress code. Instead of wearing business shirts, suits, ties, and dress shoes, workers are allowed to dress down and wear casual clothes such as jeans, T-shirts and sneakers. Casual dressing at work was initially a Friday-only occasion, but more and more companies have adopted 'business casual' attire standards for their offices. Of course, business casual can also mean different things office to office, and business to business.

As the *Wall Street Journal* notes, in the article "Business Attire: The Office Coverup" (August 5, 2006), dressing casually at work, as a recognized trend, began in the early 1990s. The article cites the Pittsburgh-based aluminum company, Alcoa, as one of the early proponents. Alcoa, it seems, let employees dress in casual clothes for two weeks in 1991 if the employees donated to the United Way charity.

Many employees followed suit, and began explicitly allowing employees to dress more casually than they typically would on Fridays. But the turn of the century has seen a polarization of the trend, with some employers encouraging employees to dress down all the time, and others explicitly requiring employees to meet a certain standard of dress at work.

The *Wall Street Journal* article noted that Lehman Brothers and Bear Stearns are among the companies to institute a business dress code. It also cited a survey of 1,400 companies by Mercer Human Resources Consulting, which found that in 2006, "some 84 percent of companies with 2,000 employees or more have a business-casual dress code, up from 79 percent two years ago." Joe Vocino, a senior consultant with Mercer, was quoted in the article as saying that "the point of these policies is not so much to encourage business casual but rather to define the limits of what can be worn."

Companies can often be grouped by industry when it comes to expectations of the kinds of clothes employees should wear. Some interpret "Casual Friday" as wearing jeans; others expect that employees who are dressing down will still appear in suits, though possibly leaving the jackets at home. Often, the way in which a company's employees dress contributes to the company's brand (*see* **Branding**). If an employee is dressed more formally, for example, the company may be trying to show customers that it can be relied upon with sensitive client information. It's no wonder, then, that law firms and financial service firms generally have a more formal dress code than do many other types of businesses.

See also: *Dilbert*; Flex-Time; Generation X, Y, and Z

Further Reading

Survey by Emily Post.com Surveys, Monday September 17, 2007, "Many businesses today have a 'Dress Down Friday' policy. Do you think this is a good idea?" www.emilypost.com/surveys.

Signs of Changing Culture: The Working Lifestyle

This makes "Casual Fridays" seem, well, obsolete:

> I'm sitting on a heated toilet in my pajamas. I'm in engineering building forty at Google on 'pajama day,' and directly in front of me, attached to the inside door of the toilet stall, is a one-page flier, printed on plain white paper, titled "Testing on the Toilet, Episode 21." The document . . . explores such subjects as 'lode coverage' and reminds engineers that even biobreaks need not interrupt their work.

The quote is from an article entitled "Search and Enjoy," by Adam Lashinsky, published in *Fortune Magazine*, January 22, 2007 (Volume 155, No. 1, page 70). The piece is all about working at Google, which is rated first on the list of *Fortune* 100 Best Companies to Work for 2007.

The article talks about how the Google "campus" is like college—how employees can do their laundry at work, or work out at a gym, or study a foreign language (just to name a few of the benefits). It also talks about how good the food is at the company's eleven free gourmet cafeterias.

And, it talks about how hard employees work, though, and how deeply engaged they are with that work—and with the company. Of course, the article also goes on to ask: "Is Google a great place to work because its stock is at $483, or is its stock at $483 because it's a great place to work?"

Time will tell.

Change Agent/Change Management

Getting an organization to "change" its practices, processes, or culture to meet fluctuations in the market, or keep up with new technologies or customer demands, is incredibly difficult. It can be especially challenging when an organization is large and established. "But we've always done things this way," is a common response when confronted with change, and one that's hard to overcome.

Nonetheless, change is necessary for survival in today's marketplace. Companies that can't adapt often don't last. What's needed are effective change agents (people who spearhead and lead change efforts) and effective change management (the approach by which the organization's leaders build consensus among employees to change, guide employees through the change, and ensure that the new processes and practices stick).

According to isixsigma.com on March 13, 2003, by Manoj Bhardwaj, "A change agent is a person who leads a change project or business-wide initiative by defining, researching, planning, building business support, and carefully selecting volunteers to be a part of a change team. Change agents must have the conviction to state the facts based on data, even if the consequences are associated with unpleasantness."

And according to a definition posted on October 13, 2006, on Whatis .com's Target Search (http://whatis.techtarget.com/definition/0,,sid9 _gci799426,00.html), change management is "a systematic approach to dealing with change, both from the perspective of an organization and on the individual level." This definition goes on to say that "change management has at least three different aspects, including: adapting to change, controlling change, and effecting change. A proactive approach to dealing with change is at the core of all three aspects. For an organization, change management means defining and implementing procedures and/or technologies to deal with changes in the business environment and to profit from changing opportunities."

Change agents are often company leaders—top executives or senior managers. But the definition of change agent is sometimes broadened to include individuals or forces outside of an organization. For example, in an article published in the *Journal of American Medical Association* on February 13, 2002 (*JAMA* 2002; 287:776), journalists are noted as change agents in medicine and health care. "In some cases, investigative reporters have exposed aspects of medicine and medical science that prompted legislative and policy changes in the health care system."

The article went on to say that, "Investigative reporters often rely heavily on anonymous sources who might jeopardize their careers for leaking damning information These "whistleblowers" also risk being sued once they trust a journalist with sensitive information about their organizations. Journalists can risk exposing their confident sources when they attempt to substantiate claims by speaking with people who oppose or disagree with the whistleblower."

See also: Benchmarking; Core Competencies

Further Reading

Change Masters, by Rosabeth Moss Kanter, Simon and Schuster (1983).
Leading Change, by John P. Kotter, Harvard Business School Press (1996).
"10 Principles of Change Management: Tools and Techniques to Help Companies Transform Quickly," by John Jones, DeAnne Aguirre, and Matthew Calderone, *Strategy+Business*, published by Booz, Allen and Hamilton (April 25, 2004), www.strategy-business.com.

Code of Ethics

A Code of Ethics is a set of rules governing the behavior of members of an organization. Most companies are explicit about these codes; setting standards for employee behavior and integrity makes it clear where the company stands and what constitutes "crossing the line."

Sometimes, a code is set not by an individual company, but by an industry. For example, the Society of Professional Journalists has a code of ethics that is voluntarily embraced by thousands of writers, editors, and other news professionals. The preamble of the Society of Professional Journalists Code of Ethics state that

members of the Society of Professional Journalists believe that public enlightenment is the forerunner of justice and the foundation of democracy. The duty of the journalist is to further those ends by seeking truth and providing a fair and comprehensive account of events and issues. Conscientious journalists from all media and specialties strive to serve the public with thoroughness and honesty. Professional integrity is the cornerstone of a journalist's credibility. Members of the

Society share a dedication to ethical behavior and adopt this code to declare the Society's principles and standards of practice (www.spj.org).

But many corporations have their own Code of Ethics that is specific not only to industry standards but to its particular context and culture. For example, the *New York Times* states in its New York Times Company Journalism Ethics Policy that the core purpose of the New York Times Company is to "enhance society by creating, collecting and distributing high-quality news, information and entertainment. The central place of our news and editorial units in fulfilling that promise is underscored by the No. 1 statement in our Core Values: Content of the highest quality and integrity: This is the basis for our reputation and the means by which we fulfill the public trust and our customers' expectations."

The Times' code goes on to stipulate expectations that include how journalists should cover the news with impartiality, and how all employees should treat sources, customers, and advertisers.

Some codes of ethics are created in-house, written by top managers who want employees to understand how they see the company fitting into the world of work. Often, such codes reflect the wording in the corporate mission statement; they can be very general. Other times, a code is very formal, prescribing specific standards and expected behaviors for a range of situations.

The National Association of Social Workers code of ethics, for example, was approved by the 1996 NASW Delegate Assembly and revised by the 1999 NASW Delegate Assembly. According to the organization's website, the code has four sections, covering broad issues, such as the core values of the profession, and specific standards to "guide social workers' conduct and to provide a basis for adjudication."

While a company may have articulated a Code of Ethics, the ethics of the organization are played out on a daily basis by the people who work for the company. The Code of Ethics may be written in black and white, but the reality is that many employees are faced with shades of gray in their decision-making. One "back-of-the envelope" ethics test is euphemistically called the "*Wall Street Journal* test," i.e., if you wouldn't feel comfortable with your actions published on the cover of the *Wall Street Journal*, don't undertake them.

See also: Enron

Further Reading

Harvard Business Review on Corporate Ethics, Joseph L. Badaracco, Harvard Business School Press, Harvard Business Review Paperback Series (July 2003).
www.amanet.org (American Management Association)
www.ethicsweb.ca/codes
www.socialworkers.org/pubs/code

Competitive Advantage

What companies sell the same types of products as your company? Which firms offer the same types of services? How can you differentiate your company from the pack, and what will establish your company as the "one to pick" in the eyes of the consumer?

Answer all of those questions and the perennial puzzle of competitive advantage will have been cracked. Competitive advantage, reduced to its essentials, means the "edge" that one company has in the marketplace that enables it to outperform other companies.

Maybe a company's edge is the quality of its customer service. Maybe it is the ability to gather and garner talent to respond to clients faster and more effectively than the next company. Maybe it's the ability to get products to market faster. Maybe it's being able to produce products at lower cost. Maybe it's the ability to position your brand as a premium offering and command higher prices. Whatever it is, the ability to find it, develop it, and use it to its potential is the key to excelling in business.

Competitive advantage is a holy grail of sorts in business today, and as such, it is studied exhaustively by industry and academia alike. Michael Porter is the leader of the Institute for Strategy and Competitiveness at Harvard Business School. He is also considered a leading—if not the leading—authority on competitive advantage, competitive strategy and the competitiveness and economic development of nations, states, and regions. Key components of Porter's work include undertaking an analysis of the competitive structure of an industry and then employing a competitive strategy leveraging a firm's competitive advantage in the industry. He offers three generic strategies: overall cost leadership, differentiation, and focus.

Beyond Porter, as noted above, competitive advantage has the attention of many other consultants and academics—and even this is a gross under-

---

Why I Do This: Independent Marketing Consultant
Andrea Harris

I'm the owner of a one-person marketing firm that helps professional services businesses and authors promote their services and books. In a typical week you might find me creating a plan for a business's new e-mail newsletter, making recommendations for an overhaul of their website, determining how to get them more targeted web traffic, rewriting their articles, and getting those articles placed on websites that their potential customers read. Because this is my own business, I don't think of it as just a job. I got started in the business after a dozen years in high-tech marketing communications. I took a year off, then started taking on freelance writing and web projects, and it grew from there. Now I've got enough work that I'm outsourcing some of the web development and administrative work to other freelancers. I generally work with the same clients from month to month, but occasionally take on new ones.

I like the freedom of deciding what kind of work I want to do—which usually means something new and interesting. When client work becomes repetitive I can often delegate it to another freelancer. If a potential client seems like they might be difficult to work with, I don't have to accept the work—I have no boss telling me what to do! Sometimes the work requires learning something challenging and potentially scary—like the first time I created a business blog for a client. I had no idea what I was doing, but I figured it out and have gone on to create them for other clients. That willingness to take a risk and do something outside your comfort zone is tough at first, but worth it in the end because it makes you grow. It's a great business for someone who can think creatively, juggle many projects, and is willing to stretch a bit and learn new things.

---

statement. Much of the literature on the subject shares common themes; much of it is rooted in or at least influenced by Porter's work.

Finding and developing a competitive advantage to its potential is devilishly difficult. Layers of management can disguise or dilute a potential competitive advantage in larger companies. In smaller companies, the ability to sustain an advantage can be a huge challenge. But consider what Jack Welch had to say on the subject. In an article on postcresent.com posted on December 10, 2006, for Fox Valley Inc., titled "Identifying, trumpeting a competitive advantage," Judy Waggoner writes: "Business guru Jack Welch has offered this succinct advice: 'If you don't have a competitive advantage, don't compete.'"

See also: Competitive Intelligence; Performance Management/Performance Meausurement

Further Reading

Competitive Strategy: Creating and Sustaining Superior Performance, by Michael E. Porter, Free Press (1998/1985).
The Concept of Corporate Strategy, by Kenneth Andrews, 3rd ed., Dow Jones/ Richard D. Irwin (1987).
www.isc.hbs.edu (Institute for Strategy and Competitiveness at the Harvard Business School)

Competitive Intelligence

No company operates in a vacuum. In order to compete successfully, a company needs to understand not only its own product and existing customers, but also the way in which the company fits into the larger business landscape. Information concerning the company's current competitors, other companies that are rising stars, ways in which the industry is changing, how customer tastes gravitate toward a new technology and what new modes of doing business are present, all relate to competitive intelligence.

All of this information, and more, according InvestorWords.com, is and composes "competitive intelligence," or data gathered and used by a company for the purpose of learning about its competition in a given market.

There are any numbers of ways to gather competitive intelligence, among them: industry and analysts' reports, customer focus groups, news articles, academic research.

In an article for *Fast Company* magazine (Issue 14) published in March 1998 titled "Competitive Intelligence—Get Smart!," a panel of experts including consultant Leonard Fuld, researcher Marc Friedman, and consultant Tracy Scott provided advice ranging from doing research on the Internet to attending conferences and networking.

In the article, Friedman was quoted as saying "Sometimes I'm really amazed at what searching the Net can turn up. One of our product lines consists of antennae for air-traffic-control systems. I got a call from our people in Canada, who needed a country-by-country breakdown of up-grade plans for various airports. I knew nothing about air-traffic control at the time. So I got on the Net. I found a site for the International Civil Aviation Organization, which had lots of great data. I also found several research companies that had done reports."

However, Scott said that she makes it a point to separate secondary information, such as what you can learn on the Internet, from "human-source information: stuff that real people tell you." As Scott said, "I always look for 'star talent' and think about what the comings and goings of those people mean. I also love conference proceedings."

Regardless of how a business gathers information, what's equally important is figuring out which information is actually relevant to the business at hand, and how to use the information once it's been gathered.

In a June 9, 2005, article entitled "Competitive Intelligence: What you don't know can hurt you" written for ClickZ Network (www.clickz.com), Heidi Cohen, a principal in the consulting firm Riverside Marketing Strategies, writes that "True competitive intelligence requires understanding how diverse audiences perceive your company. These audiences include customers, prospects, suppliers, distributors, competitors, and financial markets. To keep abreast of market activity influencing your business, start by understanding how your company is viewed as a whole, as well as how your brands, products, pricing, and customer experience are seen."

Cohen recommends: "Monitor competitors by channel, assess competitors by brand or product line, understand how target consumers talk about your company and products, and track sites containing negative information about your company."

See also: Competitive Advantage; Core Competencies

Further Reading

"Competitive Intelligence—Get Smart!" by Gina Imperato, *Fast Company* magazine (March 1998).
Competitive Intelligence Programs: An Overview, by Yogesh Malhotra, PhD. (BRINT Institute, 1996), www.brint.com.
www.loyola.edu/dept/politics/ecintel.html

Core Competencies

If companies are successful it seems clear that these companies are good at something, that they are doing at least one thing right. It is less clear, however, if successful companies necessarily have to be good at everything they do. Can companies excel by focusing on the things they do well and outsourcing the rest?

A "core competency" is something that the company does well, by itself, using its own employees. Consider a bicycle company. Its core competency could be the design of the bicycles or it could be the way in which it sells and services the bicycles. If the design is the core competency, maybe the bicycle company should sell its product through another retailer and go beyond operating stores itself. If the competency is the customer service, and the design takes a back seat (so to speak), maybe the company should consider operating stores that sell a range of bicycles designed by others.

On another level, if a company does a great job at design and at customer service then it is possible that both are core competencies. But as the company grows, its HR department may be stressed to the limit, and unable to process payroll efficiently and accurately. At that point, payroll fails to be a core competency. Here is where two possibilities are considered; whether that company should invest in developing expertise in the area of payroll operations, or whether it should contract with a payroll company—a company for which payroll is a core competency

It should be noted that although many people refer to a core competency when talking about a company as a whole, core competencies exist within various departments in an organization as well. The aforementioned HR department, for example, might excel at attracting key talent to the organization. For that department, recruitment is a core competency, and the company would do well to continue to invest in sustaining that skill, but would do equally well not to personally invest as much in payroll.

An entry posted on September 19, 2003, on Whatis.com *Target Search* says that,

> a core competency is fundamental knowledge, ability, or expertise in a specific subject area or skill set. For example, an individual who becomes certified as Microsoft Certified Software Engineer is said to have core competency in certain Microsoft systems and networks. Companies with specific strengths in the marketplace, such as data storage or the development of accounting applications, can be said to have a core competency in that area. The core part of the term indicates that the individual has a strong basis from which to gain the additional competence to do a specific job or that a company has a strong basis from which to develop additional products.

How can a company determine which competencies to focus on and which competencies are really "core?" Often, the kinds of analysis that lead to identifying a competitive advantage (*see* **Competitive Advantage;**

Competitive Intelligence) will inform the answers. According to tutor2-u.net, "The starting point for analyzing core competencies is recognizing that a competition between businesses is as much a race for competence mastery as it is for market position and market power. Senior management cannot focus on all activities of a business and the competencies required to undertake them. So the goal is for management to focus attention on competencies that really affect competitive advantage."

C. K. Prahalad, professor of corporate strategy at the University of Michigan, and Gary Hamel, professor at the London Business School since 1983, and currently Visiting Professor of Strategic and International Management there, are generally credited with developing the concept of core competency. Both Prahalad and Hamel are known throughout the world of management for their work on strategy. They wrote a series of articles on core competency, published in *Harvard Business Review;* they also published a bestselling book entitled *Competing for the Future*, which explored the concept of core competencies in the context of identifying and sustaining competitive advantage.

Importantly, a core competency is about ability, and thus, not necessarily tied to any particular product or type of service. Think back to the hypothetical bicycle company. Maybe this company had great success with their 2006 design. However, if the success of that design is an anomaly (in the sense that the designs from 2005 and 2007 were not successful at all) it's possible that "design" is not a core competency. It's also possible that the company didn't recognize design as a core competency and, in failing to recognize this, made a huge mistake in terms of investing in and supporting that key element.

See also: Competitive Advantage

Further Reading

Competing for the Future, by Gary Hamel and C. K. Prahalad, Harvard Business School Press (1994).

Core Competency Based Strategy, by Andrew Campbell, and Kathleen Sommers-Luch, International Thompson Business Press (1997).

"Stick to the Core—or Go for More?," by Thomas J. Waite, *Harvard Business Review* (February 2002), pp. 31–41.

Strategic Management and Core Competencies: Theory and Applications, by Anders Drejer, Quorum Books (2002).

Corner Office

In the modern-day business environment where employees, from administrative support to management, are working in cubicles without doors or windows, the corner office is often considered a status symbol. In terms of the bricks-and-mortar work environment (*see* **Bricks and Clicks**), it generally refers to the office occupied by the top executive.

As one retired sales executive, interviewed for this work, said: "The 'corner office' means 'the boss.'" As another sales representative said, the term conjures up "mahogany row." Well appointed, the best seat in the house, corner offices in many corporations are literally just that: in the corner. They're often large, featuring big windows on two sides. This is the literal definition and the most commonly held perception. White-collar luxury, earned by virtue of holding the position where (to use another well-known phrase) "the buck stops."

But, as culture differs company to company, in some situations, the term "corner office" has come to mean arrogance and greed. As this thinking goes, it is one thing to have an office that offers the privacy and space that a top position in a company can demand. It's another to flaunt privileges when front-line employees, for example, clearly work under less-than-ideal circumstances.

"Corner office" isn't just a corporate phrase; it's often used to describe any leadership position and can also mean the governor's office. For example, according to an article in the *Boston Herald*, when Deval L. Patrick was sworn in as Massachusetts's 71st governor on Jan. 4, 2007, he asked "citizens to join a 'common cause' of social reform that will reach from the 'Corner Office to the corner of your block.'" ("Welcome to the Corner Office, Gov: Patrick Invokes Humble Start, Rich Heritage for Inaugural," by Casey Ross, in the *Boston Herald* on Jan. 5, 2007.)

If the corner office is so favorable then it would be beneficial to know how to get to this elusive place. Interestingly, according to an article in the *Wall Street Journal* published Sept. 9, 2006, for the Journal's Executive Career Site (CareerJournal.com) titled "Path to the Corner Office Often Starts at a State School" by Carol Hymowitz, "Getting to the corner office has more to do with leadership talent and a drive for success than it does with having an undergraduate degree from a prestigious university."

The article went on to say that "most CEOs of the biggest corporations

Why I Do This: Director, Account Management, Financial Services Firm
Kathleen Sullivan

It is my primary responsibility to act as an advocate for customers, to ensure that the needs of their company and participants in Stock Compensation programs are being met. One of my goals is to increase the number of households participating, and have those individuals take action within their brokerage account. To this end I need to leverage all of our resources to educate my day-to day-contacts, as well as their participants, on the benefits of having a brokerage account. I also need to make sure they are aware of the guidance and financial planning that is available to them at no charge. Another facet of my job is to see what other recordkeeping, administrative opportunities exist within the company and try to win over that business.

A typical day for me would include preparing agendas and facilitating weekly or bi-weekly calls. I also compile minutes and conduct the necessary follow up on any action items due. A day would also include responding to inquires and logging in all activity with any given client into our Customer Relationship Model tool (that's a corporate system we have in place to keep track of what we do and whether we're accomplishing what we think we should).

I might also be traveling to a client's location, running a quarterly or annual Business Service Review or planning session, and then possibly entertaining the client at a dinner.

I didn't seek this job per se, but I was working for this company in a different area, and then someone that I knew who worked in this division suggested that this job would be a good match for me.

It's a good job; I enjoy the feeling that I am running my own business. This kind of work is good for someone who likes having tangible goals and receiving a tremendous amount of support. The "everyday" also presents a variety of challenges and learning opportunities; it's never boring.

That might come as a surprise to some people. When you say "financial services," sometimes peoples' eyes glaze over. But every day is unique, with different problems, clients, contacts, and so forth to deal with. It's really a challenging yet rewarding role. The job provides many opportunities to improve your skills with respect to negotiating, presenting, listening, facilitating, and coordinating, just to name a few. And at the end of the day, what you're trying to do is help people (the clients) make their lives a little more secure.

You might like this job if you are organized and outgoing, if you're a good facilitator, and if you enjoy being out of your "comfort zone" at least part of the time. You have to be a good team player, and you also have to be able to say "No" to people (clients) sometimes, even when it is difficult to do so. You also have to be willing to face the wrath of a client even when the problem they face was completely out of your control. You are the face of the company and thus you have to take the hit as graciously as you can.

didn't attend Ivy League or other highly selective colleges. They went to state universities, big and small, or to less-known private colleges.

"Wal-Mart Stores CEO H. Lee Scott, for example, went to Pittsburg State University in Kansas, Intel CEO Paul Otellini to University of San Francisco, and Costco Wholesale CEO James Sinegal to San Diego City College."

The article said that what matters most is whether or not a person can spot opportunity and act upon it. The CEOs interviewed for the article said that among other things, they pursued areas they were interested in at college and built strong relationships with their professors.

It is possible that the path to the corner office is different for women than it is for men (*see* **Glass Ceiling**). In an article for CNN's career website posted on May 3, 2001, titled "How do they get there? How do they stay there? Women in the corner office," author Loretta W. Prencipe examined the issue, focusing at one point on the rise of Barbara Cooper to the position of CIO at Toyota Motor Sales. Prencipe wrote: "The senior-level IT professionals attending the IS Associates Spring 2001 meeting at UCLA seemed to be in awe of Toyota's Barbara Cooper. And it was impossible not to wonder how Cooper made it to the top of the tech hill at a Japanese auto manufacturer. What was it about Cooper that put her—and more important kept her—on the path to an executive?"

Cooper's response, quoted in the same article, was: "No matter what anyone says . . . to get to the top position requires a combination of dedicated mental bandwidth and plain, old fashioned time commitment to compete with the guys who possibly have a spouse who does not work."

See also: Executive Coach; Executive Compensation

Further Reading

The Ape in the Corner Office: Understanding the Workplace Beast in All of Us, by Richard Conniff, Crown Business (2005).

The Trusted Leader, by Robert M. Galford and Anne Seibold Drapeau, Free Press (2002).

Signs of Changing Culture:
Leadership Mindsets in the Twenty-First Century

Robert M. Galford is a managing partner of the Center for Executive Development in Boston. He divides his time between teaching executive education programs and working closely with senior executives at the world's leading professional and financial organizations on the issues that lie at the intersection of strategy and organization. He has taught executive programs at the Columbia University Graduate School of Business, the Kellogg Graduate School of Management, and most recently at Harvard University. Earlier in his career, Rob was executive vice president and chief people officer of Digitas, a marketing services firm based in Boston. He was also vice president of the MAC Group and its successor firm, Gemini Consulting. He is co-author of *The Trusted Advisor* and *The Trusted Leader*.

I have been struck, over the last twenty years or so, by how much more aware many corporate leaders have become of the influence they might wield in the world.

Years ago, many of the leaders I worked with, as a consultant, or coach, or colleague, seemed much more focused on the year's performance, their company's latest and next innovations, and their competitors.

They concentrated their efforts on improving, fostering, or controlling those things. They measured their own performance against . . . well, against what was easily and readily measurable.

They still do. But now add to their plates an increasingly urgent awareness of issues that take less tangible forms: the daily lives of the people they lead, and their company's place in the world. These issues take two forms. The first is economic; the second is behavioral demographic.

Economics

More and more, at least in the circles I move in, leaders have a heightened awareness of the potential legacies they are going to leave. They are connecting the dots between the decisions they make every day, and the energy (or stress) in their employees' eyes. They are connecting the dots between their decisions and the lives, communities, and nations beyond the boundaries of their companies.

What's causing this new level of awareness? Is it a "baby boomers nearing retirement" thing? In part. But a piece of it is also that we're just plain more aware of the world's issues now than ever before. Technology has made it possible for us to see more clearly how our actions—and the actions of corporations—potentially affect the world at large.

Another piece of it is that the people in leadership positions today just seem to be more aware of whose expectations are truly driving their actions. If they are realizing that the answer is "shareholders," or "the board," exclusively, and that they themselves have only a small say, that's raising a flag.

Frankly, another piece of it is that the media and the public at large are scrutinizing leaders' actions as never before. In the wake of the white-collar scandals we've seen since 2000, John Q Public is holding leaders accountable for their actions in a way we never have before. Our level of skepticism is higher, and as a result, our expectations are higher. We're not giving anyone the benefit of the doubt, these days.

That said, though, increasingly, it does seem as if leaders want to get more personal satisfaction out of leading their companies. And that's not a bad thing.

Let me be clear—it's also not narcissistic. By personal satisfaction, I don't mean personal wealth. Or power and recognition. I mean that I see increasing numbers of leaders who want to feel good about the work they are doing, both in terms of their company's vitality and growth, and in terms of the positive effect the work of the company is having on the individuals who are employed there, and beyond.

I'm speaking (writing) in broad terms, of course. I'm sure that a great many leaders still "live by the numbers" and find their greatest satisfaction in their ability to ply ever-greater monetary gains for shareholders, and in their ability to "score another victory in the marketplace."

We've only to look at the headlines in recent years to see, in very poor lights, leaders whose primary drivers have been their own wealth, at the expense of company, colleagues, and communities.

But I've met and worked with many leaders who while driven by performance-on-paper do not find that that's enough.

What does all this mean for the culture of companies in the United States? Unfortunately, there seems to remain a fairly substantive gap between those in the corner offices and the lives of people many levels down, in many companies. "Talking" green and social consciousness and work/family balance, and leadership legacy isn't "walking" those issues. The economic disparity between upper and lower levels has become such a substantial barrier that it is hard to envision how it will be overcome unless we accelerate the potential wealth-building opportunities that come with ownership of shares of a company's stock. While the relative amounts of the interests may always be sizeable, share ownership offers faster alignment than anything else we have out there.

Behavioral Demographics

The second factor is the behavioral demographic one. By this, I mean the job and career expectations of those in the younger-age part of the workforce. For these individuals, there is little memory of a time before some combination of laptops, cell phones, and the Internet. If one applies a definition of technology as everything that was invented after you were born, then cell phones and e-mail are not even technology for those individuals. They are merely a part of everyday life, in the same way that older individuals would hardly consider television to be technology. The behavioral demographic expectation of the younger-age workforce is as follows: "Things happen fast, there is lots to look at and choose from, there will always be more changes and choices, and it doesn't matter if one likes it or not, because it can and will change, and so can I."

Whether this is narcissistic is not the point. The point is that it is realistic. One can simply observe the behavioral shift in less than two years, where e-mail traffic diminishes and is substituted by instant messaging, "Facebook" messaging, or text messaging. This also plays out in job expectations as well, where there is well-documented evidence of the time that individuals expect or intend to remain in a particular job or with a particular firm. This is not a function of affluence or a good economy. It is a clear shift in what individuals expect or tolerate in their lives before making a change.

The leadership implications of the foregoing are clear. First, it says that how we attract new people to work for and follow us can rarely be based on the long-term promise. Next is that it forces leaders to be aware that the people working for them have a shorter "follower-attention span" and higher standards for what they will stick around for. The follower value proposition thus has shorter duration and greater expectations of satisfaction than before. Finally, it says that as leaders, there is no choice but to calibrate not just our expectations, but our interactions. We have to work more quickly to build and develop trust, and to talk about it as well. It requires being explicit about that as a priority. It can't just be done by behaving in a trustworthy fashion and expecting the same. Time won't allow it, and that part of the workforce won't engage as quickly if leaders don't talk about it as well.

Corporate Social Responsibility

There is a growing perception, shared by corporate leaders and employees at all levels of companies of all kinds, that in addition to pursuing their own marketplace success, businesses must also consider the impact they are having on the persons, community and environment in general in which they operate. Corporate social responsibility is more, these days, than "green" businesses, such as those that manufacture biodegrable goods using environmentally sound methods. It is a business's recognition of the responsibility it has to the world at large.

According to Mallen Baker, development director for *Business in the Community*, a movement in the UK of over 700 companies committed to improving their positive impact on society, corporate social responsibility is about how companies manage the business processes to produce an overall positive impact on society, as he states on his website mallenbaker.net.

That same general definition is widely accepted in the corporate world, with tweaks here and there, either broadening or tightening the realm of responsibility. The World Business Council for Sustainable Development, in its publication *Making Good Business Sense* used the following definition by Lord Holme and Richard Watts: "Corporate Social Responsibility is the continuing commitment by business to behave ethically and contribute to economic development while improving the quality of life of the workforce and their families as well as the local community at large."

The idea (and the actions) surrounding the concept of corporate social responsibility does not reside within the walls of individual organizations; the issue in 2007 is on the global business and political radar as it never has been before. As Baker wrote in an article titled "Standards of Corporate Responsibility" from *Business Respect* (Issue 83, published on June 15, 2005), the International Standards Organization's summit meeting in Korea focused in part on the future development of the Corporate Social Responsibility standard ISO 26000. Baker wrote: "We should surely be enthused and excited about the prospect of a standard to define best practice in corporate responsibility into a management system that can achieve consistency."

And during the 2002 Surrey Memorial Lecture at the National Policy Association on June 18, 2002, Lorne W. Craner, assistant secretary of State for Democracy, Human Rights and Labor, remarked on promoting corporate social responsibility abroad. His speech, which can be found on the U.S. Department of State website, included the following:

"Protecting and promoting democracy, human rights and labor right is a tall order. To achieve sustainable results, we must work not only with our traditional partners . . . but also increasingly work with new partners.

"An increasing number of corporations share some of our interests in advancing human rights. They appreciate, as do we, that countries that respect human rights have more open transparent laws and financial systems, less corruption, a better-educated workforce, more stability and more security. As the leading employers and revenue source in many developing countries that are transitioning to democracy, companies are uniquely placed to lead by example where they operate."

Does wearing a mantle of corporate social responsibility make a company "good?" Well, it's all relative. Ironically, as Mallen Baker pointed out in his article, "It would be interesting to make some real progress on finding ways to identify a good company. One of the most important would surely be some reflection of the 'corporate personality.' When Enron was busy running all the best community programs and environmental management systems, the only visible signs of a problem in advance of the final collapse were the stories that appeared occasionally highlighting an aggressive marketplace style." (*See* **Enron**.)

See also: Sustainability; Value Proposition

Further Reading

Corporate Social Responsibility: Doing the Most Good for Your Company and Your Cause, by Philip Kotler and Nancy Lee, Wiley (2004).

Harvard Business Review on Corporate Responsibility (Harvard Business Review Paperback Series), Multiple Authors, Harvard Business School Press (2003).

What Matters Most: How a Small Group of Pioneers Is Teaching Social Responsibility to Big Business, and Why Big Business is Listening, by Jeffrey Hollender and Stephen Fenichell, Basic Books New Ed edition (January 2006).

Signs of Changing Culture:
It's Not Easy Going Green: Environmentalism May Help Your Corporate Image, but Will It Keep You in the Black?

Published: February 07, 2007, in Knowledge@Wharton

Reproduced with permission from Knowledge@Wharton (http://knowledge.wharton.upenn.edu), the online research and business analysis journal of the Wharton School of the University of Pennsylvania.

On February 2, a long-awaited report from the Intergovernmental Panel on Climate Change (IPCC) was released citing "unequivocal" proof of global warming caused by man-made emissions of greenhouse gases. Meanwhile, some of the biggest corporations in the world, including Wal-Mart, Ford, General Electric, and BP, have adopted highly visible "green" strategies, embracing environmentalism in their marketing and core business operations. But what does "going green" mean for the bottom line? Whether motivated by desire to do what is right, or to polish their public image and fend off government regulation, companies can profit from well-designed strategies that embrace environmental goals, according to Wharton faculty and analysts.

The IPCC report's position that humans are spoiling the atmosphere—a consensus of the world's top climate scientists—is likely to generate even more corporate interest in green business, says Wharton Marketing professor Americus Reed. "It's really getting some traction now. There's a big idea in the scientific community about global warming, and I think consumers are much more aware of these issues than they were."

At one level, green marketing is a way to differentiate a company from its competitors in the consumer market, he says. "And when you market yourself as environmentally friendly, it also implies that your competitors are not."

According to Wharton marketing professor Barbara Kahn, large companies have steadily increased their efforts to integrate environmental concerns into their marketing and core business strategies. For the most part, she says, the campaigns seem to be a sincere effort, not just a public relations ploy. "Corporations understand that part of their role is to be socially responsible, and I think that's genuinely the case. Good breeds good."

Research shows that in a competitive market, the perception that a company is socially responsible can be a major differentiation point for consumers, but it must be a sincere, deeply held element of the corporation's culture, Kahn says. "You need to have a history of this kind of social responsibility. You can't fake it. . . . It's hard to do, but that's what makes it worthwhile. If it's easy to copy, then it's no longer a competitive advantage."

Wharton legal studies professor Eric Orts, director of Wharton's environmental management program, says some companies may be motivated to promote green strategies out of fear they will be targeted by environmental organizations that could tarnish their image with consumers. Wal-Mart's recent emphasis on good environmental practices, for example, may be an attempt to generate social goodwill, particularly with upper middle-class shoppers, after the company suffered harsh criticism for its labor policies. "A lot of times a big company gets seriously burned in its reputation, [which is] what happened to Wal-Mart. Although that criticism was about employment issues, not the environment, sometimes these things all go together and you get a bad reputation that starts to hurt you," he says.

At the same time, Orts notes, many companies are growing convinced that addressing environmental problems will eventually enhance their bottom-line performance. "I think there are companies out there that believe this is a serious planetary issue, that business can't just sit on the sidelines, but must instead take a leadership role." Shell and BP are examples from the energy sector, says Orts, and GE and 3M are also examples. "But I would add that it is often difficult to ascertain how seriously particular companies take these issues. There is an important difference between 'greenwashing' and true commitment to a long-term sustainable strategy. It's not always easy for an outsider to perceive the difference, which is one argument for enhanced standards for environmental disclosure."

A Proactive Stance

Wal-Mart is not the only company hoping it can turn green into gold. According to Kyle Cahill, manager of corporate partnerships at Environmental Defense, the New York environmental advocacy group, Wall Street is also beginning to look at corporations through an environmental lens. Citigroup Investment Research has issued a 120-page report that identified seventy-four companies in twenty-one industries that stand to benefit from strategies that revolve around climate change.

Meanwhile, Lehman Bros. has released its own report titled, "The Business of Climate Change," that calls global warming a "tectonic force," similar to globalization and aging populations, that will shape economic change.

"There is a sense in the investment community that climate change brings new opportunity," says Cahill. Moreover, companies are seeing that by addressing environmental challenges, they can run their businesses more efficiently. "All pollution is waste, and waste is costly."

In addition, many companies are focusing on environmental solutions in the face of tougher regulations. The newly elected Democratic Congress and the prospect of a Democrat entering the White House after 2008 make the enactment of new environmental standards more likely, says Wharton management professor Lawrence Hrebiniak. "I'd like to think this is all springing from [executives'] hearts," he adds, "but the majority of it is probably springing from sound business sense."

Companies can choose to react to regulation, he says, or proactively shape the nature of future environmental policy. He points to efforts by Alcoa, DuPont, and major utility and oil companies to establish a cap-and-trade system for carbon emissions. Under this system, similar to one already in effect for sulfur dioxide, companies would receive a cap on the amount of harmful emissions they are allowed to make. Companies that want to exceed their cap can then trade credits for additional emissions with companies that are under their limit.

"It's inevitable. The government is going to do something. So companies can either react, or be proactive and control what's going to happen. The proactive stance is more strategic," says Hrebiniak. Government may also shape the development of companies in newly emerging industries—such as biofuels and wind and solar power—focused on solving environmental problems. The federal government is likely to provide funding and other incentives to develop new technology in these areas, he notes.

Firms operating in Europe are already used to much tougher environmental regulations, according to Orts. One example is "lifecycle" requirements, which mandate that companies find ways to recycle their products after customers are done with them.

A successful environmental strategy must be deeply integrated into a corporation's underlying culture and values, Orts notes. He points to Ford, where former chief executive William Ford, Jr., launched a visible campaign to introduce environmentalism to the company. Ford appears on television ads and installed an environmentally friendly grass roof on a showplace plant. Yet Ford's product lineup continued to rely on heavy trucks and sport utility vehicles that fell out of favor among consumers when oil prices—and concern about a sustainable energy policy—began to rise. At the same time, Toyota and Honda stood ready to profit from years of investment in vehicles with high fuel economy.

"We've known for some time that there are difficulties in petroleum supplies, but for a while the price was low and American companies were pretending it would not be a problem," says Orts. "Toyota and Honda made strategic bets that this wasn't going to go away. Now they are looking pretty smart."

Despite the commitment of Ford's CEO, the entire organization was not aligned around an environmental strategy. "It didn't go down deeply into the company. It shows it takes more than just the CEO. There were a lot of good intentions, but this is not an easy thing to do."

Orts cautions that a potential danger in building a core strategy around the environment is the possibility that one action will lead to unintended consequences that may harm the environment. Companies that promote their environmental credentials open themselves up to a public backlash if an element of their strategy is later discovered to be less than pristine. He notes that Levi Strauss has been reluctant to promote its use of organic cottons in some of its apparel for fear that it might draw attention to the way the rest of its cotton is produced.

Wal-Mart: "Not Two Worlds"

At Wal-Mart, the company's high-profile environmental strategy began in 2004 with a series of meetings with dozens of associates, customers, community leaders, government and nonprofit organizations, broadly aimed at helping Wal-Mart find its place in society.

Following Hurricane Katrina, Wal-Mart chief executive Lee Scott announced the company's new emphasis on environmental awareness. "As one of the largest companies in the world, with an expanding global presence, environmental problems are our problems," Scott told associates in a leadership speech. "The supply of natural products—fish, food, water—can only be sustained if the ecosystems that provide them are sustained and protected. There are not two worlds out there, a Wal-Mart world and some other world."

Since then, the company has begun to develop a far-flung set of environmental initiatives touching on packaging, logistics, and store operations. Most recently, Wal-Mart has begun to reach back into its supply chain to eke out waste in its suppliers' operations and products, according to Andy Rubin, vice president of corporate strategy and sustainability.

Rubin says the company did not hire outside consultants to devise a strategy for the vast retailer. Instead, the company is taking a grassroots approach. Rubin is part of a three-member team coordinating strategies and holding managers accountable, but the ideas for potential environmental strategies are rising up from operations.

For example, Wal-Mart's seafood buyer is working with fisheries to produce fish in a sustainable way. Overfishing, Rubin notes, had been driving up the cost of seafood. Working with sustainable producers will help the environment, but also keep the cost of Wal-Mart's goods down, he says, allowing the company to continue to pass along savings to consumers and maintain its long-term commitment to low price.

Rubin acknowledges the company's decentralized approach to its environmental strategies opens it up to unintended consequences, but he says that for a company that operates on the size and scope of Wal-Mart, unintended consequences come with the territory. "Anytime we make a move, there are dozens of consequences, intended and unintended. That's what makes the opportunities so great . . . Our challenge is to listen to as many people as we can so we are as aware of the consequences as we can possibly be."

So far, Wal-Mart's suppliers have been open to discussing ways to improve their own environmental strategies and are providing the retailer with feedback and insights that are helping it shape its environmental policies, according to Rubin.

To doubters who view Wal-Mart's environmental crusade as public relations, Rubin insists that time will prove his company's intentions are pure. "We've said from the beginning, 'Judge us by our actions, not by our commitment.' We're doing this because it makes sense for the business. There are a lot more people who believe us today than two years ago, and there will be a lot more two years from now."

Despite what may be a growing sense that pro-environmental strategies can be good for business, Wharton's Reed says it remains difficult for many companies to take on socially responsible policies because it is still often difficult to show a clear benefit to the bottom line.

The rewards for adopting environmentally sound policies within a corporation take a long time, if ever, to become clear, he points out. While many top executives may be focused on the big picture of improving a corporation's environmental record, front-line managers need new incentives to take actions because they are usually judged on their quarterly results.

"The barrier to proliferation of socially responsible policies is that it's difficult to show social goodwill on the balance sheet," Reed says. "There is no column or item to say, 'Here it is, here's the savings in dollars.' That's the conundrum."

Crisis/Risk Management

Every transaction or decision a business makes can be fraught with risk. Much of a business's success is due to its anticipation of the risks it takes; its plan of how to reduce or manage that risk; its ability to balance a level of risk with the potential of opportunity; and its ability to handle any negative impact, sometimes known as a crisis, that might occur. A part of managing risk is handling crises.

The Institute for Crisis Management (ICM) website (www.crisisexperts .com) defines a crisis as: "A significant business disruption that stimulates extensive news media coverage. The resulting public scrutiny will affect the organization's normal operations and also could have a political, legal, financial, and governmental impact on its business."

According to the ICM, crises are caused by: "1) Acts of God (storms, earthquakes, volcanic action, etc.); 2) Mechanical problems (ruptured pipes, metal fatigue, etc.); 3) Human errors (the wrong valve was opened, miscommunication about what to do, etc.); and 4) Management decisions/indecision (the problem is not serious, nobody will find out)."

Crisis management, then, involves an immediate response to something that has had a major negative impact on the organization in real time. According to the Business Continuity Institute (*Glossary of General Business Continuity Management Terms* Version BCI DJS 1.0 01/12/02), a crisis management plan is a clearly defined and documented plan of action for use at the time of a crisis. Typically a plan will cover all key personnel, resources, services and actions required to implement and manage the crisis management process.

As noted, crisis management is a component of the larger umbrella of risk management. Risk management, according to that same source, is the culture, processes and structures that are put in place to effectively manage potential opportunities and adverse effects. As it is not possible or desirable to eliminate all risk, the objective is to implement cost effective processes that reduce risks to an acceptable level, reject unacceptable risk and treat risk by financial interventions, for example, transfer other risks through insurance or other means.

A risk management process is the systematic and documented process of clarifying the risk context and identifying, analyzing, evaluating, treating, monitoring, communicating, and consulting on risks. Risk control is the part of risk management that involves the implementation of policies, standards, procedures, and physical changes to eliminate or minimize adverse risks.

The *Global Trade Review* (*GTR*) November/December 2004 issue took a look at crisis management vs. risk management. In the *GTR*, Cathy Duffy, senior vice-president, strategic risk management at JPMorgan Treasury Services, gave a risk manager's view of how your company can best protect itself.

> A transaction's risk management process should focus on five areas: Knowledge of your client company and product, knowledge of your customer/underwriting, structure and documentation, external risk mitigation/portfolio management, and crisis management . . . There is no single formula for determining an appropriate deal structure. The goal is to achieve a reasonable balance between positive and negative factors. Some factors can be negotiated and/or influenced by each party (amount, tenor, collateral, covenants, etc.), but others, such as industry, geography, or purpose, represent the context for the structure.

Despite the most careful preparation and strategic maneuvering, crises happen. In November 1995, Norman R. Augustine (retired chairman and CEO of Lockheed Martin) published an article in the *Harvard Business Review* entitled "Managing the Crisis You Tried to Prevent." A good source of information if the "best made plans" don't cut it.

See also: Scenario Planning

Further Reading

"Armchair Crisis Management: The 3 Big Questions," in *Business Spin*, by Jack Flack (September 12, 2007), CondeNast Portfolio.com, www.portfoli-o.com.
www.12manage.com

Cubicle

In the world of office work, not everyone can have an office. So in many companies, employees at one time sat at desks that were placed together in a large, open space. While it is possible that this layout contributes to an efficient use of space, it does not offer any privacy.

Enter the cubicle, "invented" in 1968 by Robert Propst, a professor of fine arts at the University of Colorado. His term for the concept of an office that utilized cubicles was "Action Office." Cubicles, or "cubies" as they are sometimes called, were designed to create a space-within-a-space for office workers, giving each a "wall" of sorts, and more privacy, at least in theory, than they would have had without the partitions. They were also designed to allow people to spread their work out more than they could if they had only a single desk; cubies allowed for some "counter space" or a shelf.

At the same time, the theory was that cubicles would allow for more collaboration than traditional offices with four walls and a door.

The Merriam-Webster Dictionary defines a cubicle as a "small partitioned space; one with a desk used for work in a business office." Other sources employ more colorful names; the cubie, it seems, evokes strong reactions.

Consider what Linda Tischler had to say on the subject in an article called "Death to the Cubicle!" in *Fast Company* magazine (Issue 95, page 29, June 2005). Tischler wrote: "Collaboration is great, but sometimes I'd kill for a door."

In the same article, she wrote, "Propst's vision was to give white-collar workers, then toiling amid rows of desks in huge open spaces, both more privacy and a way to individualize their space. By that measure, cubicles were an improvement. But in the hands of space-mad facilities planners, the idea was perverted to justify an officescape that resembled the Chicago stockyards."

As Tischler went on to note, in the wake of the creation of the action office, came the wildly successful and cynical office-based cartoon, *Dilbert*, by Scott Adams.

An article posted on CNN Money from *Fortune* magazine published on March 9, 2006, calls cubicles "the great mistake." That article also looked back to Propst, noting that he "invented nothing so destructive. Yet before he died in 2000, he lamented his unwitting contribution to what he called 'monolithic insanity.' "

As that article noted, "The cubicle has been called many things in its long and terrible reign. But what it has lacked in beauty and amenity, it has made up for in crabgrass-like persistence . . . Reviled by workers, demonized by designers, disowned by its very creator, it still claims the largest share of office furniture sales—$3 billion or so a year—and has out lived every 'office of the future' meant to replace it. It is the Fidel Castro of office furniture" ("Cubicles: The Great Mistake" by Julie Schlosser (03/09/2006) *Fortune* magazine).

Cubicles are often the butt of corporate jokes. As Lee Butler noted in an article entitled "Living Out Loud: Cubicles and Co-Workers; Welcome to My White Collar Zoo" (Citybeat.com, August 29, 2007): "This little box is my prison cell away from home."

Cubicles also provide "common ground" for all "cubie" workers, no matter their company. Consider the following description, in an article entitled "Shooting Messengers Makes Us Feel Better But Work Dumber," written by Jared Sandberg in the *Wall Street Journal*, September 11, 2007, page B. Sandberg was quoting a Mr. Gordon, who was describing a salesman's reaction to bad news delivered by a third party: "He then kicked his own cubicle wall, 'which in turn collapsed onto his neighbor's cubicle wall and thus started a domino effect of wrecking everyone's office in the row,' Mr. Gordon recalls."

Anyone who has ever worked in a cubicle will likely not only be able to picture this, but may also have a similar cubicle story of their own.

See also: Dilbert; Generation X, Y, and Z

Further Reading

"Cubicle Culture," a regular column by Jared Sandberg that appears in the *Wall Street Journal*, and can also be found on www.careerjounal.com, or the Wall Street Journal Online.

www.lifeaftercoffee.com

Dilbert

Dilbert is a comic strip about work life in a corporate office, but it is more than a merely entertaining read in the newspaper. The manner in which the comic strip portrays conversations among management and workers has made it so popular that, as of this writing, according to the *Dilbert* website, Dilbert.com, *Dilbert* now appears in 2,000 newspapers in sixty-five countries. The website, incidentally, was the first syndicated comic strip to go online in 1995 and is the most widely read syndicated comic on the Internet. And four original books by *Dilbert*'s creator, Scott Adams, have been bestsellers: *The Dilbert Principle, Dogbert's Top Secret Management Handbook, The Dilbert Future*, and *The Joy of Work*. According to Dilbert.com, there are twenty-two *Dilbert* books—including comic strip reprint books—with more than ten million copies in print.

Created as a doodle by the artist, Scott Adams, *Dilbert* appeared in Adams' business presentations before developing into a full strip syndicated by United Media. Adams worked for many years at a bank, and then at a phone company, where he came up with the idea for *Dilbert*. In fact, in an interview with CNN.com available online at http://archives.cnn.com/2001/COMMUNITY/08/30/adams/intex.html, Adams said, "*Dilbert* might not have been created if I had a good cubicle during my corporate jail term."

The main characters in the comic are *Dilbert*, an engineer at a high-tech firm, Dogbert, his pet (who can talk, and who is by far the more cynical of the two), the Boss (according to the website, he's "every employee's worst nightmare"), and a host of colleagues and other minor characters.

"*Dilbert* is a composite of my co-workers over the years," Adams says in his biography on Dilbert.com. "A co-worker suggested I name the character *Dilbert*. Dogbert was created so *Dilbert* would have someone to talk to."

In a 2002 interview with Scott Adams (Funny Business, *BizEd*, The Association to Advance Collegiate Schools of Business, November/December), Adams said, "*Dilbert* simply reflects the often laughable exchanges that occur between managers and their employees."

In the same article, Adams said, "The strip definitely has an effect on the small stuff that companies do every day. By that, I mean that I get a lot of reports from people who say, 'My manager was going to roll out this stupid program. Then I showed him a *Dilbert* cartoon that showed exactly how stupid that same program was and he canceled the whole thing.'"

The popularity of *Dilbert* has sparked several streams of business. It has also added to the jargon of the business world. Adams speaks at business conferences; there are scads of *Dilbert* merchandise for sale; and according to www.wordspy.com, the term "dilbert" is a verb meaning "to cause a person to become bored or cynical about work." That website lists several spottings of the verb "dilbert" in use, among them:

"Can you imagine efficient private companies still working only with paper? How many man-hours must be dilberted away? How many delays? How many flat-out frauds?—Editorial 'Man vs. Machine: The old world meets the new,' The *Arkansas Democrat-Gazette*, March 27, 2002."

See also: Cubicle

Further Reading

"Kindness Pays . . . Or Does It?" by Jessica Marquez, *Workforce Management*
     (June 15, 2007) www.workforce.com (subscription required).
www.dilbert.com

Signs of Changing Culture: Buzz Words Evolve

Always looking for new ways to connect with colleagues, reports, and bosses, people are constantly bringing new words into the business vernacular. It wasn't so long ago that the word "impact" was *not* used as a verb.

Now, according to an article by Christopher Rhoads, published in the *Wall Street Journal* on Tuesday, March 27, 2007 (page 1, column 3), the word "bucket" is hot. ("Business Types Get a New Kick Out of the 'Bucket': Executives Utter the Word To Describe Groups, Units; 'Silo' Pales in Comparison")

"Suddenly the humble bucket has become a trendy fixture of corporate boardrooms and PowerPoint presentations," Rhoads wrote. "It is pushing aside other business-speak for describing categories or organizational units, such as silo and basket."

As the article says, "bucket has outgrown its barnyard roots and moved into the business world." It goes on to say, "Bucket trumps basket, which conjures up an image of someone picking flowers in a field" and "Silo also has a negative buzz these days. It implies fiefdoms and exclusive divisions, rather than inclusiveness and working together as a team thrown together in, say, a bucket."

Diversity

Diversity in the workplace essentially means having men and women from many ethnic backgrounds and belief systems working together. Increasingly, as more companies "go global," diversity has become a desirable corporate characteristic. Top managers and shareholders are seeing the value of having an inclusive corporate culture, in which a diverse group of people can work together, contributing their different perspectives to add value to the company's offerings and help it gain an advantage in the marketplace.

But the idea of diversity in the workplace stems mostly from the need for fairness. According to the Workforce Diversity Office Ernest Orlando Lawrence Berkeley National Laboratory, "The traditional polices, programs, and legal mandates of Equal Employment Opportunity (EEO) and Affirmative Action (AA) are still the first and most important steps to achieving diversity in the workplace. But diversity is a broader concept than ethnicity, race, and gender" (www.lbl.gov/workplace/WFDO). The website goes on to note that the concept of diversity at work is "inclusive of all groups, maximizes the potential of all employees, and values the variety of perspectives all employees bring to the workplace at the scientific, technical, management, and administrative levels."

According to the online version of the Bureau of Labor Statistics Occupational Outlook Quarterly (Summer 2004, Vol. 48, No. 2), diversity in the workforce is a continuing trend. That website says:

"Equal-opportunity laws were created to ensure that workers are hired, retained, and promoted without regard to characteristics such as race and ethnic origin. Regulations aside, many employers value having a staff attuned to population diversity. These employers may consider diversity in their organizations to be sound business practice because it allows them to better serve a wide range of customers.

"A number of programs encourage the development of a diverse workforce. Some are general, such as scholarships and grants for minority students in higher education. Other programs are more specific, aimed at increasing the number of minorities in particular occupations. At Howard University in 2002, for example, Secretary of State Colin Powell introduced a $1 million grant designed to prepare minorities for diplomatic careers."

There are many resources for individuals seeking to learn more about diversity in the workplace, and diversity issues. Among them: www.ethnicmajority.com; www.affirmativeaction.org; www.aimd.org (the American Institute for Managing Diversity); www.dlaa.org (the Diversity Leadership Academy); www.diversityinc.com; www.now.org (the National Organization for Women); and the U.S. Department of Labor (www.dol.gov).

Another source of further information: the 2005 Workplace Diversity Practices Survey Report: A Study by the Society for Human Resource Management (published by the Society for Human Resource Management, January 2007).

See also: Equal Employment Opportunity Commission (EEOC)

Further Reading

www.diversityinc.com (DiversityInc Magazine)

Signs of Changing Culture: The Power in Diversity

Noted in an article entitled, "Mighty is the Mongrel" by G. Pascal Zachary, published in *Fast Company*, Issue 36, June 2000, Page 27

Diversity, Zachary writes, "is at a record level."

"In a world of deepening connections, individuals, organizations, and entire countries draw strength and personality from places as near as their local neighborhood and as far away as a distant continent. Mixing is the new norm."

Why is this the case? According to Zachary, it's because "the ability to apply knowledge to new situations is the most valued currency in today's economy."

"Divergent thinking," he writes, "is an essential ingredient of creativity. Diverse groups produce diverse thinking. Ergo, diversity promotes creativity. This logic applies to corporations, research teams, think tanks, and other groups of creators."

G. Pascal Zachary is also the author of *The Diversity Advantage: Multicultural Identity in the New World Economy*, published by Westview Press.

Dot.com/Dot.bomb

Reduced to its essentials, the term "dot.com" means a company that does business on the Internet; that is, any entity on the web whose site ends with ".com" as opposed to a nonprofit organization (.org), an educational institution (.edu), and so forth.

When doing business on the Internet was new, scores of business entities rushed to the Internet, getting ".com" status. Venture capitalists were, by and large, funding new web-based businesses right and left. The "dot.com" bubble, as it was called, lasted from about 1995–2001.

But then many of the "dot.coms" became "dot.bombs." That is, faced with competition—and troubled by the structural and managerial challenges of running a "dot.com"—many online businesses failed. For many such ventures, the cause of demise was a faulty revenue model, and/or an inability to find a necessary base of customers online.

Thus, the "dot.com" bubble burst. The term, "dot.bomb" was coined to describe all of those failed companies, or any "dot.com" that does not survive.

Jad Duwaike, an Internet entrepreneur, was just one of the entrepreneurs who experienced the thrill of the dot.com launch and the agony of realizing that a business was a dot.bomb. He wrote about his experiences on the *San Francisco Chronicle*'s website. In his May 12, 2001, entry titled "Dot-com diary: The trials and tribulations of a failed entrepreneur," Duwaike wrote, "My fourth company, Greenhouse for Startups, exploded with potential. A networking group [of] entrepreneurs, Greenhouse grew to 7,000 members with chapters in five cities and obtained a ton of press coverage. Despite numerous attempts, however, I couldn't find a revenue model for the company and, by last December, it became clear that Greenhouse was simply another dot-com dot-bomb."

The dot.com bubble caused a great deal of financial angst—and that's a gross understatement. In the last few years, however, the number of Internet businesses has increased, as has the amount of useful information available to help people lead and manage online enterprises. And many indicators point to a strong future.

For example, according to an article by Tom Abate, published in the *San Francisco Chronicle* Tuesday April 14, 2007 (found online at www.sfgate.com), "For the first-time since the state lost tens of thousands of jobs after the dot-com collapse, California companies have added tech workers to their payrolls, according to a report that tracks nationwide employment in the industry."

According to the article, the American Electronics Association, which released the report, said that the figures represent "the first net increase in jobs (here) since the tech bubble began to burst in 2000."

Another article, this one in the *San Jose Mercury News*, by Ryan Biltstein, published May 19, 2007 (found online at origin.mercurynews.com), said: "Since the dot-com bubble burst, online advertising spending has jumped from $6 billion in 2002 to $16.4 billion last year, according to eMarketer. And that number is poised to grow dramatically. The web accounted for less than 6 percent of dollars spent on ads in 2006, but it's growing as much as five times the rate of offline ads, according to Oppenheimer & Co."

The entrance barriers to online businesses, some note, are also much lower now than they were during the dot.com bubble. As online entrepreneur Guy Kawasaki, interviewed by Lee Gomes for a Portals article in the *Wall Street Journal*, said: "During the dot-com bubble, you needed $5 million to do stupid ideas. Now you can do stupid ideas for 12 grand." ("In the New Net Economy, Everyone Gets to Be Stupid for 15 Minutes," by Lee Gomes, Portals, the *Wall Street Journal* Online, May 16, 2007.)

There are, however, concerns that we are entering another dot.com bubble, and will someday (soon) experience another shake-out. As Joe Bel Bruno of the Associated Press reported in an article posted May 4, 2007 at www.signonsandiego.com/news/business (the *Union-Tribune*), "It was impossible to escape the comparisons with 2000 on Wall Street this past week. Not only did the Standard & Poor's 500 index pass 1,500, a level the market has not seen since the dot-com boom, but the Dow Jones industrial average also ratcheted higher. Rising stock prices—which come amid a slowing economy—have some on Wall Street wondering if investors are making the same mistakes they made during the high-tech bubble."

And, as Mark Walsh wrote in the May 2007 issue of OMMA magazine ("Internet IPOs: Hot or Not?" *OMMA* the *Magazine of Online Media, Marketing and Advertising*) "For anyone worried about Web2.0 morphing into Bubble 2.0, few signs could be more ominous than the return of the Internet IPO . . . Fears that we're back in helium land seem to be confirmed . . . After all, the term Internet IPO, like reality TV, had become an oxymoron in recent years, as public investors shunned the high tech sector following the dot-com collapse. Buzz-generating startups with little revenue and no profits were out, and sound business fundamentals were in again on Wall Street . . . But now stirrings of a revived pubic market are appearing."

Of note: A movie entitled *What Happened*, about the implosion of the dot.com bubble. A review of the movie by Bill Lessard in *Wired* magazine, dated February 2, 2002 (found on www.wired.com) said: "The film does a good job of chronicling the events of the past five years, from the Netscape IPO that started the whole mess until the NASDAQ crash in April 2000." The review went on to say that viewers could find the film "entertaining and enlightening, particularly in some of the comparisons it draws between the speculative frenzy of the 1920 and the late 1990s."

See also: Bricks and Clicks; Entrepreneur

Further Reading

"Dot-Com Bubble, Part II? Why It's So Hard to Value Social Networking Sites," published October 4, 2006 in Knowledge@Wharton (http://knowledge .wharton.upenn.edu).

www.ecommercetimes.com

www.nethistory.info ("History of the Internet—the Dotcom bubble" by Ian Peter)

Downsizing

When a business downsizes, it is reducing the number of people it employs. Companies downsize for a variety of reasons, not the least of which is to look as lean and efficient as possible for prospective buyers. But most companies downsize to try to become more competitive. Sometimes they're facing stiff competition and they have to find a way to do more with less, and sometimes a company's financial management is not up to par, resulting in an impending crisis—such as being unable to meet payroll.

Downsizing can often be a signal to the outside world—and to Wall Street in particular—that a company is serious about rethinking its strategy and reinvigorating the business. Layoffs, then, while bad news for employees, can be seen as good news to investors.

In April 2007, for example, according to *Computerworld Management* magazine (www.computerworld.com), Citigroup announced that it would "lay off 17,000 workers as part of a massive restructuring expected to save the company more than $10 billion over the next three years." According to the article, Citigroup Chairman and CEO, Charles Prince said in a statement that "the goal was to identify and eliminate 'organizational, technology and administrative costs that do not contribute to our ability to efficiently deliver products and services to our clients,'" Prince was also quoted in the article as saying that "the planned restructuring will put the company in a better position to grow."

Sometimes, downsizing is a permanent move; sometimes, top managers downsize a company temporarily to try to avoid a crisis. "Layoffs" are one way in which downsizing is presented to employees. But managers who find themselves having to downsize their companies also use other methods, including transfers—if the company has other divisions that are hiring—or offering attractive "early retirement" packages.

Downsizing should never be undertaken lightly. In a crisis mode, companies can inadvertently slash the jobs of the very people who might help the organization recover. What's more, when a company downsizes, the way in which it treats employees—both those whose jobs are being cut and those who are staying—can significantly influence productivity and morale.

And, some say that downsizing should be the last alternative companies consider when trying to turn things around. According to an article by F. John Reh, found on http://management.about.com, "Layoffs are done to save money. Unfortunately, they are usually a short term fix, detrimental to the company." In the article, Reh says that sometimes layoffs are made as a knee-jerk reaction to appease investors when a company misses its numbers. Reh also refers to another article on management.about.com by John Dorfman, which also discusses the downside of downsizing.

In his article "Job Cuts Often Fail to Bolster Stocks," Dorfman, a Boston-based money manager who is a regular contributor to Bloomberg News, wrote that he measured the stock performance of ten companies (including Eastman Kodak, IBM, and Boeing) for eleven months to almost three years after the company in question announced job cuts in 1996 and 1997. What he found was that "contrary to popular myth, these stocks didn't outperform the market." His conclusions were that "people think that trimming the workforce is a shrewd cost-cutting measure, that it shows toughness and resolve on the part of management and that it indicates that executives are being 'proactive' in dealing with a company's problems. Malarkey."

Dorfman noted that his sample size was too small to be scientifically significant, but he called his results "powerfully suggestive" and noted that "Companies used to at least pretend to be embarrassed and apologetic when they let people go. Today, many CEOs all but pound their chests with pride as they jettison employees. To my way of thinking, this is one of the worst cultural changes of the last twenty years. There's no need for investors to blindly encourage it."

See also: Change Agent/Change Management; Lifetime Employment

Further Reading

Downsizing in America: Reality, Causes, And Consequences, by William J. Baumol, Alan S. Binder, and Edward N. Wolff, Russell Sage Foundation Publications (March 2005).
http://humanresources.about.com/od/layoffsdownsizing/a/downsizing.htm

Drucker, Peter

Peter Drucker was one of the most important observers and influencers of the business world and business culture and strategy in the past 100 years. A management consultant, professor, and prolific author of books and articles on management, he revolutionized the concept of business management worldwide.

Born in Vienna, Austria, in 1909, Drucker received his doctorate in public and international law from Frankfurt University in Frankfurt, Germany. He then worked in London as an economist and journalist, moving to the United States in 1937.

He was on the faculty of New York University in the 1950s, and then joined the faculty of the Claremont Graduate University in Claremont, California, in 1971. The management school at the university was subsequently renamed the Peter F. Drucker and Masatoshi Ito Graduate School of Management

According to the website, www.peter-drucker.com, Drucker wrote thirty-five books in all, fifteen of which dealt with management, including *The Practice of Management*, *The Effective Executive*, and *Managing for Results*. (Other sources say he wrote thirty-nine books.) He was also a columnist for the *Wall Street Journal*, and a frequent contributor to the *Harvard Business Review*.

In 1990, the Peter F. Drucker Foundation for Nonprofit Management was established (it is now known as the Leader to Leader Institute). According to its website, www.leadertoleader.org, the institute's mission is to "strengthen the leadership of the social sector—by providing social sector leaders with essential leadership wisdom, inspiration and resources to lead for innovation and to build vibrant social sector organizations."

Harvard Business School professor Rosabeth Moss Kantor, also a well-known management thinker and prolific author, wrote this about Drucker for the Leader to Leader Thought Leader's Forum: "Peter Drucker's eyeglasses must contain crystal balls because he anticipated so many trends—defining 'knowledge workers' decades before this trend was discernable, identifying the centrality of the third sector of nonprofits to getting the work of society done, putting mission first in the understanding of a business, recognizing the power of pension funds and other institutional investors in the late twentieth century capitalism, defining entrepreneurship as finding innovations to meet unmet needs."

In that same Forum Stephen R. Covey (president of the Covey Leadership Center) called Drucker "the Renaissance Man of the field of management."

Drucker was awarded the Presidential Medal of Freedom by President George W. Bush on July 9, 2002. He died in 2005.

In an article about his death published in the *Washington Post* on page B6 November 12, 2005, titled "Management Visionary Peter Drucker Dies" author Patricia Sullivan wrote that

Drucker was often called "the world's most influential business guru" whose thinking transformed corporate management in the latter half of the 20th century . . . Drucker pioneered the idea of privatization and the corporation as a social institution. He coined the terms "knowledge workers" and "management by objectives." His seminal study of General Motors in 1945 introduced the concept of decentralization as a principal of organization, in contrast to the practice of command and control in business. "There is only one valid definition of business purpose: to create a customer," he said forty-five years ago. Central to his philosophy was the belief that highly skilled people are an organization's most valuable resource and that a manager's job is to prepare and free people to perform.

A book entitled *The Daily Drucker* (Collins, 2004) offers quotes from Drucker's work, followed by short commentaries on the implications of his words. Just one Drucker quote from that book: "Effective executives do not start with their tasks. They start with their time. And they do not start out with planning. They start by finding out where their time actually goes. Then they attempt to manage their time and to cut back unproductive demands on their time. Finally, they consolidate their 'discretionary' time into the largest possible continuing units."

See also: Learning Organization; Performance Management/Performance Measurement

Further Reading

www.leadertoleader.org
www.peter-drucker.com

E-mail

What is e-mail? Is it an indispensable tool for getting work done or a ubiquitous distraction that prevents work from getting done? E-mail—the technological tool that gives individuals the ability to send and receive messages from person to person, and office to office, anytime, and almost anywhere, has passionate supporters and equally passionate detractors.

The Merriam-Webster Dictionary defines e-mail as "[the] means or system for transmitting messages electronically; messages sent and received electronically through an e-mail system."

According to www.answerbag.com, the first e-mail was sent in 1971 between two PDP-10 computers in Cambridge (USA) by engineer Ray Tomlinson, a partner in the development of the first major computer network, ARPANET, the precursor of today's Internet. The first e-mail was addressed by Tomlinson to himself and was supposed to have contained the message "Testing 1, 2, 3." Tomlinson was also the first person to use the @ symbol in an e-mail address. His ideas were incorporated in the electronic mail software on ARPANET by the end of 1972.

In a Legends article in *Forbes* magazine (published October 5, 1998, and found on the Forbes website (http://members.forbes.com), author Sasha Cavender wrote:

> After graduating from MIT in 1965, the young computer engineer spent two years working on a doctorate, then went to work nearby at Bolt Beranek and Newman (BBN), a company that had a government contract to work on the ARPANET, precursor of the Internet. "We were building an operating system to run on bargain-basement hardware," recalls his longtime friend and BBN colleague Jerry Burchfiel, "and Ray came up with a 'Send Message' program. It worked only on a local system at first, but then he took it further and created cross-ARPANET mail."

Since those early days, e-mail has of course gone on to become standard operating equipment in just about every office. But the ability to send and

---

Why I Do This: English Instructor online (part time)
Jeanie Murphy

I teach a course I put on the books years ago for the community college where I was tenured (before I resigned) called "Introduction to Mythology." I fought for and teach two sections every quarter mostly because we get great health insurance, but it's also more fun than lots of other jobs. A day is checking in with the online platform and grading discussion, checking e-mail and grading journals. Prep these days is minimal, but in the first year or two it's even more demanding than a f2f (face-to-face) class. And it's still ongoing—continual tweaks to syllabus or extra reading or lectures (which are written).

It's also a great excuse for me to pursue my interest.

How did I find my job? I was very purposeful about finding my job and did so by figuring out quickly what course would always "go" (students love myth) and then refusing to overload the section until they gave me two.

I had developed some of the first online classes for the college on a grant, so I did have an in with all this.

What do I like about my job? Interesting material, I'm more or less my own boss, *some* of the student interaction.

What is unexpected about my job? How surprisingly well this type of class works online (not all do)—I get about twice as much work out of students at a much higher level.

Why would I recommend it? It's much lower stress than f2f teaching, once you get used to it. You also have to be comfy with computers. You're on your own clock and, if like me you have a wi-fi laptop, you can do your work anywhere, practically!

---

receive messages so easily to coworkers and one's own extended community of contacts has its pros and cons. For many people, in many companies, e-mail is an efficient way to send and receive documents, hold quick "conversations" with others in the office, and also work from remote locations with ease. E-mail also makes it easier for employees to communicate with other individuals who are working in different time zones.

But, in some companies, managers have found that employees abuse the e-mail system, and waste company time chatting about personal issues. As a result, in some companies, management has instituted rules regarding e-mail usage; companies have also monitored employee e-mails. This practice has, in turn, raised employee privacy issues.

Privacy and employees' reportedly wasted time are not the only downsides to e-mail. Some employees have complained that e-mail has caused their bosses to multi-task—attending meetings with only half their attention and frequently losing the thread of conversation because of e-mail distractions. (Cell phones and Blackberry devices have reportedly had this same effect.)

An article in *Fast Company* magazine, published in the December 2006/January 2007 issue, discusses electronic communication etiquette in today's businesses with a parody on The Bill of Rights. Author Joe Robinson, after citing a Day-Timers survey that reported a sharp decline from 1994–2006 in the number of people who feel productive, offered seven protocols, the first three of which are:

> Article 1: There shall be no assumption of unlimited e-access simply because the tools allow it. Excessive messaging shall be considered electronic littering.
>
> Article 2: The right of the people to be secure from unwarranted electronic work intrusions at home shall not be violated. Nights and weekends shall be considered unplugged zones.
>
> Article 3: The people shall have the right to switch off e-mail notification and other noisemakers and instead check messages at designated times to prevent attention deficit (*Fast Company* magazine, "An E-Tool Bill of Rights." Issue 111, December/January 2006/2007, page 54, by Joe Robinson).

The final four "articles" in the *Fast Company* article call for people to feel no pressure to respond immediately to e-mails; people to be sensitive about how long their e-mails are and how much of a waste of time short e-mails that simply acknowledge receipt of a message are; companies to come up with formal and explicit policies to establish e-mail protocols; and a plea to leave people alone (i.e., don't expect them to be e-mail accessible or responsive) when they're on vacation.

That last comment resonates with company leaders who are becoming increasingly aware of the importance of a work/life balance, which is, in some circles, becoming an increasingly elusive phenomenon.

One top executive coach, chided by a colleague for staying at a posh hotel in a foreign city and—working just about around the clock—not even once taking time to relax and visit the spa on the hotel's lower floor, vowed: "I'll go to the spa next time I'm there. I'll send you an e-mail from down there."

It should be noted that in some circles—and particularly among the generation just entering the workforce—e-mail is already considered "old school." In an article found on ABC News Online, published July 28, 2005, a Reuters report said: "E-mail is for grown-ups and U.S. teenagers now prefer instant messaging to communicate with each other online, a survey has found. Internet users from twelve to seventeen years old say e-mail is best for talking to parents or institutions but they are more likely to fire up instant messaging (IM) when talking with each other, the non-profit Pew Internet and American Life Project found. E-mail is still used by 90 percent of online teens but the survey found greater enthusiasm for instant messaging." That survey was conducted in October and November of 2004; the report noted a margin of error of 4 percent.

See also: Generation X, Y, and Z; Internet; Intranet

Further Reading

E-Mail: A Write It Well Guide—How to Write and Manage E-Mail in the Work-place, by Janis Fisher Chan, Write It Well (2005).
www.livingInternet.com
www.nethistory.info

Signs of Changing Culture: Technology-Dependence

Service for the Blackberry wireless e-mail and web-access device went down for ten hours starting at 8 P.M. (EST) on Tuesday, April 17, 2007. The reported result was complete turmoil for many Blackberry users—a sure sign that the device, sold by the Canadian company, Research in Motion, has become a firm fixture in today's culture of work.

According to a *New York Times* article by Brad Stone ("Bereft of Blackberrys, the Untethered Make Do," April 19, 2007, www.nytimes .com), the downtime "revealed just how professionally and emotionally dependent so many people had become on their pocket-size electronic lifelines."

One business executive quoted in the article said "I was running around my hotel like a freak. It's very sad. I love this thing."

Another, Stone wrote, "reacted to the severed electronic leash with several panicked calls to her office in the belief that the company e-mail system was down."

That Blackberry user was quoted as saying, "I quit smoking twenty-eight years ago . . . and that was easier than being without my Black-Berry."

Emotional Intelligence

Many people have taken IQ tests, which are intelligence quotient tests that aim to measure an individual's intellectual capacity to solve problems and perform tasks. Over time, though, the conventional thinking in the business world has come to hold that pure intellectual capacity is not the only criteria for being able to succeed and lead in organizations. That recognition has resulted in the emergence of a term called Emotional Intelligence (EQ), which is the ability to perceive, consider, and manage the emotions associated with any given situation, in addition to being able to process the relevant facts.

An article in *Fast Company* magazine ("How do you feel?" Issue 35, May 2000, page 296, by Tony Schwartz) takes a look at how "emotional intelligence" is starting to find it's way into companies, offering employees a way to come to terms with their feelings. Time was, Schwartz wrote, that emotions at work were frowned upon. But by 2000, he wrote, "companies in a variety of industries are once again exploring the role of emotions in business. This renewed interest in self-awareness is, in part, the result of the rising corporate power of baby boomers. The increasing presence of women in the workplace and the higher comfort level they bring to the territory of emotions have also nudged companies in this direction. And the arrival of the new economy has made companies realize that what they need from their workers goes beyond hands, bodies, and eight-hour days."

The theory of emotional intelligence was developed by Peter Salovey, dean of Yale College, and John D. Mayer, professor at the University of New Hampshire. Salovey, Mayer, and their collaborators developed tests of emotional intelligence ("Mayer–Salovey–Caruso Emotional Intelligence Tests") that are now in use in businesses around the world.

Psychiatrist Daniel Goleman is also well known for his work in the area of his emotional intelligence, some of which builds on the work of Mayer and Salovey. Goleman wrote the bestselling book, *Emotional Intelligence:*

Why It Can Matter More Than IQ. (The tenth anniversary edition of the book was published by Bantam in September 2006.)

See also: Corner Office; Executive Coach

Further Reading

Emotional Intelligence: 10th Anniversay Edition; Why It Can Matter More Than IQ, by Daniel Goleman, Bantam (September 2006).

Employee Assistance Programs

As its name suggests, employee assistance programs (EAP), are employee benefit programs designed to assist employees. Often offered by many public and private employers in conjunction with health insurance plans, EAPs range from helping employees deal with personal problems that may affect their work performance to providing support for additional education with tuition assistance.

The largest employee assistance program in the country is run by Federal Occupational Health (FOH), a component of the United States Public Health Service. FOH, a service unit within the Department of Health and Human Services' Program Support Center, supports more than 1.3 million federal workers each year. (Information from the Federal Occupational Health website http://www.foh.dhhs.gov/default.asp)

EAPs have evolved over time in conjunction with the challenges facing working people; moving from basic personal/emotional assistance to child care to help with elderly relatives. The *St. Petersburg Times,* for example, ran an article in January 2007 about a new EAP, designed by Neighborly Care Network, the social service agency that invented Meals on Wheels, that targets baby boomers who are trying to work and care for their aging parents. According to the article, "With its new Employee Assistance Program, Neighborly will help Pinellas employers assess the needs of their workers. The companies pay $5 per month for every employee who participates. In exchange, Neighborly provides counseling, referrals and discounts on adult day care." ("Working Caregivers Get Relief," January 7, 2007, by Lorri Helfand, *St. Petersburg Times.*)

EAPs are designed, essentially, to help employees with the challenges they face outside of work, so that when they are at work, they are better equipped to focus on the challenges at hand. In this way, EAPs can be thought of as a way to improve and sustain productivity in the workplace.

See also: Cafeteria Benefit

Further Reading

Employee Assistance Programs: Wellness/Enhancement Programming, by William G. Emener, William S. Hutchinson, and Michael A. Richard (eds.), C.C. Thomas, 3rd edition (May 2003).

Signs of Changing Culture:
Efforts Are Growing to Trim the Fat from Employees—
and Employers' Health Care Costs

Published: November 1, 2006 in Knowledge@Wharton

Reproduced with permission from Knowledge@Wharton (http://knowledge.wharton.upenn.edu), the online research and business analysis journal of the Wharton School of the University of Pennsylvania.

Perhaps it was the statement from the Centers for Disease Control and Prevention in Atlanta that more than 30 percent of all adults in the United States are obese, a number that has more than doubled since 1980. Perhaps it was the new report that obesity may cause as many as 365,000 deaths per year at a time when Americans reportedly spend over $40 million annually on books, products and programs to help them lose weight. Or maybe it was the CDC's dire prediction that "current data indicate that the situation is worsening rather than improving." For whatever reason, the latest statistics have flagged obesity as a serious health issue that corporations can no longer ignore.

Yet according to Wharton experts and others, the dramatic increase in obesity is not what's driving employers throughout the country to address the problem. This past year, these experts say, companies seem to have declared war on fat for one simple reason: Obesity is now recognized as a real drain on companies' health care costs. "I don't think the increase in obesity, the sheer numbers, are what's driving companies to take this seriously," says Peter Cappelli, director of Wharton's Center for Human Resources. "The big driver is really the cost of health care, which corporations have to bear."

"We do know that obesity is a strong predictor of medical expenses," adds Mark V. Pauly, Wharton professor of health care systems, business, and public policy. "The business case for doing something to reduce obesity is not that employees would be more productive, but that business expenses would be less costly in terms of health insurance programs." The general trend for most employers, he says, "is that sooner or later, the deal you get on health insurance depends on how expensive your workers are. And when it comes to obesity, what's made it more prominent is that it's become more prevalent. Obesity in employees and dependents is starting to get employers' attention."

A $93 Billion Medical Bill

National business advocacy groups and associations now call obesity a "preventable condition"—a word choice that both recognizes the problem and acknowledges efforts to do something about it. According to workplace surveys, the vast majority of organizations with 200 or more employees say they offer programs designed to help improve the health of employees, while about a third of smaller companies offer programs as well. The most prevalent fitness initiatives in companies today include on-site fitness centers or sponsored fitness programs, along with web-based tools for tracking wellness and information.

Yet health care experts also say that many of these programs fail to deliver long-term, significant improvements. Today's spotlight on obesity in the workplace comes at a time when companies are beginning to realize that they have to do more than offer employees access to weight loss incentive programs, fitness centers, and educational seminars. As a result, corporations like Home Depot and Dow Chemical are joining forces with major universities and The National Institutes of Health to develop environmental interventions to help people manage their diet and weight—not just pump up the workplace with gleaming, state-of-the-art fitness equipment.

Based on statistics, the task is daunting. Obesity and overweight conditions contribute as much as $93 billion to the nation's yearly medical bill, according to studies reviewed by the National Business Group on Health, a Washington, D.C.-based nonprofit organization that represents large companies. Of that amount, the total cost of obesity to U.S. companies is estimated at more than $13 billion per year—a price tag that includes $8 billion for added health insurance costs, $2.4 billion for paid sick leave, $1.8 billion for life insurance and $1 billion for disability insurance. According to recent studies on the economic cost of work-place obesity, that translates into thirty-nine million lost work days, 239 million days where work activity is restricted, ninety million sick days or days in bed and sixty-three million visits to physicians.

In October, Adam Gilden Tsai, instructor of medicine in psychiatry at the University of Pennsylvania Medical School, further refined the finan-cial costs associated with being overweight to include a per-person charge. At a conference on obesity, Tsai noted that when compared to a person of average weight, an obese person accounts for an additional $1,034 every year in doctors' visits, medications and medical proce-dures. "I don't think anyone would question that obesity is a significant contributor to health care costs," he says.

For adults, overweight and obesity ranges are determined by using weight and height to calculate a number called the "body mass index" (BMI), which correlates with their amount of body fat. For instance, ac-cording to the CDC, a person who is 5'9? and weighs 125 pounds to 168 pounds is considered a healthy weight; the same person weighing 169 pounds to 202 pounds is overweight; and the same person weigh-ing more than 203 pounds is considered obese. When statistics are tal-lied to show how many Americans are obese or overweight, more than half today fall into one category or the other.

First in Fat

Among developed countries, the United States has the most obese and overweight people, according to Jean Lemaire, Wharton professor of insurance and actuarial science. "Americans are much heavier than they were ten years ago and much heavier than other people around the world," says Lemaire. "Life expectancy in the U.S., which is among the richest countries, only ranks forty-eighth in the world. Being over-weight is comparable to having diabetes or having high blood pressure. It is a true diagnosable disease that affects life expectancy."

According to statistics compiled by the National Business Group on Health through its Institute on the Costs and Health Effects of Obesity, obesity is now considered a greater trigger for health problems and in-creased health spending than smoking or drinking. Based on statistics from a 2002 report called, "The Effects of Obesity, Smoking and Drink-ing on Medical Programs and Costs," published in the *Journal of Health Affairs*, individuals who are obese have 30 percent to 50 percent more chronic medical problems than those who smoke or drink heavily.

Specifically, the CDC notes that being overweight or obese increases the risk of many diseases and health conditions, including hypertension (high blood pressure), dyslipidemia (high total cholesterol or high levels of triglycerides), Type 2 diabetes, heart disease, stroke, gallbladder disease, osteoarthritis, sleep apnea and respiratory problems, and some cancers (endometrial, breast, and colon).

As obesity rises, the medical conditions associated with obesity have helped trigger an increase in health care costs. The National Business Group on Health notes that obesity accounts for approximately 9 percent of total medical care expenditures each year, and that 8 percent of private employer medical claims are due to overweight and obesity.

All of this begs the question: Just how big a slice of the rise in medical costs can be attributed to obesity? In 2004, the last year for which data are available, the National Coalition on Health Care (NCHC) reported that total health care expenditures rose 7.9 percent, for a total of $1.9 trillion in health care spending. When analyzing increases in medical spending from 1987 to 2001, a 2004 report called, "The Impact of Obesity on Rising Medical Spending," documented that obesity drove 27 percent of these increased costs.

There's no doubt that rising health care expenses increase the cost of medical care and health insurance for employers and workers. The NCHC notes that in 2005, "employer health insurance premiums increased by 9.2 percent—nearly three times the rate of inflation." In an effort to counter these statistics and to help employees adopt healthier life styles, employers are offering a variety of programs and benefits. For example:

- With 1,400 people working at its headquarters in Newtown Square, Pa., enterprise software company SAP "believes it is important to partner with our employees related to their health and financial well being," says Brian Shay, SAP manager of rewards and recognition. Using a specially designed software program, SAP analyzes its employee population to help determine the "biggest use of prescription drugs" and the most common medical conditions. "Then we target our wellness programs to those areas. We found that obesity is one condition that we could work on and improve." To help with that effort, the company now offers an on-site gym and outside gym discounts through its health care provider, as well as additional health and wellness programs.

In 2007, SAP will roll out what Shay calls "health risk assessments," and then work to tailor health care programs to target areas like obesity or high blood pressure. The company plans to give cash incentives to employees who take the assessments, and may offer further financial rewards in 2008 for those who successfully improve their health risk assessment. Though SAP does not have any specific statistics on how its programs may have lowered health care costs, Shay says he relies on existing analytical studies that predict a market rate of return between 3 percent and 5 percent from wellness programs. "We are hoping in the long run, say a three- to five-year period, that we will see a significant decrease in our medical costs," he says.

- Over the last decade, the University of Pennsylvania's Division of Human Resources has provided a range of health and wellness programs for faculty and staff, including discounts on month-to-month fitness club memberships, health fairs on campus during the spring to provide information and health screenings, and health and wellness workshops throughout the year that address nutrition, exercise, and ways to stop smoking. In the 2006 academic year, the division added several programs to address obesity. Among them is a holiday weight and activity maintenance program called "Maintain, Don't Gain," where participants agree to weigh in before Thanksgiving and again after the New Year to encourage themselves and each other to not gain weight during the holiday season. Other initiatives include a Weight Watchers program on campus, starting the second week of January, and a spring walking program, beginning in March. Terri Ryan, HR communications manager, also notes that the University's "medical plans are very involved with issues related to obesity." Health care plans offered through Independence Blue Cross include coverage for gastric bypasses, and promise $200 back to members who successfully participate in approved weight management programs. In addition, the University's Aetna HMO plan is in the process of adding a new Weight Management Discount Program to their portfolio of health and wellness initiatives that will allow members and eligible dependents to get discounts on Jenny Craig weight loss programs and products.

- Lorrie Reynolds, director of population health and wellness for Independence Blue Cross, notes that the region's 9,500 employees probably mirror national statistics, which means that over 50 percent of the health insurance company's workforce is overweight or obese. Though Reynolds says that the company doesn't offer financial incentives for employees to lose weight, there are numerous weight reduction challenge programs (similar to those offered to subscribers); support groups; voluntary screenings for weight, blood pressure and cholesterol; online and web-based resources, and telephone counseling for people trying to lose weight. "We really try to take a comprehensive approach and not zero in on one particular way," she says. Fighting obesity "is very difficult. We offer discount programs for participation, but they are not goal based. We realize it is a challenge, and not something [that people] are going to be successful at over night."

Carrots and Sticks

Data to confirm if and how these programs work is hard to come by. Wharton's Pauly cautions that "with wellness and fitness programs I have reviewed, the sweeping generalization is that their results are mixed in terms of effectiveness." In fact, in 2004, two-thirds of the companies surveyed by the National Business Group on Health reported that only 25 percent of their workers participated in existing fitness programs—and it wasn't even clear if the participants were already fit or chronically unfit. Pauley also cautions that programs that offer financial incentives for employees to become fit are often a "delicate issue. Even if you spin it as a carrot, it can become a stick."

This may help explain why companies like Dow Chemical are taking a different approach. As part of a four-year study being funded by the National Institutes of Health, Dow is promoting weight management and physical activity for roughly 10,000 employees at twelve work sites around the country. The study, called "LightenUP," uses environmental approaches and interventions to supplement existing individual-based program efforts.

In coordination with principal investigator Ron Z. Goetzel of Cornell University and the study team, Dow plans to work with food service and vending companies to reduce the amount of high-fat and high-sugar items offered; put up signs to encourage people to take the stairs instead of the elevator; offer weight management tracking programs, and implement walking paths and routes around the buildings. "Providing opportunities for employees to develop a healthy lifestyle at the workplace has become a more strategic focus of the company," says Goetzel, director of Cornell's Institute for Health and Productivity Studies.

Karen Tully, Dow's global health promotion leader, notes that over 60 percent of Dow employees in the United States are either over-weight or obese. Without giving a specific figure, Tully says that the 20 percent increase in health care costs for overweight Dow employees tracks the national average. By participating in programs like LightenUP, Tully argues, Dow is not only "addressing overweight and obesity is-sues" but anticipating a substantial return on investment. According to Goetzel, preliminary reports from the study indicate that if the program succeeds in reducing individual employee risk factors, the subsequent re-duction in corporate health care costs would be more than double the company's initial investment in the program, which Tully says "would be a huge return."

Although the potential benefits to individuals and companies are obvi-ous, there's something about fighting obesity in the workplace that gives Cappelli and others pause. Why? "It's another boundary that's be-ing crossed between the lives of the employees and the interest of the employers," says Cappelli. Putting the spotlight on obesity is particularly unsettling because "unlike smoking—which is clearly bad, not only for the individuals who do it, but for the ones around them—obesity has no effects on the people around you. It's just about you."

From here on in, Cappelli notes, "The door is open for employers to think about all kinds of other employee-related issues which effectively cost them money. This has not been examined critically in any serious way. People in health issues see [weight-related initiatives] as a good thing. And the current interest in curbing obesity will probably stand be-cause no one is pushing back on the employee rights' side. But if you start getting into other aspects of people's lives, you may see groups pushing back."

For instance, Cappelli says, the "next step on this continuum [of cor-porate influence] is for [activities] that might affect you and your perfor-mance at work. Some professions already prohibit their executives from participating in extreme sports. Cappelli also notes that companies may already be exerting some unspoken influence on the size of families by offering cafeteria benefits that index the costs according to the number of children receiving benefits. "You have, effectively, created the incentive for fewer kids," he suggests. "No one has thrown up boundaries to this, because it's still primarily an abstract concern for people," Cappelli adds. "And as long as employers put their toe in the water and there's no objection, others will follow."

Empowerment

Empowerment in an office setting, in a nutshell, is the confidence employees have that their voices are heard, and that their opinions count (and are counted). An empowered employee is one who feels that the organization respects them and their ability to make decisions.

Increasingly, forward-thinking companies are trying to empower their employees. But "empowerment" as a term can cover a whole range of issues, from letting employees make decisions regarding customer service within a certain bandwidth of expense, to giving employees autonomy over much larger issues regarding marketing, product development, and so on.

For example, consider a customer who asks a front-line employee to reimburse him or her for a $20 charge they felt was unfair, or for a $50 service they felt was not delivered properly. In many situations, depending on the amount of the claim, the employee might be able to make the decision to reimburse the customer without having to consult anyone higher up in the organization. That employee is "empowered" to make that kind of decision.

That's one form of empowerment. Another might be giving a group of employees the responsibility and the authority to select a consultant to run a training course.

Empowerment can also be thought of more broadly—pertaining to an organization's culture rather than tying into specific decisions or events. An organization where employees feel "empowered" might be one in which employees feel that they trust their managers, and the organization's leaders, to listen to them and take them seriously all of the time at work.

A company with empowered employees often uses—and is serious about—employee surveys. Such a company is often attentive to performance reviews, and often conducts "consensus" reviews of managers and leaders. ("Consensus" reviews meaning performance reviews that are based

> ### Why I Do This: College Professor, Psychology
> ### Karol Maybury, Ph.D.
>
> As a college professor, I have taught psychology courses, including Introductory Psychology, Social Psychology, Personality Theories, and Research Methods. But in addition to teaching, most professors conduct research. I do that as well. My research examines how accurately people read others' emotions in different situations. Other psychology professors may specialize in children's development (developmental psychologists), memory (cognitive psychologists), or animal behavior (comparative psychologists). There are many other specialties in psychology. In addition to conducting research and teaching college courses, psychology professors mentor students, write articles, and advise students on course selections and career paths.
>
> I found my job after completing a four year undergraduate degree in psychology, followed by a four year doctoral degree. I found my job through an academic job advertisement (in the newspaper *Chronicle of Higher Education*).
>
> I love being a college professor. Most professors work long hours (fifty hours per week), but are able to set our hours and select which classes we'd like to teach. There is a lot of autonomy. Most college professors teach 3–4 classes each semester. Psychology is an exciting field which is always changing. I like the fact that most students find psychology classes much more interesting and challenging than they expect.
>
> One of the unexpected aspects of the job is that you need to become comfortable speaking to large groups. This comfort comes naturally to some people. But most of us get better at it, and enjoy it more, after we have been teaching for a while. I highly recommend this career field. People who enjoy solitary work (research, writing, and computer analysis) plus collaborative work (with students, with colleagues, in classes) would find this an enjoyable career field.

on input from peers, bosses, and direct reports, rather than just being based on a boss or managers' views.)

Companies that understand the importance of empowerment often also attempt to measure their "performance" on the issue. As an article in *Fast Company* noted:

Berth Jönsson at SIFO developed the Empowerment Index for ABB Asea Brown Boveri in the United States. According to Jönsson, motivation and trust are not adequate measures; employees also need appropriate skills and tools to do the job. Thus SIFO's survey adds questions regarding employees' willingness and ability to take action, the support they receive to take action, and their access to systems and information. Categories include Motivation, Support Within the Organization, Awareness of Quality Demands, Responsibility Versus Authority, and Competence" (*Fast Company* magazine, "Trust! (but Verify)." Issue 2, April 1996, page 52, by Eric Matson).

The SIFO questionnaire, the article noted, is filled out by employees, anonymously, and then returned to SIFO for analysis. The results are then presented to the company's leaders. This survey, the article said, has been used by companies including AT&T, Skandia, Swedbank, and Microsoft.

While the concept of empowerment and its effective use can lead to dramatic and meaningful change in organizations, the actual word "empowerment" is often times dismissed in business. Through the 1980s and 1990s, the term became trivialized with overuse.

See also: Generation X, Y, and Z; Glass Ceiling; War for Talent

Further Reading

Empowering Employees, by Kenneth L. Murell and Mimi Meredith, McGraw-Hill (2000)

Enron

Enron Corp. was once a hugely successful energy company, but the giant fell in 2001, when it was discovered that the company had engaged in a massive deception centered around its accounting practices. Since the company fell, the term "Enron" has been increasingly used as a generic synonym for "corporate scandal" or "accounting scandal." The fall—and the fallout—have been huge.

In a report entitled "The Corporate Scandal Sheet" published in *Forbes* magazine August 26, 2002, Penelope Patsuris summed up the Enron scandal as follows: "Boosted profits and hid debts totaling over $1 billion by improperly using off-the-books partnerships; manipulated the Texas power market; bribed foreign governments to win contracts abroad; manipulated California energy market."

In a January 28, 2002, essay in *BusinessWeek*, author Bruce Nussbaum wrote:

There are business scandals that are so vast and so penetrating that they profoundly shock our most deeply held beliefs about the honesty and integrity of our corporate culture. Enron Corp. (ENE) is one of them. This financial disaster goes far beyond the failure of one big company. This is corruption on a massive scale. Tremendous harm has befallen innocent employees who have seen their retirement savings disappear as a few at the top cashed out. Terrible things have happened to the way business is conducted under the cloak of deregulation. Serious damage has been done to ethical codes of conduct held by once-trusted business professionals.

In the December 24, 2001, issue of *The Nation* (www.thenation.com), national affairs correspondent William Greider (a former *Rolling Stone* and *Washington Post* Editor) wrote: "An energy-trading company that Wall Street had valued at $80 billion ten months ago is now a penny stock. Meanwhile, California consumers and businesses are stuck with the ruinously inflated electricity prices that Enron rode to brief financial glory. The firm's gullible creditors include some of the best gilt-edged names in American banking—J.P. Morgan Chase, Citigroup—whose ancestral houses were big players during the first Gilded Age too. Unfortunately, then and now, these venerable financial institutions lured millions of innocents to the slaughter, unwitting shareholders who bought the exuberant promises."

And, in an article entitled "Called to Account," published in *Time* magazine June 18, 2002 (online at www.time.com), Cathy Booth Thomas wrote: "Accounting firm Arthur Andersen had already been found guilty in the court of public opinion, and paid a heavy penalty. Clients deserted; employees fled. In fact the Chicago firm was barely alive, but one question remained: What would its epitaph be, the lesson for others?" An answer came last Saturday, when a Houston jury found Andersen guilty of obstructing justice. It provided a moment of vindication for investors who lost more than $60 billion in the spectacular collapse of Enron, whose books had been audited by Andersen.

John Ellis, a New York based writer and consultant, writing for *Fast Company* in its February 2002 issue (Issue 56, page 118), summed up the scandal in the context of the new economy:

Enron's deranged notion that it could lie itself out of its pickle is emblematic of how little the company really understood the underlying principles of the new economy. Principle one is transparency. Principle two is opportunity. Principle three is speed. Enron grew at an astonishing speed. It seized a tremendous opportunity (creating a futures market for any number of basic services). But it never understood the most important principle: A business of information requires transparency. And so, Enron failed. Good riddance.

Note: Ex-Enron CEO Kenneth Lay, awaiting sentencing for fraud and conspiracy in the Enron trial, died in 2006. According to a report in CNNMoney (www.money.cnn.com) by Shaheen Pasha, published July 5, 2006, Lay "was found guilty of ten counts of fraud and conspiracy related to the collapse of Enron, the energy company he founded that eventually grew into the nation's seventh largest company before it imploded after an accounting scandal."

Pasha wrote: "It was an astounding fall from grace for the Houston businessman who was affectionately called 'Kenny Boy' by President Bush. Lay had raised funds for Bush earlier in his political career. In the Enron trial, Lay was accused of lying to investors and Wall Street about the health of Enron in late 2001 even as he enriched himself by selling millions of dollars in stock."

Ultimately, the word Enron has become synonymous with corporate greed and leaders who can't be trusted.

See also: Code of Ethics

Further Reading

"Life After Enron's Death: Preventing Another Enron Means Understanding What Really Went Wrong. That Means Understanding Transparency, Opportunity, and Speed," by John Ellis, *Fast Company* magazine (February 2002), p. 118.

www.enron.com

Equal Employment Opportunity Commission (EEOC)

The U.S. Equal Employment Opportunity Commission (EEOC) is the federal agency responsible for enforcing employment discrimination laws. Its Training Institute provides a wide variety of training programs to help employers understand, prevent and correct discrimination in the workplace.

The EEOC has five commissioners and a General Counsel appointed by the President and confirmed by the Senate. Commissioners are appointed for five-year, staggered terms. The term of the General Counsel is four years. The President designates a Chair and a Vice Chair, The Chair is the chief executive officer of the Commission. The five-member Commission makes equal employment opportunity policy and approves most litigation.

According to the EEOC website, the federal laws prohibiting job discrimination are:

- Title VII of the Civil Rights Act of 1964 (Title VII), which prohibits employment discrimination based on race, color, religion, sex, or national origin;
- the Equal Pay Act of 1963 (EPA), which protects men and women who perform substantially equal work in the same establishment from sex-based wage discrimination;
- the Age Discrimination in Employment Act of 1967 (ADEA), which protects individuals who are 40 years of age or older;
- Title I and Title V of the Americans with Disabilities Act of 1990 (ADA), which prohibit employment discrimination against qualified individuals with disabilities in the private sector, and in state and local governments;
- Sections 501 and 505 of the Rehabilitation Act of 1973, which prohibit discrimination against qualified individuals with disabilities who work in the federal government; and
- the Civil Rights Act of 1991, which, among other things, provides monetary damages in cases of intentional employment discrimination (Information obtained from www.eeoc.gov).

The EEOC's Training Institute is part of the Commission (www.eeotraining.eeoc.gov). According to its website, it provides training that can help prevent discrimination in the workplace, and also correct discriminating behaviors. The Training Institute also provides assistance for people who want to learn more about EEO law. The Training Institute has an annual conference it calls EXCEL. According to the website, this conference is for "EEO managers, supervisors and specialists, attorneys, union representatives, mediators, Alternative Dispute Resolution coordinators and human resources professionals." The Training Institute also runs regular seminars—held in major cities throughout the United States—that explore various EEO topics and clarify EEOC policies and procedures.

See also: Age Discrimination; American Association of Retired Persons (AARP); Americans with Disabilities Act; Harassment

Further Reading

www.eeoc.goc

Executive Coach

An executive coach is an individual who works with business executives to advise them on how to become better leaders and managers. Executive coaches sometimes take on the role of trusted advisor, the role of therapist, and the role of career coach simultaneously.

An article published in the *Harvard Management Update* quoted Babson professor James Hunt on coaching. "Coaching is effective for executives who can say, 'I want to get over there, but I'm not sure how to do it,'" says James Hunt, an associate professor of management at Babson College and coauthor of *The Coaching Manager* (Sage Publications, 2002). "Coaching works best when you know what you want to get done." ("Methodology: Do You Need an Executive Coach?" *Harvard Management Update*, Vol. 9, No. 12, December 2004)

Coaching, in other words, can be very effective when a manager has clear aspirations. But it can also help managers in general be more effective leaders, by helping them identify and address their weaknesses and build on their strengths. Sometimes, an executive will call on a coach when the organization is going through a crisis, or a period of undue stress. In "normal" times, possibly the executive would not need such coaching. But in the midst of turmoil, a coach can be an objective third-party, helping the executive gain and regain perspective so that they can make decisions with as clear a head as possible.

And, sometimes, a coach can be helpful when a manager is in over their head in terms of leadership issues. Sometimes, if a strong employee—say, a "rainmaker" sales person—is promoted to a leadership position, that person can flounder due to lack of experience, or confidence as a manager. A coach can often help the person develop necessary leadership and management skills faster than they would do on their own.

See also: Blanchard, Ken; Corner Office

Further Reading

"What an Executive Coach Can Do for You," by Paul Michelman, *Harvard Management Update* (published June 13, 2005), located at http://hbswk .hbs.edu.

"The Wild West of Executive Coaching," by Stratford Sherman and Alyssa Freas, *Harvard Business Review* (November 1, 2004).

Executive Compensation

Executive compensation, put simply, is what executives receive from a company in exchange for the work they do. Time was, such compensation could consist simply of a salary and a bonus. More often than not, however, the term today means more than that. According to a special report on Forbes.com in an article titled "CEO Compensation" published on April 21, 2005 and edited by Scott DeCarlo, executive compensation today means a "salary and bonus plus 'other' compensation, which includes vested restricted stock grants and 'stock gains,' the value realized from exercising stock options during the just-concluded fiscal year."

In many cases, executive compensation, beyond an agreed-upon salary, is determined in large part by how the company performs under the executive's leadership. (If the person is not a top manager, compensation might be tied to the division or function that they run.) This is common practice, although it does have critics. Another article on Forbes.com published on May 9, 2005 titled "Paychecks on Steroids" by Michael K. Ozanian and Elizabeth MacDonald, takes a closer look at executive pay. This article first says that paying executives based on company performance is a long-established practice, and notes that in 1929, Eugene Grace, president of Bethlehem Steel earned a $1.6 million cash bonus on a salary of $12,000. It then goes on to say that such pay-for-performance practices "became all the rage in the 1990s. The stock market was taking off, and stock options were the currency of choice because companies did not have to expense them. Incentive plans would typically cover two or three years and incorporate such metrics as profitability and the company's stock price."

That article notes that it is difficult to ensure that a pay-for-performance system links shareholder interests with the interests of the senior executive in question: "The proxy statement is often so vague it's impossible to figure out what targets were supposedly met by an executive to qualify for a bonus. Plus, it's easy to play with how you meet targets, especially earnings."

The article quoted Baruch Lev, an accounting and finance professor at New York University's Stern School of Business. Lev told Forbes.com: "Generally accepted accounting principles are an art, not a science. Give a smart boss the incentive to do it, and he can push the earnings envelope to the limit—or beyond."

The issue has sparked much debate—and not just in the United States. For just one more example, the Ottawa Citizen editorialized on executive pay in an article titled "There's no profit in arguing" by Mark Sutcliffe that appeared on the Ottawa Citizen website on January 6, 2007.

The article said: "It's easy to criticize rising executive pay. It's much harder to come up with a method of controlling it . . . And while it's worth exploring how, through better governance practices, the growing compensation gap between CEOs and their employees can be closed, it's fair to ask whether the exorbitant pay earned by the highest-paid executives in Canada is really a big problem for society or just a convenient target."

The article noted that according to the Canadian Centre for Policy Alternatives, the average of Canada's 100 highest-paid chief executives made more money in the first two full days of 2007 than the average Canadian will earn the entire year.

This article also went on to note that according to a report around that time in the *New York Times*, executives at major U.S. corporations "make 170 times the typical worker."

Many opinions offered in the press and by academics acknowledge that the salaries paid to the top executives of companies are far too high, especially when compared with the wages earned by employees much lower on the organization chart. Some contend that the issue continues to spiral out of control, despite the fact that most people—even most top executives—would acknowledge that something should be done to bring top manager's wages more in line with those earned by the rest of the company's employees. There has yet to be a large movement, however, towards resolution of this issue.

See also: Corner Office; Sarbanes–Oxley Act of 2002

Further Reading

"Fixing Executive Pay" by Orit Gadiesh, Marcia Blenko, and Robin Buchanan, a Bain Results Brief (February 26, 2003), www.bain.com/bainweb/publications.

Exit Interview

An exit interview is the meeting held between an employee who is leaving a company, and a representative of that company—most often someone from the Human Resources department. Exit interviews can be valuable on several levels. For example, allowing an employee to vent freely about the workplace, and about his or her reasons for leaving, can shed light on chronic management problems, or other issues at the company that should be addressed. If a company compares notes from exit interviews, managers may recognize common themes, and take steps to remedy employee relations on a larger scale—in an effort to improve retention.

Exit interviews can also be good for the employee who is leaving. If the company is truly interested in its employees as people, an exit interview can serve as a launching pad from which the employee becomes a valued "alumni" of the organization. Some businesses—notably those in the professional services field—take alumni-employee relations very seriously. A firm's alumni can be a great source of references for new business, and also word-of-mouth recommendations for future employees.

According to an article on the National Federation of Independent Business website posted on January 27, 2004, by Charles R. McConnell titled "Simple Exit Interviews Help Reduce Turnover," "Valued employees often consider changing jobs because of unhappiness with some aspect of the work situation, and often their reasons relate to how they believe they are treated."

The article goes on to say that "departing employees are most likely to speak honestly if exit interviews are conducted by someone other than the immediate supervisor, say perhaps another supervisor, the immediate supervisor's manager, or, preferably, whoever usually attends to human resource matters. Even when undertaken by a neutral party, some departing employees—usually those leaving for 'personal reasons'—may say nothing negative for fear of affecting future employment references."

The article notes that it is important for companies not to jump to conclusions based on one exit interview, but to gather information from as many interviews as it can before making any judgment calls about what's going on inside the company—or department within the company that has high turnover (http://www.nfib.com/object/4152571.html).

An article on Entrepreneur.com provides some tips on conducting a successful exit interview. The key idea, according to this article, is to offer the exiting employee a "safe" place in which they feel they can speak honestly and freely about issues at the company, or the behaviors of a certain manager. It's a good idea, the article says, to guide the conversation a bit, to touch on points including relationships with colleagues, the behavior and style of the boss, the way in which the company's different departments and functions interact, and employee satisfaction. The article also said that it can be helpful to let the exiting employee know beforehand what topics might be covered, so that they have time to think about the issues and don't feel on the spot or under pressure during the interview. ("Conducting an Exit Interview: Just why would you want to interview an employee who's decided to quit? We'll give you a few good reasons." By David Javitch. October 17, 2006. Entrepreneur.com. http://www .entrepreneur.com/humanresources/employeemanagementcolumnistdavid javitch/article169102.html)

Much like an annual employee survey, exit interviews are an excellent way to get an in-depth view of what is really happening in a business's office culture. But it is important to follow through with the person conducting these interviews. Otherwise, the interview process can become an exercise in futility, and a waste of time.

See also: War for Talent

Further Reading

"Exit Interviews: Gone with the Wind," by Mansi Dutta & Mansi Tiwari, *The Economic Times* (powered by Indiatimes) (September 11, 2007).

"Why Good Employees Leave—and How to Retain More of Them," by Gregg Gregory, *Reliable Plant* magazine (September 2007), www.reliableplant .com.

Feng Shui

The concept of Feng Shui, or "wind and water," has its roots in ancient Chinese philosophy. Essentially, Feng Shui calls for people to live in harmony with their environment; when harmony is achieved, there is a natural flow of energy, which can improve one's sense of well-being.

Many home decorators embrace the concept of Feng Shui as they set out to create calming and inviting interiors. But Feng Shui is also popular in office settings. When Feng Shui is applied at work, the goal is to reduce stress and thus encourage increased employee productivity. According to an article by Miriam Marcus on Forbes.com ("A Healthy Office, A Healthy Mind?" May 29, 2007), the use of Feng Shui is on the rise among corporate leaders.

The *Forbes* article quotes Dirk Moler, CEO of Get Logistics, a Billings, Montana transportation broker. "The crazy thing about Feng Shui is that I don't know if it was the right business timing for increased profits, the right time of the year, or the result of good Feng Shui, but it all happened at the same time, and I attribute at least some of that success to Feng Shui," Moler said.

The article went on to say that, according to Feng Shui consultant Kartar Diamond of Los Angeles, "By manipulating a physical workspace in subtle ways, such as color choice, furniture arrangement, and the use of natural building materials, Feng Shui can increase employee productivity, amplify profits by attracting more customers, cut down on office politicking and build a better corporate reputation."

Importantly, the article notes, the practice of Feng Shui is not about placing items around an office to cue people to reduce stress. More likely, applying Feng Shui in an office setting will involve rearranging the furniture to align people within the office and people moving through an office to minimize disruption and maximize individuals' abilities to concentrate and interact productively.

An article by Claire Bush written for the *Arizona Republic*, published May 30, 2007 on www.azcentral.com, concurs, noting also that a good first step is getting rid of clutter. As Feng Shui consultant Carol Johnsen says in that article: "Getting rid of clutter gets rid of the overwhelming feeling that zaps your energy. If you don't have time to take care of things in your immediate environment, don't have them in there."

Feng Shui can even apply if your office is in your home According to a Q&A by Rose B. Gilbert, posted on ParamusPost.com on Friday, June 8, 2007, the most important step a person can take to promote the concept of Feng Shui in a home office is to "get your office out of your bedroom."

A Google search for Feng Shui consultants, conducted on June 11, 2007, results in about 992,000 cites. Among the top three: The Feng Shui Directory (www.fengshuidirectory.com).

See also: Dilbert

Further Reading

"The Feng Shui Kingdom," by Laura M. Holson, *New York Times*, Late Edition—Final, Section C, Page 1, Column 2 (April 25, 2005).

"SQUARE FEET: BLUEPRINTS; Where Comfort Is Obvious, and Wiring Less So," by Claire Wilson, *New York Times*, Money and Business/Financial Desk Late Edition—Final, Section 3, Page 24, Column 1 (December 17, 2006, Sunday).

www.amfengshui.com (American Feng Shui Institute)

Flex-Time

Flex-time is a work schedule that allows employees to work hours that are not within the standard 8 A.M. to 5 P.M. range. Employees working a "flex-time schedule" for example, might put in a few hours early in the morning, then take time to take their children to school, and then return to work at 10 A.M. Alternatively, other employees might start their workday later in the morning, and stay later into the evening, or work a "short day" and then put in extra hours at night or over the weekend to make up the time.

Far from being an altruistic move, most employers who offer flex-time arrangements do so to get the most out of valued employees who are trying to balance the demands of work and family, and contribute the most they can in each venue. These employees have found that the stress of trying to balance work and family are significant, and that it erodes their ability to do their best work.

A report on FoxNews.com posted on Dec. 20, 2006, titled "Stressed-Out Parents Cost Companies $300 Billion in Lost Productivity," points to a survey completed by researchers at Brandeis University and Catalyst, a New York-based nonprofit, which found that of 1,755 working parents nationwide, one in twenty said they were severely impacted by concerns about after-school childcare.

"Stress over after-school care is an 'equal-opportunity issue,'" Ilene Lang, the president of Catalyst, said in a statement in that report.

The study noted that companies are increasingly able to create work environments that are amenable to flex-time arrangements. E-mail, video and phone meetings, and networks on which employees can share documents all facilitate people who are working flexible hours, but expect—and are expected to—meet a high standard of full-time performance expectations. Technological aids can also allow employees to toggle back and forth between home and work life with minimal disruption.

In the workplace, shared offices, cubicles, or other work-spaces are another way to facilitate flexible schedules. Such arrangements may also result in savings associated with renting or maintaining office space. If employees are using laptops, and can easily access a robust intranet, it is easier to work effectively in multiple locations without a lot of ramp-up time.

The study recommends that companies be proactive about facilitating flexible schedules by creating environments that are conducive to telecommuting, flex-time and "flex-space." It recommends that companies also educate managers about the needs of flex-time workers, and take steps to ensure that employees are aware of the ways in which the company can support a flexible schedule.

According to the study, the results are worth the effort. "More than 75 percent of respondents said greater flexibility to arrive at work later or leave earlier, or take half-days when necessary, significantly cuts down on stress."

If company leaders are leery of embracing flex-time arrangements, they might take note of an article in the *New York Times*, which cited a survey by the Association of Executive Search Consultants, a professional group based in New York. This survey found that more than half of senior executives responding would turn down a promotion if it meant losing more control over their schedule (*New York Times*, "Flex Time for the Rest of Us," by Lisa Belkin, Dec. 17, 2006).

Companies hesitant to offer flexible schedules might also consider the cost of losing employees they have invested in—particularly to a more flexible competitor. Time was, flexible hours were considered a perk. But in a marketplace where so many companies compete on the knowledge and talent of their employees, flexibility is necessarily and strategically moving more towards standard operating procedure.

Unfortunately, as the *New York Times* article noted, although more companies are professing to offer flexible schedules, work-life balance has worsened for employees. The article said that the survey authors noted that "flexibility in more than name only is still a long way off."

See also: Job Sharing; War for Talent

Further Reading

"Employers Find Balance with Flex Time for All," by Joyce M. Rosenberg, Associated Press article as published September 2, 2007 in www.thenewstribune .com.

Signs of Changing Culture:
Men, Women, and Household Activities

"American Time Use Survey Summary" by the Bureau of Labor Statistics (BLS) of the U.S. Department of Labor, July 27, 2006. http://www .bls.gov/news.release/atus.nr0.htm

On an average day in 2005, 84 percent of women and 65 percent of men spent some time doing household activities, such as housework, cooking, lawn care, or financial and other household management.

Women who reported doing household activities on the diary day spent 2.7 hours on such activities while men spent 2.1 hours.

On an average day, 19 percent of men reported doing housework— such as cleaning or doing laundry—compared with 53 percent of women. Thirty-seven percent of men did food preparation or cleanup versus 66 percent of women.

The 4Ps

The "4Ps" are the four "essentials" that a marketer has to think about when planning a strategy for any product or service. Though different academics and practitioners have changed the terms associated with the "Ps" to suit their work over the years, the generally agreed upon "4Ps" are: Product, Price, Promotion, and Place.

Product is the "what"—what is being sold and can be a thing or a service. Price is, as the word implies, the amount that the customer must pay to get the product. What will the company charge for its product or service? Will the offering be part of a bundle? Will it be a monthly fee? Promotion has to do with how the product is marketed. In what context is the product sold? To what target customers? How is it marketed?

Finally, place has to do with distribution. Place deals with how a customer gets a product—whether the purchase takes place in a store or online or both. This aspect also deals with whether a store in which an item is purchased is owned by the company and even covers details of distribution, manufacture (or creation of service), and delivery to the customer.

According to the American Marketing Association website (www .marketingpower.com), the "most common classification of these factors is the four-factor classification called the "Four Ps"—price, product, promotion, and place (or distribution). Optimization of the marketing mix is achieved by assigning the amount of the marketing budget to be spent on each element of the marketing mix so as to maximize the total contribution to the firm. Contribution may be measured in terms of sales or profits or in terms of any other organizational goals."

Here's another definition of the 4Ps, or the Marketing Mix, this one according to www.marketingteacher.com:

The marketing mix is probably the most famous phrase in marketing. The elements are the marketing "tactics." Also known as the "four Ps," the marketing mix elements are price, place, product, and promotion. The concept is simple. Think about another common mix—a cake mix. All cakes contain eggs, milk, flour, and sugar. However, you can alter the final cake by altering the amounts of mix elements contained in it. So for a sweet cake add more sugar! It is the same with the marketing mix. The offer you make to you customer can be altered by varying the mix elements.

Marketingteacher.com goes on to note that some people choose to use five "Ps," adding "people" to the mix, and asking marketers to think more closely about who is going to be buying or using the product. And some marketers use even more "Ps," trying to emphasize, for example, "process," or the whole "experience" of buying and using a product.

The "experience" of buying and/or using a product or service has lately factored largely in the traditional "mix." B. Joseph Pine II and James H. Gilmore's book *The Experience Economy: Work is Theatre and Every Business a Stage,* explores the concept in great detail. Consider this short anecdote from their book:

> Immediately on arriving in Venice, Italy, a friend asked a hotel concierge where he and his wife could go to enjoy the city's best. Without hesitation, they were directed to the Café Florian in St. Mark's Square. The two of them were soon at the café in the crisp morning air, sipping cups of steaming coffee, fully immersed in the sights and sounds of the most remarkable of Old World cities. More than an hour later, our friend received the bill and discovered the experience had cost more than $5 a cup. Was the coffee worth it, we asked? "Assolutamente!" he replied.

Considering "experience" can allow a company to alter the "mix" significantly, and please the customer while reaping increased profit.

The term "4Ps," was reportedly coined by Neil H. Borden in his article "The Concept of the Marketing Mix" in 1965. That's more than forty years ago, as of this writing, of course. So fast-forward to a slightly more recent year, 1985, when Benson P. Shapiro, another venerable Harvard Business School professor, wrote another key article on the topic, published by the *Harvard Business Review*. This article, called "Rejuvenating the Marketing Mix," reviewed the essential elements, but honed the subject, talking about how to tailor the "mix" depending on company strength, the competition and the greater context of the market. The marketing mix as a concept has stood the test of time, and is still relevant in the "new economy," and the age of the "knowledge worker." Companies that get it right, do well.

See also: One-to-One Marketing; Relationship Marketing

Further Reading

"The Keys to Growing Brands," by John Blasberg and Vijay Vishwanath, *Marketing Magazine* (October 6, 2003), located at http://www.bain.com/bainweb/publications.

The Toyota Way Fieldbook: A Practical Guide for Implementing Toyota's 4Ps, by Jeffrey Liker and David Meier, McGraw-Hill (2005).
http://marketing.about.com/od/marketingplanandstrategy
www.marketingpower.com (American Marketing Association)

Signs of Changing Culture:
The New Age of Marketing

Glenn Rifkin

Glenn Rifkin is a business journalist and author based near Boston. He is a regular contributor to the *New York Times* and is the co-author of *Radical Marketing: From Harvard to Harley; Lessons from Ten That Broke the Rules and Made It Big*. This article is used courtesy of Glenn Rifkin.

On October 23, 2006, a string of seemingly unrelated stories made the business news pages of various publications. Among the most compelling:

- *Shares of Google* stock topped $480 a share, an incredible price for a company that had been in existence for less than eight years. Much of the recent surge in the stock price stemmed from Google's decision to buy YouTube.com for $1.6 billion, which had been announced the week before.
- *Apple celebrated* the fifth anniversary of the launch of the iPod. Despite early sluggish sales of the innovative product, the iPod quickly became an icon product in the new millennium. By this date, Apple had sold 68 million iPods for $14 billion and experts predicted that the 100 millionth iPod would be sold before the end of the year.
- *CBS announced* that it was canceling a promising new drama named *Smith* after just three weeks on the air. This came less than a week after NBC announced it would no longer produce "scripted" shows (i.e., sitcoms, dramas, and anything that isn't reality TV) for its once coveted 8 P.M. timeslot.
- *Ford Motor Company announced* a third-quarter loss of $5.8 billion, the largest in fourteen years.
- *Jeffrey Skilling, the former CEO* of Enron, was sentenced to

133

twenty-five years in prison for his role in defrauding investors
and bringing the giant corporation to bankruptcy.

In fact, these stories, chosen on a random day in a chaotic business
year, demonstrated the dramatic changes taking place in the world of
business and media. Fundamental shifts in thinking about once inviolate
markets have been underway for several years and it has become increasingly obvious that there is a new order in the world in terms of
news, entertainment, advertising, marketing, and the movement of information in all our lives.

A company like Google, founded in a Silicon Valley garage in 1998,
has quickly become the major technology player in the minds of marketers trying to reach a broader audience. In what seems like an instant,
Google changed the landscape of the Internet, not just for search engines but for the wide dissemination of information around the globe.
In fact, the name Google quickly became a verb in the technology-
driven lexicon of a new generation.

Its latest acquisition, YouTube.com, a popular website for video postings, was even more of a lightning rod for the new media. Less than
two years old, this site had quickly become a destination location for
Generation Y'ers and a harbinger for the future of Internet marketing.
With no profits and few revenues, the $1.6 billion price tag that Google
paid for YouTube was reminiscent of the mindless spending for overin-
flated ventures during the dot.com era of the late 1990s. Yet YouTube
has obviously struck a chord with a growing audience and marketers
could no longer afford to ignore its influence. No one could point out
the exact tipping point for YouTube, when it crossed the line from upstart to cool, but once that occurred, the rush to corral that audience
was on.

Symbolizing the massive shift in media, Apple's iPod quickly became
more than a well-designed MP3 player. It has become a platform for
layers of media including television programming and movies and it has
been the catalyst for a new, potent form of communication dubbed Podcasting. Apple's iTunes website simply changed the music business, creating a new model for pricing and distribution of music.

These and other powerful new media have begun to change the landscape for traditional media outlets. The major television networks, such
as CBS and NBC, have been forced to reconsider their content offerings
as well as how they will attract audiences among new generations of

viewers. New TV shows have just a few weeks to attract an audience or they will be canceled. Expensive dramas and sitcoms are being replaced by cheap to produce reality shows, and the audience for television in general seems to be dwindling as the demographics get younger.

Tectonic shifts in economic trends and markets have created tremendous pressures on traditional corporate powerhouses such as the Detroit automakers. Finding appealing new products is now only the first step in the quest for greater profits. Reaching an audience that is not responding as past audiences have is creating challenges that corporate marketers struggle to overcome. Giant companies like Ford find themselves in a quandary over how to incorporate the new media in order to sell products. The old ways clearly are not working. Several large companies experimented with using the Internet to encourage customers to create their own advertising. Chevy discovered the concept was a mixed blessing as its Chevy Tahoe SUV was lambasted by creative neo-advertisers with a barrage of ads portraying the Tahoe as a gas-guzzling, environment killing vehicle that buyers should avoid.

And the Skilling verdict was a reminder that the stakes in this economic drama remain high enough for players to be tempted to scam the system, seeking fraudulent ways to market their message, bolster the numbers, and garner personal riches. The new economy, fueled by the digital revolution, is likely to be fertile ground for nefarious means to dubious ends.

The foundation for all these changes actually began in the 1980s with the advent of the personal computer, followed by advances in telecommunications technology and the birth of the Internet in the 1990s. With the confluence of several remarkable technologies in the early part of this decade, there was a perfect storm of world-changing events. The great leap forward in computing power and speed coupled with the explosion of the Internet around the planet collided head-on with the widespread adoption of broadband connections to the online world. Suddenly, almost without warning, the Internet began to attract hundreds of millions of users around the planet and the technology opened the door for new applications of video, audio, and online commerce. A new virtual world, which had been much discussed and anticipated for two decades, suddenly came real.

In the midst of this great transition, the old and the new have bumped up against each other, leaving corporate marketing executives, advertising professionals, and consultants in a quandary as to how to proceed. Traditional marketing methods such as print and broadcast advertising are under tremendous pressure to demonstrate the kind of return on investment that justifies the billions of dollars of spending that continues today. For example, an estimated 12 million American homes now have digital video recording (DVR) devices installed, including the pioneering technology TIVO. Although that remains a relatively low number, the implications of the technology are great. Viewers armed with DVRs can record their favorite programs and simply eliminate the commercials. Even those homes without such devices have changed their viewing habits dramatically, zapping to other channels when commercials appear. So what must corporate clients do to reach their target audiences with their marketing messages in a world where that message can be easily ignored?

In ten years, for example, radio, a medium long favored by advertisers, has seen a dramatic drop in teenage listeners. According to Edison Media Research, the average weekly time spent listening to the radio among 12–17 year olds has dropped from 15.75 hours to 12.75 hours. Listening hours have also dropped 21 percent for 18–24 year olds during this same period.

Indeed, television viewing in these demographics has dropped nine percent in recent years as a wide array of new media is drawing this young audience away. Teenagers spend far more time on cell phones, online blogging at such social networking sites as Facebook and MySpace.com, or instant messaging with friends. Video games continue to be a major attraction and an emerging world of virtual communities such as *Second Life*, where members take on digital alter egos called avatars, is growing rapidly in popularity. Marketers such as Toyota, Starwood Resorts, and Nissan are already placing ads in these three-dimensional digital worlds with the hope of attracting a new audience.

Never before has the world faced such rapid and dramatic change. When Marshall McLuhan uttered his famous edict in the 1960s that "the medium is the message," he was presaging the world of today, where media advancements and market shifts occur at breakneck speed and new trends unseat current trends before most companies can react. The Internet is indeed a medium that is also the message and those who can decipher the message most effectively will be the winners.

The solution appears to be a new corporate archetype built upon flexible, diverse marketing efforts led by (usually) young, creative forward-thinkers who stay in close touch with shifting trends and technologies.

At the same time, companies cannot get ahead of themselves and presume the early and untimely death of traditional marketing techniques. Television and print, for example, remain potent conveyers of messages to a wide audience, including the economically powerful baby boom generation that is just now turning sixty. This target audience has massive buying power, long memories, and media habits that date back several decades. Although they are generally open to embracing new technologies, they have not abandoned long favored connections such as newspapers, radio, and television viewing.

Like so many corporate challenges, this is all about the journey, not the destination. The winners will be companies like Nike, Apple, Toyota, Yahoo, and others that recognize and embrace new technologies while sustaining long-held ties to traditional media.

Free Agent

Free agents are people who work independently, and are often hired by larger companies for their expertise. As individuals, their input keeps a great many companies running more smoothly than they otherwise would. As a group, they are growing in number and impact on the world of work.

They often work from home, or from very small offices—sometimes quite untraditional in nature and location. And they are known by a variety of monikers, among them: "free agents, freelancers, elancers, solo practitioners, independent consultants, and home-based business operators."

In December 1997, Daniel H. Pink wrote a *Fast Company* article entitled: "Free Agent Nation." In it, Pink wrote:

> It's out there, from coast to coast, and it's growing every day. The residents of Free Agent, USA are legion: Start with the fourteen million self-employed Americans. Consider the 8.3 million Americans who are independent contractors. Factor in the 2.3 million people who find work each day through temporary agencies. Note that in January the IRS expects to mail out more than seventy-four million copies of Form1099-MISC—the pay stub of free agents.

Pink subsequently went on to write a book entitled *Free Agent Nation: How America's New Independent Workers are Transforming the Way We*

Live (Warner Books, 2001). A quote from that book: "The Free Agent Org Chart is fluid. And because it's fluid, it's less hierarchical. Your peer on one project could be your boss on another. Today's subcontractor could be tomorrow's customer. In this sense, the Free Agent Org Chart resembles a traditional organization chart less than it resembles the human brain . . . This is one reason that free agency might—just might—be more attuned to human nature than the typical twentieth-century employment structure."

There are growing numbers of formal networks and associations devoted to facilitating the world of the free agent. Many of these are specific to a given profession, but some are more broad in nature, Free Agent Boston (www.freeagentboston.com), for example. According to its website, "Free Agent Boston is an informal network of people working solo in the greater Boston area organized by Susan Kaup. The project got its start in December 1999 when Susan invited a couple of free agent friends to get together for lunch. Since then Free Agent Boston has hosted dozens of networking, educational, and social events for people working outside the corporate 9–5 world who want to exchange ideas, collaborate on projects and see someone during the day other than the mailman."

Elance.com is another. Elance links website designers, writers, programmers and other professionals with people and companies searching for independent contractor expertise. According to the website (albeit advertising copy), "Elance's self-service staffing model allows businesses to remain nimble while getting work done quickly and cost effectively, simultaneously bringing great work opportunities to a global network of talented service providers."

It is important for tax purposes—for both the employer and the person being hired to work—to determine, at the outset of any job, whether the relationship is employer/employee or employer/independent contractor/free agent. On this topic, the website of the Internal Revenue Service (www.irs.gov/businesses/small) says:

Before you can determine how to treat payments you make for services, you must first know the business relationship that exists between you and the person performing the services. The person performing the services may be—

An independent contractor
A common-law employee

A statutory employee

A statutory non-employee

In determining whether the person providing service is an employee or an independent contractor, all information that provides evidence of the degree of control and independence must be considered.

It is critical that you, the employer, correctly determine whether the individuals providing services are employees or independent contractors. Generally, you must withhold income taxes, withhold and pay Social Security and Medicare taxes, and pay unemployment tax on wages paid to an employee. You do not generally have to withhold or pay any taxes on payments to independent contractors.

Caution: If you incorrectly classify an employee as an independent contractor, you can be held liable for employment taxes for that worker, plus a penalty."

The website goes on to say that: "A general rule is that you, the payer, have the *right to control or direct only the result of the work* done by an independent contractor, and *not the means and methods of accomplishing the result.*

Example: Vera Elm, an electrician, submitted a job estimate to a housing complex for electrical work at $16 per hour for 400 hours. She is to receive $1,280 every two weeks for the next ten weeks. This is not considered payment by the hour. Even if she works more or less than 400 hours to complete the work, Vera Elm will receive $6,400. She also performs additional electrical installations under contracts with other companies, that she obtained through advertisements. Vera is an **independent contractor**.

The IRS website offers a great deal of other information for independent workers/free agents. Other good resources include the United States Small Business Administration (www.sba.gov), the National Small Business Association, and the American Small Businesses Association.

See also: Flex Time; Job Sharing

Further Reading

"Free Agent Nation," by Daniel H. Pink, *Fast Company* magazine (December 1997), p. 131.

Free Agent Nation: How America's New Independent Workers Are Transforming the Way We Live, by Daniel H. Pink, Warner Books (2001).

General Electric (GE) Workout

General Electric is often used as an example of a well-run, highly successful company. As a result, the tools and techniques that General Electric has used are widely studied, and have been tailored for use in many other organizations. One of these techniques is the "GE Workout," which was developed under the leadership of Jack Welch. Essentially, the GE Workout is an approach to decision-making and problem solving in which larger groups of employees, along with their managers, identify problems or decisions that need to be made, and then smaller groups of employees—sans the higher-level managers—gather to figure out solutions. (This phase is often accomplished with the help of an outside facilitator. The goal is to push beyond "the way things have always been done," and find new and innovative ways to address the issues at hand.) These smaller groups, armed with an idea, then meet again with the higher-level managers in a town meeting-like setting to vet their ideas.

According to "Adapting General Electric's Workout for Use in Other Organizations: A Template," published in the Management Development Forum (Willam S. Schaniger, Jr., Stanley G. Harrish and Robert E. Niebuhr, Volume 2—No. 1[99]), the GE Workout "was as much a philosophy and approach to problem solving as it was a technique." The article goes on to say that the Workout approach—together with benchmarking best practices and mapping processes, have been the fundamental keys to GE's success.

The article, and other sources, note that the GE workout is a process, not a one-off event. It must be embraced at all levels of the organization, or it will not work.

An article on www.isixsigma.com published on Feb. 11, 2004, called "Six Sigma and Workout: Building a Better Tool Set for Accelerating Change," by Rick Tucci also discusses the evolution of the GE Workout. As Tucci noted, the GE Workout marked a striking departure from other organizational tools and approaches designed to help companies improve performance. For example, he noted, the GE Workout differed from the

Total Quality Management (TQM) approach to continuous improvement by calling for action as soon as the "town meeting" agrees upon a solution (TQM, by contrast, incorporated more time for analysis). What's more, Tucci wrote, the Workout could be used by anyone—or any group—with knowledge of the problem at hand. Other methodologies, including TQM, require statistical and analytical expertise.

As Jack Welch noted, in an interview in the *Harvard Business Review* in October 1989, "Work-out is absolutely fundamental to our becoming the kind of company we must become . . . The ultimate objective of Work-out is clear. We want 300,000 people with different career objectives, different family aspirations, different financial goals, to share directly in this company's vision, the information, the decision-making process, and the rewards" ("Speed, Simplicity, Self-Confidence: An Interview with Jack Welch," by Noel Tichy and Ram Caran, *Harvard Business Review*, September–October, 1989).

See also: Action Learning; Learning Organization; Six Sigma

Further Reading

The GE Work-Out: How to Implement GE's Revolutionary Method for Busting Bureacracy & Attacking Organizational Problems, by Dave Ulrich, Steve Kerr, and Ron Ashkenas, McGraw-Hill (2002).

Jack: Straight from the Gut, by Jack Welch with John A. Byrne, Warner Books (2005).

Winning, by Jack Welch with Suzy Welch, Collins (2005).

Generation X, Y, and Z

Why does U.S. society in general—aided and abetted by marketers—label generations of people? There's the "Greatest Generation" of people who were young during World War II. Then there are the Baby Boomers—born in the period after World War II, and up until about 1964. Then there are Generations X, Y, and Z.

One reason for the tendency to label generations is that such labels imply a certain set of common characteristics. As different as the individual people are who were born throughout the baby-boom years, for example, they can still be identified—in broad strokes—among larger groups of people because they lived through the same national and global historical events that shaped the years during which they grew up.

For companies considering their market, this is a boon because it helps them tailor offerings to certain age groups. For companies considering their employees, it can also be a boon; it can help them better understand where their staff members are "coming from" and what might constitute their "comfort zones" with regard to office culture norms. Again, though, this is a very broad-stroke assumption; it establishes commonalities that might not prove true if researched thoroughly.

When employees of different generations find themselves at odds with one another, they often blame the "generation gap," which is thought to be the differences in values, styles and approach between one generation and another. In her book, *Retiring the Generation Gap: How Employees Young and Old Can Find Common Ground* (Jossey-Bass, 2006) author Jennifer Deal, however, pushes back at that conventional wisdom. Deal's research suggests that when employees find themselves in conflict with one another, and blame the "generation gap" for that conflict, what's really happening is simple miscommunication. She writes, in her introduction: "Fundamentally, people want the same things, no matter what generation they are from," and "You can work with (or manage) people from all generations effectively without becoming a contortionist, selling your soul on eBay, or pulling your hair out on a daily basis."

Deal begins her book, in fact, with an eye-opener of a quotation: "Children today are tyrants. They contradict their parents, gobble their food, and tyrannize their teachers." This quote is attributed to Socrates, who lived from 470–399 B.C. She also writes: "The so-called generation gap, is, in large part, the result of miscommunication and misunderstanding, fueled by common insecurities and desire for clout—which includes control, power, authority, and position."

All that said, the labels exist. To go back, those born between 1925 and 1945 are considered the "silent generation" if for no other reason than the publicity that the Baby Boomers, who followed, have garnered

Baby Boomers were born between 1946 and 1963 or 1964, depending on whom you ask—and can be classified as either early- or late-boomers. Generation Xers birthdates begin in 1964 (or 1965) and range through the mid-1980s. Interestingly, in the post–baby-boom years, the start and end-dates of generational labels are fuzzier, with more sources in disagreement.

Focusing on Generation X and beyond, according to an article entitled "Generation X Defies Definition," by Jennifer Jochim, published in the *Nevada Outpost* (copyright 6/1/97 Nevada Outpost http://www.jour

.unr.edu/outpost), "Generation Xers were brought up on television, Atari 2600s, and personal computers. They are the generation that was raised in the 1970s and 1980s, and saw this country undergo a selfish phase that they do not want to repeat."

In that article, Jochim quotes Jackie Shelton, a thirty-one-year-old advertising executive, as saying: "Generation X grew up in the 'me generation' of the 1980s, and now they are able to see that it is not all it is cracked up to be."

Jochim explains in her article that "Generation X" was coined as a label in 1991 by author Douglas Coupland, in a novel about three people he describes as "underemployed, overeducated, intensely private, and unpredictable." Jochim writes: "Coupland took his book's title from another book *Class*, by Paul Fussell. Fussell used X to describe a group of people who want to pull away from class, status, and money in society. Because the characters in Coupland's book fit that description, he decided on the title 'Generation X.'"

People in Generation Y were born, predictably, after those born in Generation X. Some are children of the oldest baby boomers; others are children of Generation Xers.

According to a *USA Today* article posted on www.usatoday.com on November 6, 2005 ("Generation Y: They've arrived at work with a new attitude," by Stephanie Amour), Generation Yers comprise as many as seventy million people. "This age group," Amour writes, "is moving into the labor force during a time of major demographic change, as companies around the USA face an aging workforce." The article goes on to say that the "new job entrants are changing careers faster than college students change their majors, creating frustration for employers struggling to retain and recruit talented high-performers."

Amour's article refers to research by Bruce Tulgan, a founder of a company called RainmakerThinking, which studies the lives of young people. The article says, "Unlike the generations that have gone before them, Gen Y has been pampered, nurtured, and programmed with a slew of activities since they were toddlers, meaning that they are both high-performance and high-maintenance, Tulgan says. They also believe in their own worth."

Generation Z, as of this writing, may still be in elementary school. Sources on the web differ as to what constitutes the first year of Generation Z individuals. Some sources identify Generation Z as those born after 2000. Others cite dates as early as 1993, or before. Some indicate the early

1990s. For example, an article by Thomas Hoffman entitled "Job Skills: Peparing Generation Z" published August 25, 2003 in *Computerworld* (www.computerworld.com) says that corporate CIOs responding to a survey indicated that they were concerned that colleges and universities are by and large doing a poor job of preparing current college students for company life. That article's title indicates that the piece is written about Generation Z.

According to that article, "The survey, plus interviews with CIOs, indicated that the shortcomings are in the areas of business skills, troubleshooting skills, interpersonal communication, project management and systems integration."

All of this information may be daunting, but consider Deal's theory, which came out of an extensive research project done by the Center for Creative Leadership, and which surveyed people born between 1925 and 1986. And recall another quote she cited in her book, this one by Alexandar Dumas, 1824–1895: "All generalizations are dangerous, even this one."

See also: War for Talent

Further Reading

Beyond Generation X, by Claire Raines, Crisp Learning; 1st ed. (1997).
Generation X: Tales for an Accelerated Culture, by Douglas Coupland, St. Martin's Griffin; 1st ed. (1991).
Managing Generation Y, by Carolyn A. Martin, HRD Press (2001).
Retiring the Generation Gap: How Employees Young and Old Can Find Common Ground, by Jennifer J. Deal, Jossey-Bass (2006).
www.ccl.org (Center for Creative Leadership)

Signs of Changing Culture: Good Job, You!

How do you know when you're doing a good job at work?

According to an article by Jeffrey Zaslow, published in the *Wall Street Journal* April 20, 2007 (page W1), young people joining the workforce today expect a lot of praise. And, it seems, companies are wiling to go to great lengths to deliver.

Specifically, Zaslow writes, companies are "hiring consultants to teach managers how to compliment employees using e-mail, prize packages and public displays of appreciation." One company, Zaslow noted, calls one staffer its "celebrations assistant." This person's job includes throwing confetti and passing out balloons.

"There are benefits to building confidence and showing attention," Zaslow writes. "But some researchers suggest that inappropriate kudos are turning too many adults into narcissistic praise-junkies."

Times have changed, noted one law firm partner quoted in the article. Early on in his career, he said, "If you weren't getting yelled at, you felt like that was praise."

Glass Ceiling

The term "glass ceiling" was coined by *Wall Street Journal* writers to describe the barriers that prevent women from reaching leadership positions in companies. As of this writing, it has come to mean women and also any other group of people prevented from reaching corporate leadership positions due to discrimination of any kind. But it is most commonly associated with women in business.

The glass ceiling has been studied and written about a great deal. A federal commission was established in 1991 to study and report on the topic. The glass ceiling has also been considered extensively in individual fields—the glass ceiling in medicine, the glass ceiling in high tech industries, and so forth. Much of the writing focuses on pay gaps, and on ways in which women can "break" the ceiling to attain leadership positions. But there are also some controversial views. According to a 2006 Forbes.com article by Hannah Clark, titled "Are Women Happy Under the Glass Ceiling" (Forbes.com, March 8, 2006) women may not be as unhappy with the consequences of the glass ceiling as they once were. The article cites a study of 1,200 executives in eight countries, done by consulting firm Accenture. The study reports that about "70% of women and 57% of men" believe that the glass ceiling exists. But, as Clark's article goes on to say: "If women are unhappy about making 77 cents for every dollar earned by a man, it's not reflected in Accenture's statistics. Globally, the same percentage of men and women—58%—felt they were fairly compensated. In the U.S., 67% of men were happy with their salaries, compared with 60% of women. But American women were almost as satisfied as men with the professional levels they had achieved."

Why I Do This: Director, Career Development and Placement Graduate School
Carol R. Anderson

My job is to prepare students pursuing masters degrees at a professional graduate school to find internships and jobs in their fields of study. I help them identify their professional assets (skills, education, experience that differentiate them from competitors) and learn how to find opportunities, present themselves effectively to prospective employers, how to interview, negotiate salary, choose between multiple offers. My work is varied: I counsel students individually, run resume and strategic workshops, organize job fairs and recruit companies, nonprofits, and government agencies to participate, bring in alumni to talk to students, coach working students on career issues, survey alumni on their career progression.

I did not find this job; I was invited to apply for it by a colleague at my previous job in outplacement (counseling professionals who lost their jobs on finding new ones) who was on the school's search committee and recommended me. Most jobs (70–80%) are found through such introductions, not through ads or online or through employment agencies. I segued into this field as a second career, when I was over fifty, but you can start as soon as you complete graduate school. Good preparation while you're in high school and college: camp counselor, being a Big Brother or Big Sister, tutor, sports coach, acting (trying on different lives, role play), Toastmasters, a summer job in an employment agency, any job that involves customer service, advocacy, being an exchange student overseas or hosting one, shadowing people who do jobs you find interesting, any experience that allows you to broaden your horizons by trying something (legal, ethical, and safe) about which you know nothing, psychology courses.

I have a passion for this work, and I am good at it, two criteria for any successful career. My success is vicarious: the satisfaction comes when graduates get the job they've dreamed of, or are chosen by prestigious organizations for competitive programs, such as the United Nations Young Professionals Program or the Presidential Management Fellows program in the federal government. As director I have a great deal of autonomy in planning my work, choosing what my office provides to students and alumni and when, another factor that contributes to my career satisfaction. Three "unexpected" elements of my work are the amount of writing and editing I do in it (workshop handouts, resumes, cover letters, a newsletter), the depth of my relationships with students and alumni, and the path that led to it. While many career services jobs in academe require an MA in counseling, I have an MBA in finance and a BA in English, and prior careers in book publishing and financial management on Wall Street. To enjoy this kind of job, you need what we call the "service gene," a strong desire to help others, as well as patience, cross-cultural sensitivity, and the ability to inspire others.

Resources for more information include: www.ethnicmajority.com, www.breaktheglassceiling.com, www.feminist.org, www.womensleadership .com, the Center for Women's Leadership at Babson College, and the Institute for Women's Leadership at Rutgers University.

See also: Corner Office

Further Reading

A Glass Ceiling Survey: Benchmarking Barriers and Practices, by Ann M. Morrison, Carl T. Schreiber, and Karl F. Price, CCL Press, (1995), www.ccl.org

Golden Parachute

A golden parachute, according to investorwords.com, is a clause in an executive's employment contract specifying that he/she will receive large benefits in the event that the company is acquired and the executive's employment is terminated. "These benefits can take the form of severance pay, a bonus, stock options, or a combination thereof."

Golden parachutes are "golden" because they're very large. Consider a BusinessWeek.com article published Dec. 22, 2006 titled "The Golden Parachute Club of 2006: Top executives who left their companies this year were rewarded with rich pay packages. But is this the last hoorah?" This article, by Moira Herbst, describes some of the rewards received by CEOs, and discusses how the size of the "parachutes" are being received by shareholders:

On Dec. 21, Pfizer revealed that (then CEO Hank) McKinnell, who did give up the CEO post in 2006, is getting even more money than originally thought. He'll receive a total of $122 million in retirement, as well as deferred compensation worth an additional $78 million.

The sum total of $200 million isn't going over too well among investors. "It's not reasonable to pay someone who failed as CEO this much; he's the poster child for pay-for-failure," says Daniel F. Pedrotty, director of the investment office of the AFL-CIO, whose member unions' funds hold about $568 million in Pfizer shares. "Unfortunately, once you've negotiated this and gotten it wrong, it's hard to fix."

In Corporate America, the article goes on to say, "the road for even the bitterest of goodbyes has long been paved with sweet financial rewards. Continuing a long-term trend, 2006 saw many companies parachuting executives into soft post-employment landings, whether leaving with head held high, like ExxonMobil chief Lee Raymond, or in a cloud of controversy like McKinnell (www.businessweek.com).

Indeed. MarketWatch.com published a report on its website on January 3, 2007 about the $210 million golden parachute departing Chief Executive Robert Nardelli received from Home Depot. According to that article, "Some corporate governance experts said that Nardelli's pay package was not entirely out of line with other companies of that size that cut ties with top managers, and there could be others like it down the road unless shareholders enact reforms."

The article went on to quote Sydney Finkelstein, professor of management at Dartmouth University's Tuck School of Business, as saying "It's clearly an outrageous number but one that was preordained from [Nardelli's] employment contract," said. "I think it's a sign of the new rule for CEOs" (MarketWatch.com. "Don't Expect Reforms in Wake of Nardelli Parachute: Experts Say Large Home Depot Packages Could Continue; Others Could Follow," by Russ Britt, January 3, 2007.)

See also: Executive Compensation; Sarbanes–Oxley Act of 2002

Further Reading

"Executive Pay: A Special Report; More Pieces. Still a Puzzle," by Erich Dash, *New York Times*, Late Edition-Final, Section 3, Page 1, Column 2 (April 8 2007).

Hacker

A hacker is a computer expert who can access and manipulate computer programs, applications, systems, and more in "unorthodox" ways to achieve his or her goal. Initially, the term *hacker* was a derogatory term, meaning someone who was unlawfully breaking into a computer system they were not supposed to have access to. It is still used that way. But the meaning of the term has evolved and expanded.

Consider the following, quoted from a "Portals" column by Lee Gomes in the *Wall Street Journal* ("How a Young Turk Spared Hackerdom from Respectability," Wednesday, October 4, 2006, Marketplace Section, page B1): "Hacker, of course, used to mean 'computer-connected bad guy.' That's still how the word is used on TV. In tech circles, however, it has shed its nefarious undertones and now stands for 'computer enthusiast.' (Although, in more rarified programming circles, it has come full circle and is pejorative once more; here a hacker has only a superficial knowledge of programming and gravitates toward quick but impermanent solutions. Think duct tape.)"

Gomes writes, "The pro-hacker aesthetic is now so ascendant that the mere whim of [a] hacker is valued more than even the most studied plan of someone else, such as a marketing dweeb."

The term, then, changed mostly for those people who do not understand the inner workings of computers, the Internet, and cyberspace. Consider this as well, from the website www.catb.org, in an article by Eric Steven Raymond entitled, "How to Become a Hacker":

There is a community, a shared culture, of expert programmers and networking wizards that traces its history back through decades to the first time-sharing minicomputers and the earliest ARPANET experiments. The members of this culture originated the term 'hacker.' Hackers built the Internet. Hackers made the Unix operating system what it is today. Hackers run Usenet. Hackers make the World Wide Web work. If you are part of this culture, if you have contributed to it and other people in it know who you are and call you a hacker, you're a hacker.

That article goes on to say that there is "another group of people who loudly call themselves hackers, but aren't. These are people (mainly adolescent males) who get a kick out of breaking into computers and breaking the phone system." The article says that "real" hackers call those people "crackers," and goes on to say that according to a real hacker, "being able to break security doesn't make you a hacker any more than being able to hotwire cars makes you an automotive engineer." The article laments the fact that the media generally uses the work "hacker" when "cracker" would be more appropriate. "Hackers build things," the article says, and "crackers break them."

Raymond is the editor of *The New Hacker's Dictionary*. The book's third edition, in paperback, was published by the MIT Press in October 1996. Even though more than a decade has passed since the book's publication, its information still engages readers because hackers *do* have their own language, as noted by Hugh Kenner in his review of the dictionary in *Byte* magazine. Kenner, as quoted from the Amazon.com website, wrote:

> My current favorite is "wave a dead chicken." New to you? You've waved a dead chicken when you've gone through motions to satisfy onlookers (suits?), even when you're sure it's all futile. Raymond's book exhilarates. . . . *The New Hacker's Dictionary*, though, is not for skimming. Allot, each day, a half hour, severely timed if you hope to get any work done.

Good guys or bad, hackers, whether we adhere to the Gomes definition or the Raymond, are the people who understand computers, applications, systems, and more much better than most.

See also: Killer App

Further Reading

Gray Hat Hacking: The Ethical Hacker's Handbook, by Shon Harris, Allen Harper, Chris Eagle, Jonathan Ness, and Michael Lester, McGraw-Hill Osborne Media, 1st ed. (November 9, 2004).

Hacking Exposed, by Stuart McClure, Joel Scambray, and George Kurtz, McGraw-Hill Osborne Media, 5th ed. (2005).

www.hacker.org

Signs of Changing Culture: Privacy Increasingly Formal

Noted in *The Financial Times*, November 14, 2006, page 8
"Business Slow to Act on Data Protection and Privacy," by Philip Stafford in London

Stafford, in this article, has tacked the tough topic of privacy. Citing an Ernst & Young study, Stafford notes that more companies are realizing that they need to pay more attention to protecting their data.

Stafford cited an Ernst & Young Global Information Security Survey of 1,200 public and private sector organizations in 48 countries. He wrote, "For the first time in the study's nine-year history, organizations have cited privacy and data protection as a significant issue."

The article quoted Richard Brown, head of technology and security risk services at Ernst & Young, as saying, "Businesses are only just waking up to the dangers of having little or no privacy policy in place for managing sensitive data."

Stepping back and considering the big picture, it's interesting to note that companies are becoming more vigilant about protecting their data even as many probe more deeply into employees' information. The issue of where employee privacy boundaries reside continues to spark heated debate.

Harassment

The Federal Communications Commission describes harassment as any form of discrimination that violates the Civil Rights Act of 1964. It is classified as unwelcome verbal or physical conduct based on race, color, religion, sex, national origin, age, disability, sexual orientation, or retaliation.

The U.S. Equal Employment Opportunity Commission describes sexual harassment as

> Unwelcome sexual advances, requests for sexual favors, and other verbal or physical conduct of a sexual nature [that] constitute[s] sexual harassment when submission to or rejection of this conduct explicitly or implicitly affects an individual's employment, unreasonably inter-

feres with an individual's work performance or creates an intimidating, hostile or offensive work environment.

Sexual harassment can occur in a variety of circumstances, including but not limited to the following:

- The victim as well as the harasser may be a woman or a man. The victim does not have to be of the opposite sex.
- The harasser can be the victim's supervisor, an agent of the employer, a supervisor in another area, a co-worker, or a non-employee.
- The victim does not have to be the person harassed but could be anyone affected by the offensive conduct.
- Unlawful sexual harassment may occur without economic injury to or discharge of the victim.
- The harasser's conduct must be unwelcome.

The commission's website notes that victim's should inform the harasser that the conduct is not appropriate and not welcome, using whatever system the employer has available for such complaints. The website goes on to explain that the EEOC, when investigating allegations of sexual harassment, considers the context of the alleged offense and the nature of the alleged offense, and makes its judgment based on facts, on a case-by-case basis.

When investigating allegations of sexual harassment, the EEOC looks at the whole record: the circumstances, such as the nature of the sexual advances, and the context in which the alleged incidents occurred. A determination on the allegations is made from the facts on a case-by-case basis.

Retaliation and Backlash

Under the law, retaliation against a victim or complainant is illegal. Unfortunately, retaliation is still pervasive.

Victims who speak out against sexual harassment are often labeled "troublemakers" or "attention seekers." As is too often the case in rape or sexual assault, the victims often become the accused, and their lives and motives come under sharp scrutiny. They risk hostility and isolation from colleagues, supervisors, teachers, fellow students, and even friends. They may be passed over for promotions that they deserve.

Training in the Workplace

The position of the EEOC according to its website, www.eeoc.gov, is that "prevention is the best tool to eliminate sexual harassment in the workplace. Employers are encouraged to take steps necessary to prevent sexual harassment from occurring. They should clearly communicate to employees that sexual harassment will not be tolerated. They can do so by providing sexual harassment training to their employees and by establishing an effective complaint or grievance process and taking immediate and appropriate action when an employee complains."

A column in the Baltimore Sun discusses sexism and harassment in the country in 2007 and notes,

It's also true that the United States may have gone further than any other country to protect women's right to equal treatment in the workplace. Laws against sexual harassment and discrimination are broad and reasonably effective. Further, this country has advanced the cause of justice for rape victims ("Lingering Sexism Impedes Women's Path to Highest Level of Power," by Cynthia Tucker. *The Baltimore Sun*, January 8, 2007).

Many published sources discuss the difficulty that an accuser/victim of harassment has in making the issue public. According to these sources, many victims feel as if they must prove their innocence, and are thus reluctant to come forward. Other sources also note how difficult it is from a manager's point of view, to handle claims of harassment fairly and fully, highlighting again the need for formal employee policies, and procedures. A *Harvard Businses Review* (HBR) case, "The Case of the Hidden Harassment," by Daniel Niven, published March 1, 1992, discusses the issue of harassment from a third-party managerial point of view in a fictional setting. Another fictional HBR case study, "Will She Fit In?" by Joan Magretta discusses the issues of gender, harassment, and leadership. HBR cases, fictitious scenarios designed to highlight managerial issues, include commentaries from experts on the topic at hand. For more information, go to www.hbsp.harvard.edu.

See also: Age Discrimination; Code of Ethics; Diversity; Glass Ceiling

Further Reading

http://library.uncg.edu/depts/docs/us/harassment.asp (University of North Carolina, Greensboro, Libraries) http://www.fcc.gov/owd/understanding-harassment.html (Federal Communications Commission)

www.catalystwomen.org

www.eeoc.gov

Harvard Business Review

The *Harvard Business Review* (HBR) is a venerable business magazine published by Harvard Business School Publishing. It is owned by the Harvard Business School. Since its founding in 1922, HBR's contributors have comprised a veritable "Who's Who" of business thought. Many of the groundbreaking articles in business theory and research have been published in HBR including work by Clayton M. Christensen, Peter F. Drucker, Theodore (Ted) Levitt (both a marketing scholar and HBR editor), Michael E. Porter, Rosabeth Moss Kanter, and Robert S Kaplan. Its worldwide English-language circulation is about 240,000 and there are eleven licensed editions of the magazine.

For some, HBR fills a unique niche by bringing the work of academic theory into the real world application of business and creating a resource for practitioners at the cutting edge. While the format has changed over the years, the magazine usually offers a combination of articles, an HBR interview with a thought leader, and HBR Case Study, a "Different Voice" article—that offers the viewpoint of a leader outside the business main stream—and a Best Practice piece. At times, too, issues will feature a "Classic" article—an article whose contents have stood the test of time, and whose insights are considered as valid upon reprinting as they were when first voiced.

In 2006, *Harvard Business Review* was included in the list of publications licensed for digital uses inside organizations, according to a press release on BusinessWire.com titled "*Harvard Business Review* Joins Copyright Clearance Center's Digital Licensing Program" on December 11, 2006.

With *Harvard Business Review* content now available through CCC's Annual Copyright License, employees of licensed companies are allowed to internally share HBR content in electronic formats.

The announcement follows major additions to CCC's digital repertory earlier this year of *Science*, the *British Medical Journal*, the *Jour-*

nal of the American Medical Association and the *New England Journal of Medicine.*

Harvard Business Review is the leading monthly magazine of management thought and practice, with a circulation of 242,000. HBR publishes for the global business leader, with articles written by management experts on new thinking in strategy, negotiation, innovation, leadership and other topics. It is published by Harvard Business School Publishing (HBSP).

With demand for electronic content growing daily, we are pleased to work with CCC to make HBR articles digitally available to its corporate license customers," said Allan Ryan, Director of Intellectual Property at HBSP. "Joining the digital repertory will encourage lawful digital use of our valuable content within corporations."

"We are proud to broaden our ties with Harvard by adding more of their titles to our digital repertory," said Bob Weiner, CCC Senior Vice President, Licensing. "And we know our corporate customers will be pleased to license *Harvard Business Review* content in digital formats."

According to the *Harvard Business Review* website, "you can rely on *Harvard Business Review* for ideas that truly make a difference to your organization—ideas on leadership, motivation, managing change, innovation, and more. Every monthly issue of HBR will help you run your business more successfully." The site goes on to say that "you'll be impressed by the influence HBR's insights with have on you, your team, and your entire organization."

Harvard Business Review is published monthly except for a July/August issue which counts as two issues.

See also: Blanchard, Ken; Drucker, Peter

Further Reading

www.hbsp.harvard.edu

Headhunter

Barron's, a weekly publication for investors, from the publisher of the *Wall Street Journal*, describes a headhunter as an independent employment service—or individual—that seeks out personnel for high-level executive positions; formally known as an executive search company. Headhunters are generally used by companies that are looking outside their present staff to fill executive positions. (*Dictionary of Marketing Terms*, Copyright 2000 by Barron's Educational Series, Inc.)

Fast Company magazine interviewed a headhunter to give job seekers tips on how to succeed during the job interview process. Headhunter Nick A. Corcodilos covered the basics of a successful hunt and showed readers how to "deliver the one, surefire thing that every employer is looking for—proof that you can do the job, and do it profitably."

"Headhunters know that a résumé rarely gets you inside a company," Corcodilos said in the interview. "A résumé can't defend you or answer questions about you. All that a résumé can do is outline your past, and your past is largely irrelevant, because it doesn't demonstrate that you can do the work that the hiring manager needs to get done.

"A résumé leaves it up to employers to figure out how you can add value to their organization," says Corcodilos. "That's no way to sell yourself. Headhunters deal with a company's human-resources department only when they're filling a highly visible position, such as president or CEO. Otherwise, they avoid HR whenever possible. So should you" (*Fast Company* magazine, "Interview with a Headhunter," by Bill Breen. Issue 21, December 1998, page 154).

An article on the *Wall Street Journal* Executive Career Site titled "Find Good Career Advice From Headhunter" by Frederick C. Hornberger posted on February 10, 1999, says that when looking for career advice, ask an executive recruiter.

Executive recruiters are specialists who find, evaluate and select talent for employers. Throughout the selection process, they evaluate a broad variety of candidates and career-success stories. They also counsel employers on the structure, benefits and presentation of their job opportunities so they'll attract quality candidates. This knowledge of the employer's perspective makes executive recruiters an invaluable source of career advice.

Why I Do This: Senior Managing Director, Management Consulting Firm
Sam Hill

I am a management consultant, and I work on strategic projects at what is called the C-Level, working for CEO, COO, CMO, CFO, CIO. (That's Chief Executive Officer, Chief Operating Officer, Chief Marketing Officer, Chief Financial Officer, and Chief Information Officer—the top levels of a company.)

What that means is that a CEO or COO calls me when they have a really complicated problem, usually involving marketing strategy, since that is my specialty. These problems arise either because something has changed or is about to change with markets or competitors, or because their organizations have attempted something and struggled. I sit down with them and their staff, listen, and then develop a work plan to answer the question. If they agree that the work plan makes sense, they hire me and my team.

A consulting team is usually three to five people, some of whom are full time on an assignment and some of whom are part time. Typically, there are two or three junior people whose job is to gather data, do analysis, etc. A mid-career manager who guides the work, checks the quality of the analysis, and tries to understand what it all means, and me. My job is to make sure the team stays on track and answers the question we were hired to answer (it's easier than you think to go off course) and leads the communication with the CEO and COO. We have to be very careful in what we say and how we say it, since our advice will change people's lives and involve hundreds of millions of dollars.

Yesterday was a typical day for me. At 7 A.M. I met with a CEO in Detroit for an hour and a half, briefing him for a board meeting. From 9 to 11 or so, I read client documents. Over lunch I worked on the outline for our next report. Early in the afternoon, I had a conference call with my team to review a very complicated analysis that will tell us how effectively the client is spending its huge marketing budget. At 3, I scheduled five interviews with the R&D group to discuss their thoughts on marketing and worked with the CEO's assistant to schedule our next major report. At 4 I reviewed a workplan for a different client we will be meeting with on Monday in New York. From 5 to 6, I made a half dozen phone calls, some related to internal administration, and some trying to help another part of my consulting firm prepare for a meeting they have with a BOD (board of directors in consulting slang.) Today I will spend in the office writing reports between conference calls, and tomorrow I will be back in Detroit doing the interviews I scheduled yesterday.

You'll really like this job if you are very smart, easily bored, quantitative, able to think in a structured way, flexible, aren't afraid of flying, and like to work hard. If you love working with people, like a well-defined schedule with a well structured day and lots of time for your friends, and if you find algebra a chore, this might not be the right choice.

This article says that employers help executive recruiters by being forthcoming with them about internal corporate issues, personalities, and preferences when it comes to types of employees. This information, in turn, can be very helpful when a job seeker is looking for a company where they'll "fit."

The only caveat about searching for a job (or an employee) via a headhunter, or a career counselor, is that it is important for the employer (or the job-seeker) to be comfortable with the expert, and trust in their judgment. If a manager does not establish a connection with the headhunter (and in fact, doesn't get along with them, or doesn't understand them), how can that manager, by extension, expect the headhunter to turn up a good fit for the organization?

Put another way, if you can't stand the real estate agent, is it going to be easier or more difficult to find a house that you like? If you keep saying you love staircases, and the agent keeps showing you ranch houses, that should tell you something—the same goes for a headhunter.

See also: War for Talent

Further Reading

"The Role of the Board in CEO Succession," by Ken Taylor and Keith Meyer in *Director's Monthly*, September 2006 (Volume 30, Number 9).

Herman Miller Furniture

Herman Miller, Inc. produces office and healthcare furniture and accessories for businesses and home offices. It also offers services for furniture management, strategic facilities consulting and leasing, according to its website. Net sales of $262,000 in 1923 grew to $25 million in 1970, the year the company went public. Net sales in fiscal year 2006 were $1.74 billion.

Business Ethics ranked Herman Miller, Inc. among the "100 Best Corporate Citizens" in America in 2006. Herman Miller has also been ranked as the "most admired" company in its industry in *Fortune* magazine's annual survey.

Our founder, D.J. De Pree, committed Herman Miller to "modern" furniture in 1936 partly because he saw a moral dimension to Gilbert

Rohde's clean designs, honest materials, and lack of ornamentation. In 1984, a major impetus behind Bill Stumpf and Don Chadwick's Equa chair was a desire to give a reasonably priced, comfortable, good-looking chair to everybody in offices—not just the higher-ups. These are but two examples of some of the best work done at Herman Miller. Our people and the designers we work with are concerned with larger issues of humanity and equality and bettering the world we work in. What arrives on the truck is furniture. What went into the truck was an amalgam of what we believe in: innovation, design, operational excellence, smart application of technology, and social responsibility (Information from www.hermanmiller.com).

According to a second-quarter report (discussing the company's second-quarter ending December 2, 2006), Herman Miller's "strong sales growth, coupled with improved financial leverage, drove the highest quarterly earnings per share ever recorded by the company. Sales for the quarter increased 13.9 percent and orders increased 22.1 percent from the year-ago period. Operating earnings expanded to 11.8 percent of sales based on improvements both in gross margin and operating expenses as a percentage of sales. Net earnings were $36.6 million, or $0.56 per share, an increase of 31.2 percent over net earnings of $27.9 million for the same period in the prior year." As of this writing, they're doing something right (*Furniture World Online Magazine* [www.furninfo.com]. "Herman Miller, Inc., Reports 22.1 percent Order Growth and Record Earnings Per Share," December 21, 2006.)

See also: Feng Shui

Further Reading

"Forum Focuses on Sustainability, " by Shandra Martinez, The Grand Rapids Press (located at www.mlive.com, Thursday, September 13, 2007).

"Furniture Desk Set," by Rebecca Ascher-Walsh, *Wall Street Journal* (September 15, 2007), Page W8.

"So You Want Ivy Around Your Desk?," by Elizabeth Olson, *New York Times* (Sunday, November 19, 2006), Style Desk Late Edition—Final, Section 9, Page 12, Column 3.

www.hermanmiller.com

Horizontal Organizations

The term "Horizontal Organizations," also known as flat organizations, refers to an organization with few or no intervening levels of management between the top executive and the workers, according to the American Marketing Association Dictionary of Marketing Terms. "It presents a stark contrast to the classic hierarchical organization and bureaucratic organization with their layers of managers each of whom supervises a lower layer, leading finally to the supervision of workers. The underlying concept of the flat organization is that trained workers with assigned goals, and with the authority to achieve the goals in their own way, will—working individually or in groups—be more productive than workers who are closely supervised by managers."

The idea of a horizontal, or "flat" organization, lends itself to a world of work in which employee empowerment and creativity are valued. But horizontal organizations are not easily created, or sustained.

An article entitled "Working in FLAT Organizations: An Idiot's Guide," by Vijay Bhat, published on Ezinarticles.com, offers a sometimes cynical view of the horizontal organization, including:

> If you are a Mid-Level manager—Flat means there is no more room for you to go up. They have replaced the corporate ladder which you were climbing with a stool and you are already standing on top of it. The people above you are actually above the ceiling.
>
> If you are a Senior Manager—Flat means your responsibilities will be now given to smarter and younger staffers probably even trainees who do the same work at much lower pay, so that you become redundant before you retire.

Another article, this one entitled "The Corporate Ladder is Here to Stay," by Ethan A. Winning (1999, www.ewin.com/articles) offers this insight:

> Okay, so we'll get rid of the hierarchy. There'll just be two levels in the company: the President and everyone else, 'cept we know that there are sub-layers which remain because we can't all be chiefs. But, we take away the titles. Still, there are those with offices with windows and carpeting, and there are those with cubbyholes and lineloleum, and there are those with a wood desk, and those with no desk at all.

Of course, we have those making $200,000 a year and those making $20,000 a year. Do we have a hierarchy? You bet we do.

So, ultimately, then, are horizontal organizations really "flat?" No. A better term, according to the American Marketing Association (http://www.marketingpower.com/mg-dictionary-view4001.php), would be "flatter." According to that website, a "flatter organization" would be one in which there are as few layers of management as possible, and employees have more autonomy—and more responsibility—than they would in a corporate culture with many layers of management. Importantly, the website notes that in the case of a business—particularly where stock is issued to the public—the hierarchy cannot be dispensed with entirely. The corporation is charged with many fiduciary and legal requirements. Consequently, top management must provide policies, direction, and controls to ensure that managers and workers at all levels understand and comply with these requirements."

Another way to think about it would be to consider the prominent features of a horizontal organization. A paper by Dr. Joe H. Mine (The Horizontal Organization: MIT Course 16.852J/ESD.61.J—Fall 2002), summarizes the principles of organizing horizontally as follows:

- Organize around cross-functional core processes, not tasks or functions
- Map processes, eliminate waste
- Re-deploy personnel and resources
- Install "process owners" who have responsibility for an entire core process
- Make teams, not individuals, the basis of organizational design and performance
- Empower individuals and teams to make decisions directly related to their activities in the work flow; provide essential training and education
- Ensure cross-trained work teams
- Retain down-sized functional units as "centers of excellence" for expertise and career-path "homes" for professionals
- Measure for end-of-process performance objectives (which are driven by the value proposition)

That paper goes on to say that horizontal organizations are commonly characterized by their team structures, by their propensity to have groups of people organized by "core process," and by their focus on the company's "value proposition" to customers.

Are "flat" organizations "better" than hierarchical organizations? They can be. But a company can also lose much in the attempt to become flat. A *BusinessWeek* Playbook audio, dated October 26, 2006, which sites BMW as an exemplar of the horizontal approach, sums up the dilemma in this way: "BMW is an idea machine, driven by a culture that listens to entry-level workers and rewards the risks they take. As others try to repeat that feat—ideas flow better in more cooperative, flat organizations—chaos has the potential to reign." The Playbook seems to suggest that there is a fine line between collaboration and chaos, and that if the flat organization is to succeed, managers have to find "a way to cut through the clutter and new ways to stay better aware of their organization's collaborative cultures."

An article entitled "Micromanagers Take Root in 'Flat' Organization," published on May 2, 2003, by Debbie Heuer, in the *Cincinnati Business Courier*, put it this way:

It seems that many companies adopted only a part of the innovation but lost sight of its full intent. Flatter organizations were rapidly adopted largely because they appealed to the cost-cutting instincts of organizational leaders; the lure of the dollar, like a siren's call, distracted leaders from the goal of dispersing decision-making to the most appropriate organizational level.

In theory, flat organizations were intended to eliminate unnecessary decision-making tollgates and the faithful trolls who guarded them. Unfortunately it appears that, too often, the trolls were eliminated, but the tollgates remained viable and accessible to other aspiring trolls.

See also: Empowerment

Further Reading

Built to Change: How to Achieve Sustained Organizational Effectiveness, by Edward E. Lawler, III, and Christopher G. Worley, Jossey-Bass (2006).
"Going Horizontal," Title Annotation: Process Management: A New Leaf; case

studies on process-based organizations; Date: May 1, 1996; Publication: Chief Executive (U.S.); (found at www.thefreelibrary.com).

The Horizontal Organization, by Frank Ostroff, Oxford University Press (1998).

"Managing for Results: Using Strategic Human Capital Management to Drive Transformational Change" (A Statement of David M. Walker, Comptroller General, United States General Accounting Office, Testimony before the National Commission on the Public Service, July 2002) (located through www.brookings.edu).

Innovation

Innovation. New ideas. The next big thing. The "different" product or service that will be all the rage, and hopefully, become an integral part of the way people live or work. This is all part of the battle to attract, and retain, customers and marketshare. It's all part of the battle to make a profit, please shareholders, and go home confident that the company will live to see another day and that your job is secure.

When companies "innovate," they're coming up with new ideas. The question is whether that innovation will have the desired result—success in the marketplace. Can it help a company gain and keep a competitive advantage?

According to an article entitled "Don't Look to New Ideas for Growth," in BusinessWeek.com posted January 17, 2007, by Jeneanne Rae, "innovation isn't necessarily the panacea that many companies hope it will be." Rae writes: "In the annals of corporate innovation history, 2006 should go down as the year of 'idea management.' As innovation is more widely recognized as a new business discipline, executives are lining up to implement idea-management systems and software intended to harness the considerable insight and talent within their corporations."

But then she writes: "Too many times, however, idea management is the end of the discussion on innovation." She notes that managers are too often content to create some "buzz" around innovation and new ideas, but that the follow through is sorely lacking. "Considering the energy that goes into creating and vetting these insider contributions, relying on new ideas as your primary source of innovation is, in itself, a very bad idea."

Rae goes on to note that the challenges associated with generating new ideas are many. Among them: there are too many ideas being generated internally, and companies aren't able to sort or prioritize or thoroughly vet any one of them; the ideas are not generated with any sort of strategy in mind; and growth platforms—innovations that can lead to multiple streams of products and marketplace successes—are very difficult to identify.

Erich Joachimsthaler would likely agree. The Preface of Joachimsthaler's book, *Hidden in Plain Sight: How to Find and Execute Your Company's Next Big Growth Strategy* (Harvard Business School Press, 2007) begins: "We live in a world of innovation overdrive, overloaded by consumer choice and excruciatingly tough commercial realities, realties that include the rapid commoditization of markets, technology shifts, margin pressures, and relentless fragmentation of consumer and business markets."

He then goes on to note that companies "with any talent" continually try to grow by generating new ideas. The problem, he writes, is that when a company grows, its organization necessarily becomes more complex. Success breeds "hierarchy, structure, processes, systems, and policies that . . . can inch the company further away from the very people [it] has been serving." Joachimsthaler calls this complexity "a kind of smokescreen" that makes it "very difficult to see the biggest opportunities for innovation and growth, even though they are right there, hidden in plain sight."

Joachimsthaler's take on the challenge to innovate is that companies need to get out into the "daily routines" of the people they want to serve. They have to (at least figuratively) "forget" what business they're in, and what their strategy has been and instead consider the "dynamic and complex ecosystems" of customers' lives. Only by doing so can they truly innovate successfully.

According to an article by Joyce Wycoff, entitled "The Big Ten Innovation Killers and How to Keep Your Innovation System Alive and Well," published on www.thinksmart.com, there are ten reasons why most innovation initiatives fail:

Not creating a **culture** that supports innovation
Not getting buy-in and **ownership** from business unit managers
Not having a widely understood, system-wide **process**
Not allocating **resources** to the process
Not tying projects to company **strategy**
Not spending enough time and energy on the **fuzzy front-end**
Not building sufficient **diversity** into the process
Not developing **criteria and metrics** in advance
Not **training and coaching** innovation teams
Not having an **idea management system**

To home in on one, "Idea Management Systems" (also mentioned above by Rae), Wycoff writes:

Idea Management System—Many innovation projects have died on a sticky-note covered wall as participants lost energy trying to figure out what to do with those yellow pieces of paper fluttering to the floor. Having an effective system that captures ideas and engages people in developing, modifying, enlarging, and evaluating those ideas is just as critical to innovation as accounting systems are to the financial health of an organization.

It's hard to get innovation right. That much everyone agrees on. And that's why, as Joachimsthaler says, so many companies find themselves saying, "Why didn't I think of that!" It is of great benefit to the companies that do this.

See also: Competitive Advantage; Entrepreneur; Killer App

Further Reading

Catalyst Code: The Strategies Behind the World's Most Dynamic Companies, by David Evans and Richard Schmalensee, Harvard Business School Press (2007).

"Communities of Creation: Managing Distributed Innovation in Turbulent Markets," by Mohanbir Sawhney, and Emanuela Prandelli, *California Management Review*, Summer 2000, 24–54.

Hidden in Plain Sight: How to Find and Execute Your Company's Next Big Growth Strategy, by Erich Joachimsthaler, Harvard Business School Press (2007).

60 Trends in 60 Minutes, by Sam Hill, Wiley (2002).

"The 12 Different Ways for Companies to Innovate," by Mohanbir Sawhney, Robert Wolcott, and Inigo Arroniz, *MIT Sloan Management Review*, Spring 2006.

Signs of Changing Culture: Adapting to New Technology— As Always, Easier for Some . . .

Noted in the *Wall Street Journal*, Tuesday, November 14, 2006, Page 1, Column 4

"To Uneasy Riders, Buttonless Elevators Have Ups and Downs: Schindler's Lifts and Otis's Promise a Swifter Trip; Miscues at the Marriott," by Julia Angwin

One way to think about culture is to consider what a company's norms are. What is considered typical behavior? What technologies are second nature? Some practices or habits that might be "business as usual" at your company could cause friends at other organizations to raise their eyebrows, couldn't they?

Time was, many people viewed ATMs with suspicion. Today, they're ubiquitous. Time was, "push button" elevators were new. People who had the luxury of riding in an elevator were accustomed to asking an "elevator operator" to take them to their desired floor.

And so it goes. Consider what Julia Angwin writes about the new "buttonless" elevators, which, apparently, are taking some riders some time to get used to: "Elevator riders enter their floor number on a key-pad and are directed by the display to a particular car that will stop at their floor. You can't change your mind about where you're going after the doors shut."

Angwin noted in her article that elevators "joined the computer revolution" in the 1970s. Before that, she wrote, they had been operated manually from the lobby. But this new evolution came about in 1990, the brainchild of Joris Schroder, an engineer at Schindler. Schroder thought of using microprocessors to make banks of elevators more efficient.

The first "destination elevator" was installed in Germany in 1990, Angwin wrote. The first such elevator in the United States was launched in Indianapolis, in the Ameritech building. "When the new elevators arrived," Angwin wrote, "the building hired mimes to show tenants how to use them."

Signs of Changing Culture: Successful Innovation?
You Might Not Know Until You Try It

Noted in a feature entitled "How to Succeed in 2007," published in *Business 2.0*, located online on November 30, 2006.

What is the best advice that notable business leaders can offer in today's world? Well, it depends. In this article, *Business 2.0* offered advice from fifty highly successful people, among them Chad Hurley, co-founder of YouTube.

Hurley said that in order to succeed with a start-up business, entrepreneurs would do well to: "1) Test first, 2) Seek outside feedback, and 3) Give partners what they want."

Specifically, Hurley noted, "Launch your product or service before you have funding. See how people respond to it before you have a PowerPoint and business plan—have something people can use, and go from there . . . Don't assume that you know all the answers. . . . We saw YouTube as a powerful way to add video to auctions, but we didn't see anyone using our product that way, so we didn't add features to support it . . . Approach your business partners with concepts that they can get their heads around."

For more information and to see the entire *Business 2.0* feature, go to http://money.cnn.com/popups/2006/buz2/howtosucceed.

Intangibles

When people talk about sports teams and their performance they often refer to the intangibles—the leadership, the interaction between players, the will to win among certain athletes—the list of things that are hard to quantify, but when put together, create a winning formula. In business, there are intangibles too.

Intangible Property is property that has value but cannot be seen or touched, according to the Internal Revenue Service United States Department of the Treasury. The Internal Revenue Service (IRS) says it includes things such as: goodwill, business records, a patent, a license, and a covenant not to compete.

Investopedia calls an intangible asset one that is not physical in nature. The website Investopedia.com says, "An intangible asset can be classified as either indefinite or definite depending on the specifics of that asset. A company brand name is considered to be an indefinite asset, as it stays with the company as long as the company continues operations. However, if a company enters a legal agreement to operate under another company's patent, with no plans of extending the agreement, it would have a limited life and would be classified as a definite asset."

This source goes on to note that intangibles "can prove very valuable for a firm and can be critical to its long-term success or failure. For example, a company such as Coca-Cola wouldn't be nearly as successful were it not for the high value obtained through its brand-name recognition" (Copyright © 2007 Investopedia, Inc.). Brand strength, or brand equity, is in fact a powerful intangible asset.

Jack Keen, president of The Deciding Factor and coauthor of *Making Technology Investments Profitable: ROI Road Map to Better Business Cases,* writes in an article published in the Sept. 1, 2003 issue of *CIO Magazine* titled "Don't Ignore the Intangibles," that an astute handling of intangibles, "those goals that can't be easily measured in dollar terms," can provide a big boost for your business.

Keen goes on to say that "more than 25 percent of the value of enterprises is now based on intangible assets, such as brand image and market share, according to economists." He notes, however, that many managers do not yet understand (or accept) the implications of "this financial reality." He writes:

> Burned by failed project implementations, and noting that such projects had a heavy dependence on intangible benefits, they jump to the erroneous conclusion that all intangibles are bad. Unfortunately, when business cases are devoid of intangible analysis, projects vital to the enterprise go unfunded because intangibles can't add to the hard number ROI. Strategically marginal projects showing a high ROI (often because the investment is small) get the money. Such misguided project investments can undermine critical strategic goals, such as improvement of market share and sharpening of competitive advantage.

Intangibles must be taken seriously; they can and do affect the bottom line. As such, their importance must be realized, not only by managers and employees, but also by directors and shareholders. Jane Davidson, writing in *Accountancy Age* (June 21, 2007, www.accountancyage.com), notes the need to convey the importance of intangibles in a company's annual report ("Why Every Picture Tells A Story in an Annual Report"):

> The need to effectively communicate "intangible assets" means the presentational aspects of company reports have never been more important. Intangible assets could include elements such as a company's products, management, or brand. It is believed by some financial commentators that when Procter & Gamble acquired Gillette in 2005

for $56bn (£28.4bn), up to 97 percent of the price was for Gillette's intangible assets.

In that same article, Davidson notes that traditional accounting methods don't "adequately deal with the recognition, measurement, and disclosure of intangible assets." She suggests that although pictures and text have long been thought of as "lightweight elements of the annual reporting package," they are in fact "heavyweight ingredients, both in the richness and variety of their messages, and in their potency."

As an aside: the idea of "intangible" value has also made its way into business-school curriculum. In that venue, it may not mean quite the same thing as an "intangible asset" of a business, but the concept is similar. Consider what Peter Walker wrote in an article for CNN entitled "Learning to be Creative," posted on www.cnn.com February 9, 2007:

> Professor David Sims, who teaches organizational behavior at London's Cass Business School, aims to teach students the seemingly intangible virtues of imagination, inspiration, intuition, and improvisation. He does this by taking students choosing his elective on themed exercises, for example going to London's National Portrait Gallery to look at pictures of leaders with the help of an art historian.

In an age where the knowledge worker is rising in importance, where "flat" organizations call for innovative thinking from all employees, and where the purchase "experience" can make the difference between winning and losing customers, it's no wonder "intangible assets" are critical, even if they're not visible.

To sum up that point, consider an article in *Fast Company* magazine titled "Intangible Assets Plus Hard Numbers Equals Soft Finance" by Bill Birchard (Issue 28, September 1999, page 316). This article takes a look at how hard assets and intangibles add up.

> "Hard questions about soft assets are driving finance professionals to develop new measurements, new reporting forms, new tools and techniques for an economy based on intangibles," Birchard writes. "At Macromedia Inc., for example, a San Francisco-based Web-software company, CFO Betsey Nelson finds herself calculating value based on how close the company can get to its customers. "We're looking at the value over time of a relationship," she says.

Birchard also looks at Silicon Valley Bank in Santa Clara, California. He quotes Ken Wilcox, the bank's president, chief operating officer, and chief banking officer, who "leads his loan officers in equating company value with the value of people networks inside and outside the company: 'A management team that can change fast is of the greatest importance,' says Wilcox."

See also: Knowledge Management; Knowledge Worker

Further Reading

Brand From the Inside: Eight Essentials to Emotionally Connect Your Employees to Your Business, by Libby Sartain, and Mark Schumann, Jossey-Bass (2006).

Intangibles: Management, Measurement, and Reporting, by Baruch Lev, Brookings Institution Press (2001).

Intellectual Capital

Closely linked to an "intangible asset" is a company's "intellectual capital." Intellectual capital is knowledge that can be exploited for some money-making or other useful purpose. According to SearchCRM.com (2000–2007, TechTarget):

> The term combines the idea of the intellect or brain-power with the economic concept of capital, the saving of entitled benefits so that they can be invested in producing more goods and services. Intellectual capital can include the skills and knowledge that a company has developed about how to make its goods or services; individual employees or groups of employees whose knowledge is deemed critical to a company's continued success; and its aggregation of documents about processes, customers, research results, and other information that might have value for a competitor that is not common knowledge.

Certified Professional Accountant Barry Brinker writes in his executive summary titled "Intellectual Capital: Tomorrow's Asset, Today's Challenge" (1998, 1999, 2000 AICPA [American Institute of Certified Public Accountants]) that "we are still working toward a universal definition of intellectual capital." In his article he describes intellectual capital as assets currently valued at zero "on the balance sheet" including items such as "human brainpower, brand names, trademarks, assets booked at historical costs that have appreciated over time into something of much greater value."

Other experts define intellectual capital, he says as the "combined intangible assets which enable the company to function" or "the sum of human capital and structural capital." Brinker adds that, however it is valued, the gap between a company's market value and the value of all its tangible assets has widened significantly over the last two decades. Market-to-book ratios are rising demonstrably, and so are price/earnings ratios. Simultaneously, corporate investments in tangible capital stock have been declining."

Brinker writes that traditional accounting measures, then, cannot really calculate the true value of a company. The strength of a company's intellectual capital can have a great bearing on a company's ability to develop and implement viable strategies and deliver on its goals.

One comprehensive source of information about intellectual capital? Thomas A. Stewart's book *Intellectual Capital: The New Wealth of Organizations* (Currency/Doubleday, 1997) discusses the impact of intellectual capital on business, and the importance of the concept to managers.

See also: Knowledge Management; Knowledge Worker

Further Reading

The Leadership Pipeline: How to Build the Leadership-Powered Company, by Ram Charan, Stephen Drotter, and James Noel, Jossey-Bass (2000).
"Who Owns the Concept if No One Signs the Papers?," by Jason Pontin, *New York Times* (located on www.nytimes.com, August 12, 2007).

Internet

The Internet has become an almost indispensable tool in the business world (from the company point of view and from the consumer point of view) in just a few short years. It has had an enormous influence on how business transactions are completed, how customers purchase goods and services, how banking gets done, bills get paid, used cars get sold, jobs get found, job candidates are evaluated, students select possible careers, and research gets conducted.

While its influence is felt, it is still difficult to define the Internet. According to (SearchVb.techtarget.com, 2000–2007 TechTarget), the Internet (also referred to as the "Net") is "a worldwide system of computer networks—a network of networks in which users at any one computer can, if they have permission, get information from any other computer—and sometimes talk directly to users at other computers." It was conceived by the Advanced Research Projects Agency (ARPA) of the U.S. government in 1969 and was first known as the ARPANET. The original aim was to create a network that would allow users of a research computer at one university to be able to "talk to" research computers at other universities. A side benefit of ARPANET's design was that, because messages could be routed or rerouted in more than one direction, the network could continue to function even if parts of it were destroyed.

An article in *Fast Company* magazine ("Power Partners," by George Anders. Issue 38. August 2000. Page 145), explores the early Internet economy and other "ambitious" online players. The article said that the future belongs to partnerships. It used Wells Fargo as one example.

> What is especially striking about Wells Fargo's push to embrace the Web is how much work is being done in close partnership with Internet startups. These young allies bring ingenuity and urgency beyond what the big bank could create on its own. Yet Wells Fargo, with its 148-year heritage and $222 billion in assets, provides vital strengths that a dotcom couldn't conjure up. Not only is Wells Fargo chock-full of banking expertise and a history of relationships with financial regulators, but it also enjoys a time-tested brand name.

That article went on to describe how many Internet start-up companies "vowed to remake entire industries and send corporate 'dinosaurs' to the graveyard." Written in the wake of the collapse of the NASDAQ index, however, the article also discussed how the "dinosaurs" (big companies) were finally gearing up to innovate and succeed with web-based business initiatives. "These pragmatic companies," the article said, "are taking pointers from the new mind-sets, the new practices, and the new energy levels of the startup world. Step inside such diverse companies as Ford Motor Co., Hewlett-Packard, and UPS, and you'll find veteran managers teaming up with Internet startups."

According to the Computer Industry Almanac's press release (January

4, 2006) the number of people that used the Internet was one billion in 2005, with the largest numbers of users in the United States, China, Japan and India. Overall penetration in the leading countries was 65–75 percent.

Another good source of information about Internet use is the U.S. Census (www.census.gov). The report entitled "Computer and Internet Use in the United States: 2003" notes that "In 2003, 70 million American households, or 62 percent, had one or more computers, up from 56 percent in 2001. In 1984, the proportion of households with a computer was 8 percent."

That report goes on to say that "Sixty-two million households, or 55 percent, had Internet access, up from 50 percent in 2001, and more than triple the proportion of households with Internet access in 1997 (18 percent). Most households with a computer also had Internet access (88 percent). In 1997, less than half of households with computers had someone using the Internet."

Whether it is attracting customers or making their businesses more efficient, companies are discovering almost daily new ways to leverage their performance via the Internet, and the Internet continues to have an increasingly strong influence on corporate culture.

See also: Hacker; Killer App

Further Reading

"DIGITAL DOMAIN; All the Internet's a Stage. Why Don't C.E.O.'s Use It?," by Randall Stross, *New York Times* (Sunday, July 30, 2006), Money and Business/Financial Desk Late Edition—Final, Section 3, Page 3, Column 1.

Signs of Changing Culture:
Behind the Scenes in the Blogosphere:
Advice from Established Bloggers

The following excerpts of this study are reprinted courtesy of Nora Ganim Barnes, Ph.D., Chancellor Professor of Marketing and Director, Center for Marketing Research at University of MA Dartmouth.

Blogs will make or break your business. They have the power to disseminate information and host global conversations on any topic. Every publication from *BusinessWeek, Forbes*, and the *Wall Street Journal* to online white papers from Marqui (www.marqui.com/blog) warns businesses that blogging is not an optional endeavor. Those that don't will not survive. With over 40 million conversations going on twenty-four hours a day, the question becomes, how does a business enter and thrive in the blogosphere?

The answer to this question is that smart businesses will seek guidance from the experts. The talented and generous bloggers in this study candidly offer thoughts and ideas on how to succeed in the blogosphere, how to promote your blog and even what characteristics they feel will make you a great blogger. These innovators share their view on how to get noticed in the online world.

The seventy-four bloggers included in this study represent some of the biggest and best in the business (or the most successful independent blogs). The blogs in this study have been operating an average of 2–3 years. Seventy-three percent of these bloggers have been running their weblogs for over a year, including 20 percent who have blogged for more than three years. Fifty (68 percent) of the bloggers in this study have direct or indirect ties with a corporation or business. The independent blogs are some of the most established in the blog community. These are amazing statistics given that blogging began in 1998 and corporate blogging is only a few years old.

Each of our seventy-four respondents listed key words that describe their blog. We searched using their keywords on Google to see which blogs appeared in the results. Twenty-six of the blogs in this study (36 percent) come up in the Google top ten using their key words search and sixteen ranked first or second.

This report is based on the most experienced, business savvy and respected bloggers who are at the forefront of innovation in the blogosphere. In this report, they talk about everyday challenges of running a blog and how they deal with them. Behind the Scenes in the Blogosphere (www.umassd.edu/cmr) looks at the time it takes to run a blog, feelings about a public policy for comments and how blogs tie into existing business websites, products and promotions. Take their advice on the best way to promote a blog and hear about the next set of changes these blog leaders plan to make to stay competitive in the blogosphere.

This report, like the blogospere itself, is based on conversation. Through extensive written comments, phone interviews, and numerous online exchanges, rich data was collected that provide statistics as well as a plethora of anecdotal information. Those researchers who are veterans of blogger studies know what I have now learned; bloggers are generous, helpful, unselfish, and friendly. Discover what these experts have to say, and move your business into the blogosphere.

Two hundred and ninety-eight bloggers were contacted for this study using published lists to locate business or corporate blogs. Through the assistance of many of the early participants who posted or linked to the survey, seventy-four bloggers provided information for this report. Many offered to be interviewed, and were. Most provided links to other articles or studies they felt would enhance this project.

In many ways the data in this study was blogger driven. Respondents offered comments on the wording of questions, suggestions for new questions, and help in disseminating the survey to be filled out. The final version of the survey presented here is more personal and revealing thanks to the bloggers who wanted the findings to be meaningful, useful, and unique in perspective.

Blogosphere Truths

1. Blogs Take Time and Commitment

Initially many of the bloggers in this study did not anticipate the time their blog would take. A good blog is one where posts are fresh and new posts are frequent. Researching interesting new things to share with your audience takes time. One blogger noted, "The worst blogs are those that are updated infrequently." He cautions others with, "Be prepared to spend more time than you think."

If your posts have to be vetted by legal or discussed with others in your organization, there will be additional time demands on the blogger, and delays on posting. A business blogger in the study advised, "The corporate communications team needs to commit to rapid turnaround of items submitted for pre-posting."

In this study, 49 percent of bloggers reported the time a blog takes as the major drawback to running one. Two-thirds of the bloggers report spending less than one hour a day on their blog, while 31 percent spend 1–3 hours a day. One blogger writes, "Look on it as a learning experience (you will get back as much as you give). Once you start, don't stop." Another warns, "Make sure you have time and resources dedicated to supporting it."

Some of the time commitment is due to bloggers spending more time posting. Thirty-eight percent have increased the number of posts to their blog since they began. Overall, bloggers feel that the time investment is worth it with 95 percent reporting their blogs are successful. Some measure success in links, some in income, some in self-satisfaction, and some in the quality of human connections they have made.

2. Blogs Must Be Part of A Plan

It is unlikely a successful business or a new venture would be lacking a business plan. As part of that plan, or in addition to it, most businesses and organizations developed mission statements long ago. Many have added customer service mission statements to guide their customer service component. These plans and mission statements are created to focus peoples' efforts and capture the purpose of the organization and its relationship to its customers.

One blog author was adamant about the need for a business plan for creating and running a business blog. "Like anything else in business, a blog requires a plan. Without a plan, the blog is going to fail within three months. Period."

Another adds, "Create a business plan. Since this is intended to make money, a full business plan was created for it and we are still tweaking it a bit (you might say it is in Beta right now)."

Bloggers decide on a focus for their site. Surveyed bloggers say, "Have a purpose in mind and method for measuring success. Don't do it just because everyone else is."

"Define your audience and that will help in defining the voice and direction of your blog."

As a new communications tool, blogs are essential for communicating with your target audience. Blogging can help to mitigate problems as well. One business blogger offered: "In a company environment blogs can be used as a tactic to solve a number of communications issues so don't blog just for the sake of having a blog."

Blogs can be internal, external, or both. They can be used in conjunction with websites, or in some cases instead of them. Blogs can be used to gather data, disseminate information or both. They can be official business blogs or can be affiliated or sponsored by a business. The purpose of the blog will determine who should post, how often, and how the blog should be directed.

To maximize the potential of a blog, it must be viewed as part of the overall package and voice of the organization. If it is not part of an integrated strategy, it will lack focus and a following. The plan should also address policies on reader comments, directing traffic to the blog from company websites, products and advertising.

In this study, 18 percent of blogs reported having a public policy regulating conversation on their blog. These policies range from the formal disclaimer and creative commons license to the very informal directive on comment forms. Policies are found on front pages, FAQ section, or in comment fields on blogs.

Fifty-eight percent of bloggers reported their company website directs visitors to their blogs. In all cases the link was on the company site home page. Additionally, 39 percent reported their company packaging, labeling, or promotion directs people to the blog.

3. A Blog is a Conversation

Author Robert Scoble (http://scobleizer.wordpress.com) calls it "naked conversations." Early blogger Dave Winer (http://www.scripting .com) calls it "come-as-you-are conversations." Some marketers call blogs "2-way marketing." The point is the same in all cases—participation is essential in the blogosphere. One respondent says, "Don't start a blog unless you have people in your organization ready to post to it daily in an open, friendly, and excited tone. A blog is a conversation. Don't open the line unless you're ready to really talk."

A blog is an invitation to debate, discuss, and exchange. It is what makes blogging different than websites. The responsive nature and human connection pull people in. Consumers want to talk about products and services. If they can't talk to the vendor or the manufacturer, they will talk to others online.

The plethora of articles being published on Web 2.0, speak to this new paradigm. In the first generation of online experiences, the web provided a vehicle for mostly one-way communications. Websites were static. Many are not updated. E-mail allows us to speak to a certain designated person or group. We now have the ability to go beyond this and disseminate information in a more personal and timely way.

A survey respondent cautioned against blogging with a traditional mind-set: "Don't think of a blog in terms of publishing metaphors—it's not a newsletter replacement. Blogs are a great communication tool. But when you set one up to serve as a "corporate voice" it's as effective as spam. Find human beings to blog—don't set up a blog and try to find someone to manage it. It will fail if you do."

It is important not to be afraid of giving up the mono-directed control that usually characterizes an organization. One respondent offers, "Blogs are conversation rather than one-way speech. Allowing that conversation actually strengthens your base.

Blogs, facilitated by increased access to the Internet, high-speed connections, RSS feeds, a selection of easy to use blog software, and new blog search capabilities, now allow businesses to speak to current and potential customers in real time. Equally important, consumers can talk back in real time. Bloggers say, "It's a great way to get closer to your users, customers, and other critical stakeholders." "There is no downside to getting to know your customers on a more personal basis."

"The opportunities for businesses to test new ideas, discuss product lines, introduce brands, or conduct online research are infinite. The prerequisite for success however, is that the business blog accepts the premise that the blog is a conversation, not a monologue or an infomercial." This is what our seasoned business bloggers had to say about the essence of a blog conversation: "The 'popularity' of your blog is directly related to frequent posting, open and honest dialogues."

4. Transparency, Authenticity, and Focus are Good. Bland is Bad

Consumers know when they are being talked at, played, or deceived. Respondents say, "Be authentic. If you can't, don't blog." "Don't focus on execs, the public wants to hear from people they can relate to—the average worker. Pick a "short fuse" topic to get started, with a definite start and end date, before you start an indefinite blog."

Consumers want corporate/business blogs to talk honestly and candidly about their products, services, ideas, and plans. Consumers want more than to be on the receiving end of commercials. Bloggers warn, "Write it yourself, no PR guys on it. Comment broadly on your industry. Don't just summarize your press announcements."

People are looking to talk to someone in authority about their experiences, ideas, and suggestions. If they have something negative to say, they expect (on a blog) that their comments will be heard. A recurrent theme with the bloggers studied was honesty and openness. They advised, "Be transparent and authentic." "Make it genuine, make it interesting, have guest authors talking about all aspects of your business." "Make it real. Have the right people talking about product innovation, not the PR people."

Keep in mind that conversations will happen outside your blog that relate to your products or industry. You need to be aware, current, and honest in dealing with those conversations too. One business blogger wrote, "Monitor the blogosphere closely, both for discussions about your brand, and for comments about your blog. Respond with comments to those outside blog posts. The blogosphere respects participation, so respond."

Consumers who feel like a business blog is authentic, honest and interesting will contribute to it and support its products. These contributions, and the resultant conversations, provide a rich new data source for companies as well as great new relationships. One experienced blogger summed it all up for a company thinking about starting a blog: "Be honest and don't pander. Readers can tell."

Blog Growth and Development

A blog is constantly evolving, growing, and developing. Bloggers are looking for new and better software, exciting and innovative information to post and for new links to increase their presence on search engines. The bloggers in this study are doing all this and more. Fifty-four percent of those surveyed are planning to make changes to how their blogs function.

Corporations encourage blogging. Some corporations are encouraging employees to start blogs. Of those some are choosing to focus on products or product applications. These product-oriented blogs are particularly successful in targeting niche markets that may not warrant major corporate expenditure. Other employees blog about R&D as well as upcoming product releases. Employees using a blog to discuss general happenings in the industry are also contributing to the corporate presence. The blogs give the corporation a human face and allow multiple ways to communicate with the company.

As additional bloggers are added, the blog may need to adapt. One blogger plans to do that and says, "As we add bloggers, we will need to change the layout to accommodate so it doesn't become cluttered."

Blogs serve as barrier breakers. Some companies are running (or considering) blogs in other languages to reach markets where traditional marketing may be costly and difficult. These are particularly good to "introduce" products without the expense or risk of a full campaign.

Blogs evolve. Bloggers surveyed also plan to add more video, introduce new media/mobile technology, add podcasting, and expand the number of visitors to their sites. Here are some of the responses that address these kinds of changes:

"I am thinking of doing a podcast that I would append to the blog, probably covering and expanding the same topics, but maybe doing some interviews."

"Getting us listed on more blog engines, having our associates post comments to other blogs and linking those posts to ours, incorporate images in our posts."

"I may add more advertising and affiliate stuff—I am interested in how it works and this is a good place to explore these areas. I may replicate more of my posts to the corporate site. I may look for more discussion and responses."

Most of the bloggers in this study spoke of redesigning their blog and changing their software. One offered, "I'd like a better index—TypePad says they are planning to introduce this soon." Another said, "I will be moving the blog from Blogger to its own domain name in WordPress soon. The charge will allow significantly increased functionality over the free blogspot.com set up currently used."

For the bloggers in this study redesign includes the appearance as well as content changes. Bloggers indicated they were planning to "offer a dynamic style sheet for users to pick their favorite style layout" or "become more topical with events in our industry as other process manufacturers, trade press, automation suppliers, join in the blog conversation."

Adding additional authors. Many of the bloggers spoke about adding authors, more information on authors, more channels, and more frequent posts. In this study, 38 percent have increased posts on their blogs since they began them.

Blogging begets blogging. When asked how to grow readership and promote a blog, our respondents were very clear. One blogger wrote, "The best way to promote a blog is by commenting on other people's blogs in the same niche and industry." Another offered, "Grow your blog by being cited by other more popular blogs." The theme continued with, "Get linked to by talking about issues of importance to bloggers with high PageRank."

Publicize yourself. Many of the bloggers in this study suggested using a link in your e-mail to direct others to your blog. They suggest talking about your blog in your e-mails and encouraging people to visit. Beyond that, send e-mail blog posts to people who might find them interesting. One business blog author said they "constantly reinforce the blog within the membership, mentioning it every chance we get, in every e-mail we send out and at every meeting we have."

You need to connect. Ultimately the growth of a blog will depend on the quality and quantity of posts on it and on what one blogger calls "blogger relations." One blog author attributes growth to, "Consistent quality postings coupled with relevant comments adding to the conversation on other blogs over the long haul." Another says, "Provide useful information, post regularly, be honest, and be user-oriented." In classic blogger form, we get advice that is both humorous and probably true: "Be brilliant, pick a fight."

The Human Factor

People are important. The ultimate success of any blog depends on the person that manages and posts. Blogs are a human endeavor, a personal conversation, a sharing of thoughts and ideas. Readers form relationships with bloggers that are very real. Communities are formed and friendships are made. One of the blog authors tells us, "I bump into strangers who know my dog's name." There is a real person that entertains, provokes, and responds. In many ways, blogs are a place to go for all that is missing in today's off line world.

Blogs have not stolen the hearts and minds of consumers. Consumers have gone willingly in search of a more meaningful relationship. Most business communication is impersonal and one way. Customers do not feel they are valued by organizations that have built multiple walls between them and those they supposedly serve. They cannot get a human voice on the phone, an option that fits their problem, or a call back. Now, with the Internet, customers can know more about any business than the business itself is willing to tell. Employees, ex-employees, past customers, and industry experts are no more than a click away, and your customers are indeed clicking.

Businesses are no longer the soul source of product information or new product development underway. People are getting the information they need to make purchase decisions from other people. Remember, there are over forty million blogs with a new one springing up every second. If only one-tenth of one percent of those can impact your market, you have 40,000 new voices talking to your customers as we speak.

It is the humanity of the blogoshpere that makes it an enormous threat to business as usual. The only way for businesses to survive this new consumer movement is to understand what makes blogs successful. We asked our prestigious group of bloggers to tell us what characteristics make a good blogger. Many offered lists of personal traits including:

"Dedicated, opinionated, inquisitive"
"Disciplined"
"Intelligent, diligent, and patient"
"Personality, commitment, networking ability"
"Responsible, honest"
"Being true and real at all times"
"Passion, engagement, sincerity, authenticity, to be coherent, to an-

swer comments (even the negative ones), to post regularly (even if only once per week)"

Others offered more extensive comments on what makes a blogger or blog successful:

"Above average conversational or writing skills, creativity, persistence, complete honesty and integrity (if you aren't honest you'll be found out quickly); the ability to separate yourself from your blog. The worst bloggers are those that identify so thoroughly with their blog that conversation and debate can't occur—they are just seen as personal attacks."

"Short and concise postings, blogging is not about really long articles, powerful useful tips of information, a good search feature, a tad bit of humor but also knowledgeable on the subject matter. Sharing of cutting edge info rather than old news."

One well know business blogger wrote, "The blogosphere has changed forever how people share information and what their takes are on just about any topic under the sun. The net result being the world which was getting flat is now even flatter and you are a couple of clicks away from smart people with first hand knowledge and insight into all kinds of ideas that you care about."

In typical blogger form, some sent links to other blogs that have compiled lists of highly effective bloggers, others sent things they have written or have seen on the subject. This is typical blog behavior . . . people helping people.

Intranet/Extranet

The intranet is a private network that is contained within an enterprise, according to SearchWebService.TechTarget.com (2001–2007TechTarget). The intranet may consist of interlinked local area networks and use leaded lines in the wide area network, the site states. "Typically, an intranet includes connections through one or more gateway computers to the outside Internet. The main purpose of an intranet is to share company information and computing resources among employees. An intranet can also be used to facilitate working in groups and for teleconferences."

An extranet, on the other hand, is designed for companies to engage with clients. Also a private network, and also reliant upon the Internet, an extranet allows companies to share information with individuals and businesses "approved" by the company—clients, suppliers, and so forth.

According to SearchNetworking.TechTarget.com, "An extranet can be viewed as part of a company's intranet that is extended to users outside the company."

A February 26, 1996, issue of *BusinessWeek* has an article titled "Here Comes the Intranet: And It Could be the Simple Solution to Company-wide Information-on-Demand," by Amy Cortese, which explores how intranets have revolutionized the workplace. In that article Cortese writes that "the Web, it turns out, is an inexpensive yet powerful alternative to other forms of internal communications, including conventional computer setups."

What are the advantages? According to Cortese, an intranet can cut down on paper use by allowing a company's internal documents—manuals, training materials, and so forth—to be electronically stored, updated, and accessed.

That isn't all the good news, though, writes Cortese: "Intranets can do something far more important. By presenting information in the same way to every computer, they can do what computer and software makers have frequently promised but never actually delivered: pull all the computers, software, and databases that dot the corporate landscape into a single system that enables employees [to] find information wherever it resides."

The article quotes Tom Richardson, marketing manager of Digital Equipment Corp.'s Internet Business Group, as saying: "When the Internet caught on, people weren't looking at it as a way to run their businesses. But that is in fact what's happening."

A *Fast Company* article also looks at how intranets are boosting efficiency and creativity in the workplace ("Inside Job," by George Anders, Issue 50, August 2001, page 176). Anders writes that Intranets are helping employees communicate and collaborate with one another in more productive and efficient ways than they previously could.

In May [2001], for example, IBM convened 52,600 of its employees online for what it called WorldJam. Using the company's intranet, IBMers everywhere swapped ideas on everything from how to retain employees to how to work faster without undermining quality.

It's not just IBM-like giants that are taking advantage of this technology; smaller enterprises are doing so as well. At organizations of almost every size, well-run intranets are transforming clerical chores and making it possible to accomplish routine tasks faster, better, and cheaper. Internal websites are also making it easier than ever to transmit up-to-the-minute company and industry news to employees. And they are opening up new ways for business associates in far-flung locations to brainstorm together.

The very success of the intranet has made it vulnerable. Because information is so readily shared, companies have been under attack from hackers anxious to gain access to intranets and the wealth of information contained in them. As a result, increasing levels of security have been put in place to try and prevent access from outsiders.

See also: Generation X, Y, and Z; Internet

Further Reading

"UNDER NEW MANAGEMENT; The Silent May Have Something to Say," by Kelley Holland, *New York Times* (Sunday, November 5, 2006), Money and Business/Financial Desk Late Edition—Final, Section 3, Page 5, Column 1.

J

Job Sharing

The U.S. Department of Labor (DOL), defines job sharing as when two or more workers share the duties of one full-time job, each working part time, or two or more workers who have unrelated part-time assignments share the same budget line. Job sharing is a matter of agreement between an employer and an employee. Job sharing is an attractive way to recruit new employees and retain current ones. "In order for a job sharing arrangement to be successful, however, both individuals must be able to handle the position as efficiently as one person."

The pros of job sharing are clear. But the practice offers unique challenges. Consider this short article excerpt from the January 1996 issue of HR Magazine:

> According to an April 1994 Conference Board survey of 131 companies offering flexible options . . . the greatest challenges to instituting job sharing include management resistance and skepticism, corporate culture, and the specific nature of the job. Those who lack experience with job sharing often worry about compensation and benefit costs, management of an extra employee, and consequences if the arrangement fails. The study did not find significant problems based on resentment from co-workers, scheduling difficulties, duplication of work, or union negotiations. Difficulties did arise, however, from job sharers' differences in work styles, communication styles, and quality standards (*HR Magazine*, "Job sharing offers unique challenges—Tools from the HR Desk," by Elizabeth Sheley, January 1996).

Monster.com also looked at the pros and cons of job sharing in an article by Monster contributing writer Alyson Preston titled "A New Trend in Alternative Work Arrangement" (Monster, 2006) This article said: "One type of flexible schedule particularly geared toward parents is the job share—two employees essentially split one job's functions, each working part-time. According to a 1999 survey of 1,020 U.S. employers conducted by Hewitt Associates, a leading global management consulting firm, 28 percent of employers offer job sharing.

The Monster article also noted that job-sharing can be difficult, but rewarding when it works. It also noted that employees should take responsibility for figuring out how their own arrangements might work before suggesting a job-share arrangement. The article counseled employees who want to share jobs to try to anticipate all of the questions managers would have about the arrangement.

See also: Flex-Time; War for Talent

Further Reading

"The Pros and Cons of Job Sharing. Thinking About Implementing a Job-Sharing Program? Here's What You Need to Consider Before You Do," by David Javitch, www.entrepreneur.com (November 10, 2006).

Signs of Changing Culture:
Plateauing: Redefining Success at Work

Published: October 4, 2006 in Knowledge@Wharton

Reproduced with permission from Knowledge@Wharton (http://knowledge.wharton.upenn.edu), the online research and business analysis journal of the Wharton School of the University of Pennsylvania.

As an executive coach who works with corporations, Monica McGrath has her ear to the ground. And what she is hearing is this: A number of men and women in middle management are increasingly reluctant to take the next step in their careers because the corporate ladder is not as appealing as it used to be, and the price to climb it is too high. "These people are still ambitious, and they are still driving. They just aren't driving for the same things they were driving for fifteen years ago," she says.

What may be happening, suggest McGrath and others, is that people are setting career paths based on their own values and definitions of success. They are not burned out or dropping out; they are not going back to school and changing careers; they are not having a mid-life crisis. Instead, they are redefining how they can keep contributing to their organizations, but on their own terms. Rather than subscribe to the "onward and upward" motto, they are more interested in "plateauing," un-hooking from the pressure to follow an upward path that someone else has set.

A number of oft-cited trends in the workplace contribute to this phenomenon: Technological advancements are breaking down the barriers between work and non-work hours, adding to the pressure to constantly be on the job or on call. Strategic decisions like restructuring, downsizing, and outsourcing are adding to job uncertainty at all levels and reducing the number of promotions available to mid- and upper-level managers. The continuing influx of women into the workforce keeps raising the level of stress when it comes to work/life balance issues.

Lois Backon, a vice president at Families and Work Institute (FWI), a New York-based nonprofit research organization, points to a report FWI does every five years entitled, "National Study of the Changing Work Force." The latest one was released in 2003. One of their areas of research relates to what the organization calls "reduced aspirations" among various sectors of the workforce. "This is an incredibly important issue, and it offers some of the most troubling data out there for corporate America," she notes.

For example, in one of its latest reports, "Generation & Gender" (2004), which uses data from the national study to determine differences among generations, FWI found that fewer employees aspired to positions of greater responsibility than in the past. Among college-educated men of Gen-Y, Gen-X, and boomer ages, 68 percent wanted to move into jobs with more responsibility in 1992, versus only 52 percent in 2002. Among college-educated women of Gen-Y, Gen-X, and boomer ages, the decrease was even higher: 57 percent wanted to move into jobs with more responsibility in 1992 versus 36 percent in 2002. (Generation Y is typically defined as those born between 1980 and 1995, Generation X as those born between 1965 and 1980.)

"We then did a more focused look at leaders in the global economy," Backon says. "We took the top ten multinational companies—such as Citicorp and IBM—and conducted in-depth interviews with the top 100 men and top 100 women. Of those leaders, 34 percent of the women and 21 percent of the men said they have reduced their career aspirations."

This plateauing is part of a bigger phenomenon in the workforce—

one that also includes people putting higher priorities on activities outside their jobs, from family to volunteer work to hobbies. For example, in the FWI study, the reason that the majority (67 percent) of these leaders gave for their response was "not that they couldn't do the work, but that the sacrifices they would have to make in their personal lives were too great," says Backon.

"We call it 'negative spillover from their jobs to their homes,'" Backon adds. "The whole issue of overwork, of needing to multitask, of having to deal with numerous interruptions during their work day" affects employee attitude, not just toward their jobs but also their free time. "Based on our research, we know that 54 percent of employees are less than fully satisfied with their jobs, 38 percent are likely to actively look for new employment in the next year, and 39 percent of employees feel they are not engaged in the work they are doing." Most employees "do want to feel engaged by their jobs. The term 'reduced aspirations' does not mean they are not talented or not good at what they do. They are. But in focus groups, they also say things like, 'I need to make these choices because my family is a priority,' or 'I need to make these choices to make my life work.'"

One way to look at this phenomenon, adds Wharton management professor Nancy Rothbard, is that some employees "still derive some sense of identity from their jobs but they have, or are seeking, other ways to get that fulfillment." They are no longer pushing for the bigger raise, the larger staff, the more prestigious title; "they are taking energy that had been focused primarily on goals defined by the corporation and focusing it elsewhere."

Fewer Promotions, Fewer Pensions

Peter Cappelli, director of Wharton's Center for Human Resources, has done extensive research into the changing nature of the workplace. As he and others have noted, companies no longer promise job security, generous benefits packages or even pensions, and employees no longer feel loyal to their employers or obligated to stay for long periods of time. Employees are responsible for managing their own career track and seeking out the mentors and training they need to move on in their current company or, just as likely, in a new company.

Cappelli agrees that organizations "don't have quite as much influence over people as they used to in terms of shaping their goals and aspirations, in part because people come to these jobs at an older age and change jobs more frequently than in the past. Does that necessarily mean people are on their own career path? It depends what you mean by that. I'm not sure it means they are eschewing corporate success. But they are looking outside their current employer's definition of success, more so than in the past."

Cappelli cautions, however, that it's unlikely employees can go on cruise control and still hope to be retained and valued by their employers. "It used to be you could just lie low and wait for the pension. That doesn't happen much any more." And while some employees may not pay as much attention to the goals that their companies want them to pursue, they "continue to work hard because they are afraid of being laid off. . . . Companies systematically go through and fire people who are not pulling their weight. The ability to punish people into appropriate behavior is one of the great and unpleasant lessons of the 1980s. Employee morale sank and productivity stayed up because people were afraid of being fired," Cappelli notes, adding, however, that this dynamic changes in a tight labor market.

Wharton management professor Sara Kaplan "could imagine a scenario where people have discovered that there is not too much point being loyal to their employers, and then go on to say, 'Okay, I have gotten where I am going to get, and I am going to focus on the other part of my life. I will keep working but won't invest all my energy in my job.'"

But Kaplan also thinks "everyone needs something to be passionate about, so it would be hard for me to imagine that people would simply ramp down on their job without having a crisis or without having found something else" to interest them. Indeed, in today's economy, she adds, "you can't keep your job unless you are engaged, to a certain extent. Corporations don't want people who don't want to go higher. They don't want people who won't strive. You can't plateau; there are always people biting at your heels."

Directly related to the issue of job satisfaction is the question of job design. "Management scholars have been studying this for a long time," says Wharton management professor Sigal Barsade. "Whenever a company designs a job, it must take into account how employees view that job, whether their goal is to get ahead, whether work is central to their lives, and so forth. A company can make a real error trying to redesign a job to be more enriched if the employee doesn't want that," especially if the new job definition requires them to work harder.

What is crucial, Barsade says, "is good job fit. Is the person doing what the company needs done? If the answer is 'yes' and the person also is good at what they do but simply doesn't want to do more, then that could actually be a good situation, especially for jobs that don't include room for promotion." This is applicable in particular to customer service positions where people need to be engaged while they are providing the service, but are not expected to be thinking of ways to redesign the whole customer service system. "So the fit needs to be between what the organization needs and what the employee wants and values. If that fit isn't there, that's when you are going to have a problem."

When should employees who have no interest in advancing or taking on higher challenges worry about losing their job? "I think as long as these employees are working diligently and competently and are willing to change—whether that means learning a new technology or adapting to a new work process—they should be safe," says Barsade.

Making Tradeoffs

Kathleen Christensen, who directs The Program on The Workplace, Work Force and Working Families at the Alfred P. Sloan Foundation, suggests that plateauing in one's job "is a completely natural part of a career, but we ignore it because we have this notion of a steep trajectory." Psychologists, she says, "talk about different stages of human development. One stage may be that as people reach middle age, there is the idea of generativity—a willingness at this point to start giving back, perhaps start cultivating others rather than just" focusing on your own achievements. Plateauing can be desirable, she says, in that employees "are likely to have a great deal of institutional knowledge. They can be the ones who know the processes, can share them and guide others. If everyone is always out for themselves, it goes counter to developing the team culture that every company wants."

No matter how people define their jobs, Christensen adds, "they still must have performance goals, and be evaluated in terms of how well they meet those goals. But we should also recognize that at different points in people's lives, they may define their performance goals in slightly different ways—they may move at different tempos—and still be well within what the company needs in order to achieve its business goals."

Plateauing cuts across all boundaries, Christensen suggests, and it could be the result of certain events in people's lives—like the birth of a child or the need to care for a sick parent—which lead an employee to decide, "I'm going to hold my own but not try to climb." But it would be "a mistake to assume that all the factors that lead to different tempos are due only to outside forces. It could just be an employees' own decision not to try to climb" in the organization. It doesn't mean they are slacking off. "Someone can be working hard and still be plateauing in a career," Christensen says.

She emphasizes the need for employer and employee to communicate expectations and goals. Any decision to plateau, for whatever length of time, should be a "deal that is structured to meet both sides' needs. It's a danger if employees think they can make these decisions based only on what they want to do. It's also a danger for the company if it doesn't take into account what the employee needs in order to do his or her best. It comes down to principles of good management."

At Deloitte & Touche USA LLP, senior advisor Anne Weisberg is involved with a pilot program called mass career customization, which allows employer and employee together to customize an individual's career "along a defined set of options." It's a realization, she says, that "the 'one size fits all' approach no longer works." In the pilot program, which started in June with a practice group of 400 people and will run for a year, "we have unbundled the career into four dimensions: role, pace, location and schedule, and work load." Under the role dimension, employees can specify, for example, whether they want an external role involving significant client interaction, an internal role without that client service aspect, or a role somewhere between the two. Under pace, the issue is how quickly an employee wants to move up. Under location and schedule, issues such as part-time hours, working at home and willingness to travel are included, while work load looks at variables like the number of projects an employee is willing to undertake at any one time.

"There are tradeoffs to these choices," Weisberg emphasizes. "A totally internal role has a different compensation structure and advancement route. But the tradeoffs are articulated and an employee can move from one set of options to another. It's a recognition that people need to fit their work into their life and their life into their work over the course of their career, which is forty years. No one solution will work" for all that time. (Interestingly, she notes, the pilot program so far has found that "rather than dialing down on their careers, most of the practice group is choosing to dial up," reflecting, in part, the fact that 65 percent of Deloitte's employees are under the age of thirty-five.)

Companies can't redefine the corporate ladder "with a different model that is just as rigid," Weisberg adds. "We need to replace the corporate ladder with a corporate lattice"—a term implying a more adaptive kind of framework which allows an individual to move in many different directions, not just upward or downward. "I know in many companies, employees are evaluated on the basis of how much time they spend on the job or how many sacrifices they make. That paradigm has to shift so that you look at performance and contribution separate from sacrifice."

Weisberg, senior advisor to Deloitte's Women's Initiative, says that when the initiative was started in 1993, it was concerned primarily with women's career paths, which are very different from men's. (For example, the vast majority of women, about 80 percent, do not work full-time continuously throughout their career, whereas the vast majority of men do, she notes.) "But we quickly realized these issues affect many groups other than women, including men, members of Gen X and Gen Y who perhaps want to accelerate early and then decelerate later, and the baby boomers" who are trying to adjust their workloads to accommodate interests or responsibilities outside of work. What's been missing, she says, "is a way to approach all these different people with a consistent set of options." On the micro level, she adds, "it is fundamentally a negotiation between the employer and employee," which is why it is so important to develop "the right kind of negotiation framework."

In scanning the 2006 employment landscape, Weisberg says she sees a "heating up of the war for talent. If you look at the demographics, there is a huge shortage in many of the knowledge-based industries. That is going to be with us for a long time." She cites a recent statistic that women now make up 58 percent of college graduates, a trend that should affect even more how jobs and careers are structured. "Smart employers don't want to drive their employees so hard that they burn out. That is very expensive. The estimates of the cost of turnover keep going up, in large part because of this issue of the shrinking skilled labor force."

In the past, she says, "we used 150 percent of salary as the cost of turnover. We are now using 200 percent of salary." Some experts say that for knowledge-based companies, that figure is 500 percent. "Turnover is a huge cost. One of the major reasons for doing mass career customization is to improve retention."

Weisberg, too, suggests the need for transparency in any decisions related to the work environment. When both employer and employee are clear about the choices being made, "then both sides are more satisfied with the arrangement. If choices are never discussed, you can end up with mismatched expectations, which can lead to stress on both sides."

Wharton management professor Stewart Friedman, who teaches Wharton Executive MBA students, among others, agrees that "people are struggling with this issue of, 'What do I really care about and how do I measure success?' My sense is that more people, not just middle-aged employees but younger people as well, are raising this question in ways they didn't twenty years ago. If so, is it because more people are hitting the pyramid and accepting the reality of lowered expectations caused by less upward mobility, or is it that they are part of a larger swing in our culture that is more focused on other definitions of success besides economics? I think it is probably both."

What makes leaders in an organization effective, says Friedman, is that they realize employees can have different values than your typical workaholics—those who enjoy working eighty hours a week—and still contribute to the organization. "But it's hard to change norms and cultural values that are deeply embedded." What Friedman describes as "the excesses of the overworked generation" have reached a point "where more and more people are starting to question their total dedication to work. We are seeing more people pursuing creative alternatives. The big question twenty years ago was, 'How early did your power breakfast start?' Now the big question is, 'Where and how far did you go on your vacation?'"

Disappearing Flex-Time

It's not clear how managers in organizations might react to employees who redefine their positions as jobs rather than as vocations or callings. "They could worry that people simply decide to 'work to rule'—i.e., do exactly what is specified and nothing more," says Rothbard. "Companies are terrified of that happening: They know things will break down at that point because you can't specify everything that has to be done in a particular job. But I think if employees' identities are still tied up in their jobs, this won't happen."

Another consideration is how to continue to motivate people if none of the traditional rewards are available—such as a promotion or a bigger office. "A company may, in fact, want employees to have other sources of fulfillment, and so will try to build in things that matter to them," says Rothbard. That could include flex-time, job sharing, job sabbaticals, or the sponsorship of charity events that are meaningful to employees.

Some people question the sincerity of programs like flex-time or sabbaticals that let people pursue interests outside of work. "I don't think companies are paying a lot of attention to people's passions. There are programs to address this but, frankly, it doesn't happen that much," says Kaplan, who notes that companies will try to institute flex-time benefits during times of economic growth, but "the minute the crunch happens, then all those programs go away." And even when companies implement such procedures as flex-time or job sharing, adds Barsade, "it doesn't really address the bigger issues of the tremendous amount of work people these days are expected to do on the job."

One of those bigger issues relates to work/life balance and job commitment. McGrath recently taught an executive education course for women in the middle management ranks of a pharmaceutical company to explore "ways to build relationships with, and support each other, as they attempted to take on the next level of responsibility. It's because the companies were finding that women were not willing to step into the high-potential pool of employees" for a number of different reasons, including in some cases, wanting to make sure they had time for their families. "These women were at the vice president level. They weren't lacking in ambition and they wanted to make a difference in their jobs. It was just a question of, 'How much more responsibility can I take on?'"

Rothbard continues to find it ironic that employees who want to "opt out" of their jobs for a short time get less pushback than women who want flex-time "so that they can pick up their children from school at 4:30 instead of 5:30 every day." Rothbard cites Arlie Hochschild's book

The Time Bind, which notes the exceptions available to high-potential men who want to take a sabbatical and travel around the world. In one chapter, Hochschild relates how two men had asked their supervisor for time off to do underwater photography of coral reefs. The supervisor granted them an educational leave to pursue their project. Why, the author asks, can't the company offer flexible schedules to parents who want to pick up their children early from daycare?

Rothbard also points to research on the phenomenon of "multiple roles, and the fact that there are physical as well as psychological benefits to people" who have more than one area in their lives that engages them and requires their attention. An example would be a woman who has responsibilities both at her job and with her family at home. The research discusses "the buffer hypothesis, which says that if something goes wrong in one area, you then have another area that buffers you," says Rothbard. "In other words, work/family roles enrich, rather than deplete, each other."

Stress in the workplace, many experts have noted, can be intensified by technological advancements that make it harder for people to ever totally disconnect from their jobs at appropriate moments, like vacations. As McGrath notes, "there are no boundaries around employees' time. They are always available." McGrath has worked as a coach in five large corporations over the past year and at all of them, she observed workloads that were, in her opinion, unmanageable. Some employees, she says, react by trying to set strict limits on their accessibility—for example, not answering their Blackberry from 6 P.M. to 6 A.M. "They have come to some sort of peace with the fact that they will never get everything done and keep everyone happy."

Just-in-Time

Just-in-Time (JIT) is a manufacturing organization philosophy that attempts to eliminate storage costs and overstocking of parts by meeting demand for parts, components, and the like as closely as possible with supply. When the factory needs a certain component, if it is adhering to JIT practices, that is when the component will be delivered, in the amount needed at the time. By eliminating overstocking and overproduction, the philosophy aims to reduce storage costs, and cut down on wasted action.

Why I Do This: CMIR Fellow,
Surplus Asset Investment Recovery Manager
Paul F. Wengert

Inevitably, businesses and corporations generate equipment that they no longer need. "Surplus, excess, or obsolete" equipment and material is generated because businesses change. Businesses replace older equipment, develop new ways of doing whatever they do, grow or get smaller, build or teardown. The purpose of this job is to recover what remains of the original value (or cost) of the no longer needed equipment. It is, in a sense, recycling the asset.

This job involves identifying where the equipment is, conducting inventories to catalog and list the equipment in electronic databases (so that the equipment can be reused somewhere else in the company), marketing, selling, donating, or scrapping.

I was offered this job by a major corporation to manage their surplus equipment. After fourteen years I started a company that provides these services to companies that did not have people to do that work. We employed 26 people doing that for companies.

Do I like this job? I like it very much!

What is unexpected in this job: The most unexpected part of this job is finding out that corporations waste so much money by not reusing surplus assets or selling the assets that they no longer need.

This is a challenging and rewarding job that is new and changing every day. It involves working with lots of different people in different places. There is a great deal of satisfaction in this job.

What kind of person would enjoy this job? This is a job for someone who likes to be creative, wants to show initiative, wants responsibility, and is a "self starter."

If you want to know more about this career go to the Investment Recovery Association website (www.invrecovery.org).

To sum up using an old adage, JIT could be thought of essentially as the manufacturing interpretation and implementation of "waste not, want not."

According to ValueBasedManagement.net, "just-in-time" was pioneered by Taiichi Ohno in Japan at the Toyota car assembly plants in the early 1970s. "JIT cuts waste supply by supplying parts only when the assembly process requires them. At the heart of JIT lies the kanaban, the Japanese word for card. This kanaban card is sent to the warehouse to reorder a standard quantity of parts as and when they have been used up in the assembly/manufacturing processes . . . The target of JIT is to speed up customer response while minimizing inventories at the same time. Inventories help to respond quickly to changing customer demands, but inevitably cost money and increase the needed work capital" (2006 Value Based Management.net, last updated September 27, 2006) (http://www .valuebasedmanagement.net/methods_jit.html).

According to the Department of Labor's 1999 "Report on the American Workforce," prepared by the Bureau of Labor Statistics, U.S. Department of Labor:

> Both the automobile industry and the help supply industry have each, in their own way, adopted "just-in-time" strategies in an increasingly competitive economy. The motor vehicles and equipment industry throttled down labor costs during the current economic expansion. In three major segments of the industry—motor vehicle assembly, parts manufacturing, and automotive stampings—unit labor costs were lower in 1998 than in 1991. From 1991 to 1998, unit labor costs of motor vehicle assemblers declined 0.9 percent per year. During the same period, parts manufacturers cut unit labor costs by 2.0 percent annually, on average. The automotive stampings industry had even greater success in cost-cutting, reducing unit labor costs by 4.4 percent per year.
>
> The auto industry has leveraged the impact of these changes with strategies of lean manufacturing and just-in-time production throughout the supply chain. As a result, there has been a change in the structure of the industry: The number of people working up-stream in the automotive parts industry first surpassed the number in final assembly in 1981. Their lead has widened since 1987, as the industry shifted many design, development, and supply management functions to suppliers" (Monthly Labor Review Online, October 1999, Vol. 122, No. 10. "Research Summaries: The 1999 Report of the American Workforce").

JIT has helped manufacturers across many industries improve their bottom line. One source for more information on JIT is www.strategosinc .com, which offers a history of "lean manufacturing." Another is www .inventorymanagementreview.org. An article published November 8, 2005 on that website discusses JIT in the context of fast food (preparing the food long before customers order it and keeping it warm under food lamps, versus using a JIT approach and identifying an efficient way to prepare the food as needed) and also in the context of computer production. The article cites Dell Computers as an exemplar of low inventory levels and the JIT approach.

See also: Made in Japan; Six Sigma

Further Reading

"A Revolution That Came In a Box," by Joe Nocera, *New York Times* (Saturday, May 13, 2006), Business/Financial Desk Late Edition—Final, Section C, Page 1, Column 1.

Improving Production with Lean Thinking, by Javier Santos, Richard A. Wysk, and Jose M. Torres, Jossey-Bass (2006).

"Thanks to Detroit, China Is Poised to Lead," by Keith Bradsher, and Jeremy W. Peters, *New York Times* (Sunday, March 12, 2006), Money and Business/Financial Desk Late Edition—Final, Section 3, Page 1, Column 3.

Transforming Your Go-To-Market Strategy: The Three Disciplines of Channel Management, by V. Katuri Rangan, Harvard Business School Press (2006).

Kaizen

Kaizen is a Japanese term that means continuous improvement. It is taken from the words "kai," or continuous, and "zen," or improvement. According to www.valuebasedmanagement.com, "kai" literally means change, and "zen" means to become good.

According to that website, the *Kaizen* method is a Japanese management concept that consists of "five founding elements: teamwork, personal discipline, improved morale, quality circles, and suggestions for improvement. Valuebasedmanagement.com also notes that the *Kaizen* philosophy, or approach to management, provides the foundation for many other Japanese management concepts, including Total Quality Control.

In practice, the *Kaizen* approach calls for never-ending efforts for improvement involving everyone in the organization—managers and workers alike, according to 100ventures.com. *Kaizen* management, that site says, has two major components: maintenance and improvement.

Under the maintenance function, the management must first establish policies, rules, directives, and standard operating procedures (SOPs) and then work towards ensuring that everybody follows SOP. The latter is achieved through a combination of discipline and human resource development measures. Under the improvement function, management works continuously towards revising the current standards, once they have been mastered, and establishing higher ones. Improvement can be broken down between innovation and *Kaizen*. Innovation involves a drastic improvement in the existing process and requires large investments. *Kaizen* signifies small improvements as a result of coordinated continuous efforts by all employees.

The site points out that encouraging employees to suggest ways to improve processes and procedures is an important part of the *Kaizen* approach. It also says that one of the ways that top managers evaluate a company that is embracing a *Kaizen* philosophy is by keeping tabs on how

---

Why I Do This: Minister
Rev. Catherine Torpey

I am responsible for the day-to-day running of the church. I write newsletter columns, meet with parishioners who want to try something new in their lives, or who need someone to talk to. I meet with other members of the community and learn about local, national, and international social injustice issues so that I and my congregation can make the world a better place.

I have the best job in the world. I tell people what's on my mind and heart each week, in the hope that perhaps it will help them in figuring out how to make their life as meaningful and fulfilling as possible. I help people both in times of crisis and joy (funerals and weddings, for instance), and I get to help them find ways to make the world more compassionate and just. I get to sing in the choir, and go to New Orleans to help rebuild houses. I get to hang out with children and teenagers at church camps and overnights. I get to hone business skills as a leader of a nonprofit institution. In other words, I get to do everything I love in life, in such a way that it brings meaning to others. I get to use my gifts and encourage others to use theirs.

Running a church is truly a team effort. I'm the paid member of the team, a kind of coach, really. Most of the real work is done by the members of the congregation, with me helping to guide and cheer. I don't have to be the expert at everything; I just have to figure out what I'm good at, and find others who have a passion for other aspects of church life, so that we can co-create one small beloved community in this crazy world.

I'd recommend becoming a minister if you love helping others to find meaning in life. You don't have to be better, kinder, or smarter than anyone else; you just have to envision a world where we can all become a little better, kinder, and smarter.

---

many employee suggestions are made and followed up on, resulting in higher standards and improved performance. The more suggestions made by employees, the more involved they are in the work of the company, the better practices become, and the more closely the company is aligned with the Kaizen method (http://www.1000ventures.com/business_guide/mgmt _kaizen_main.html).

Silvia Hartman writes about *Kaizen* in her essay "*Kaizen*, The Exclusive Or & How To Escape From The Black and White Universe" (Silvia Hartman, 2001) on her website, silviahartman.com.

I think the most soothing aspect of the *Kaizen* philosophy is the up front presupposition that whatever you do, and no matter how well you do it, it can never be perfect . . . Yet even from this state of imperfection, there is no need to be dismayed, or afraid, if you follow the *Kaizen* principle. Here, we strive TOWARDS perfection—we do the best we can to make things better, every way, and every day, to move towards perfection in an evolution of simple endeavours, all the time.

Many companies have adapted a *Kaizen* approach to evaluating their processes, with a goal towards improving performance. Consider the Ariens Company, based in Brillion, Wisconson. Ariens manufactures outdoor power equipment for commercial and home use. An article published on www.landscapemanagement.net on June 21, 2007, notes that the Ariens company "recently conducted [its] 1,000th *Kaizen* event aimed at reducing waste within the operation." That article goes on to quote company president Dan Ariens as saying "Employees have not only created a culture of continuous improvement, they have sustained it."

Toyota Motor Sales USA is one of the higher-profile companies that embraces the *Kaizen* approach. And not only does the company pursue the *Kaizen* method internally, it also annually recognizes a large carrier company for its ability to embrace *Kaizen* concepts. According to a press release dated June 5, 2007, on businesswire.com, the 2006 Large Carrier of the Year award went to J.B. Hunt Transport Services, Inc.

The release said, "J.B. Hunt embraces the Toyota Way, and the DNA of their culture is much like ours," said Jane Beseda, Group Vice President, general manager for the Toyota Customer Services Division. "For both companies, 'there is no best . . . only better.'"

Each year, Toyota asks employees from its Corporate Logistics department, plants, and distribution centers to vote on the winners based on each carrier's performance in various categories of cost control and quality. Criteria for selection include on-time delivery and pickup, problem solving capabilities, damage prevention, professionalism, equipment availability, and enroute delays.

In addition, Toyota scores each carrier on its ability to embrace and culturally implement *Kaizen*, Toyota's methodology for continuous improvement. J.B. Hunt has taken significant steps to eliminate waste from its own operations and further improve Toyota's supply chain processes by ensuring the production facilities receive the right amount of product at the right time. This is accomplished by utilizing a unique blend of intermodal and traditional truckload movements that provide Toyota with an on-time percentage greater than 99 percent.

An article by Jewel Gopwani, published on www.freep.com (The Detroit Free Press) June 4, 2007, discusses the result of a survey of companies that supply automakers with parts, and notes that Toyota has been a perennial favorite of the parts suppliers. The article says: "At Toyota, the results reflect what the industry has come to know as the Toyota Way, a business philosophy based on mutual respect and *Kaizen,* or continual improvement."

"We will never believe that there is not room for improvement," said Gene Tabor, general manager of purchasing at Toyota's North American manufacturing headquarters in suburban Cincinnati. "That's *Kaizen* in its purest form."

See also: Lean Manufacturing; Six Sigma; Total Quality Management (TQM)

Further Reading

Kaizen: The Key to Japan's Competitive Success, by Masaaki Imai, McGraw-Hill/Irwin, 1st ed. (November 1, 1986).
One Small Step Can Change Your Life: The Kaizen Way, by Robert Maurer, Workman Publishing Company (June 1, 2004).

Killer App

First, know that "killer app" is a nickname, short for "killer application." A killer app is a computer program that becomes so successful, that it has its own "brand equity." That is, it is known and explicitly recognized for the value it creates by using, or building on, existing technology. E-mail is one of the "killer apps" on the Internet. According to the 1998 bestseller, *Unleashing the Killer App,* by Larry Downes and Chunka Mui (Harvard Business School Press; the book text also appears on www.killer-apps .com): "Over the last two years, electronic commerce . . . has been touted as the killer app that will redefine the entire manufacturing-distribution-

Why I Do This: Editorial Director, Global Management Consulting Firm

Barry Adler

I manage a group of writers and editors who produce a variety of publications about matters of interest to senior executives throughout the business world. The consultants at my firm work on a wide range of projects, and my job is to help them—via our writers and editors—capture what they've learned, and differentiate us from other firms.

Some of the materials we produce are short articles, some are longer reports, and a few projects even turn into books. All are used to market the firm to clients and prospective clients, and to give us a presence in the mainstream and industry press. The idea is that we help build and sharpen our brand in the marketplace by publishing pieces that convey the firm's thinking and that showcase our areas of special expertise and focus. At the same time, we have to be very careful not to breach our pledges of confidentiality to our clients.

In a typical day, I'll get 100 e-mails or so, and a bunch of phone calls. I might also have several conference calls. In many ways, this is a virtual organization, so I find that I'm dealing with writers, editors, and consultants from offices all over the world each day. They're all involved in various stages of developing, writing, or editing pieces. It's my job to orchestrate the process and make sure that we have the resources we need to produce the materials on schedule.

Put another way, I take an oversight role in most of the editing. I also broker many of the arrangements between the consultants and the editorial group. When consultants have ideas they want to get "out there," they're naturally looking to get something written as quickly as possible. I'm the keeper of the schedule, in the sense that I have to set realistic expectations all around to ensure that the trains run on time and arrive at the right stations in good shape.

I have to work closely with our production manager and his crew to make that schedule succeed. They do the design work and produce the galleys that eventually lead to a finished publication. I also work closely with marketing and media specialists to help coordinate and plan press campaigns when the publications are ready for distribution.

I'm a manager at this point in my career. I have extensive editorial experience, but what I'm really doing is bringing that experience to bear to make this complicated process run smoothly. I have less and less time to edit things myself. But because of my background, if need be, I can jump in and do any of the jobs that are done by the people I manage. (Although they might argue that I don't do their work quite as well as they do.)

I like managing this process—but I certainly couldn't have predicted that this would be the kind of work I would be doing. With writing and editing, it seems that you start out in a certain way, and then as you develop, people either like your work or they don't, and certain doors open as you go, based on your style and the people you work with . . .

I was at the *New York Times* for fifteen years, as an editor in the business section. And of course, that's a great name-brand place to be, so a lot of doors opened for me. One person I knew, for example, went off to the *Harvard Business Review*, and from there, he moved into the consulting world. He called me when he started a magazine at one consulting firm, and I made that move. I made another move with him when he started a small publishing unit within a big educational company. And then I was called a few years later by someone else I knew to come over to this firm, and I did. I was ready for all of these changes, and here I am.

You might like this kind of work if you like keeping an awful lot of details in your head at the same time—who's doing what, when, why, with whom, what do they need, when will they be finished, what will be next . . . You have to like, or at least tolerate, working with things that aren't necessarily very neat. Schedules change, messages aren't clear. You have to be comfortable dealing with all that and then figuring out what went wrong and how to fix it.

You also have to be able to think thematically. This is important, because the job is really not just about making the trains run on time. To do the deeper part of this job, a person needs to be able to evaluate the various pieces individually, but also put them into a greater context of what the firm as a whole is doing. What are the messages we're sending? Are they consistent? Do they build upon one another? Do they move us forward? This is where the brand-building comes in; it's also a good internal measure of the work of the firm.

A lot of what I do depends on how much I can get from the people I work with. So in order to do this job, you have to genuinely like interacting with people. That may sound strange, but a lot of people really do not like working with others. I have to understand what various individuals are good at, what motivates them, how fast they work, whether they can take stress, whether they *enjoy* stress . . . In that sense, I'm part rabbi and part therapist and part diplomat as well as manager and editorial advisor. There's never a dull moment—and hardly ever a free one.

retail-finance business cycle, creating gigantic new markets while it undermines existing ones."

But keep in mind, killer apps can be created on any sort of technology. As Dr. William Burke, a New York pediatrician, was credited with saying, "You never know where a blister will rise." As Downes' and Mui's book goes on to say: "It is easy . . . to find examples of killer apps from history that demonstrate just how unpredictable and indirect their impact can be." In Medieval Technology and Social Change, for example, historian Lynn White, Jr., studied several inventions from the Middle Ages that revolutionized not only the activities they were intended to affect but society as a whole.

Perhaps the most important of these medieval killer apps was the stirrup, which the Franks—Germanic tribes who ruled central Europe after the fall of Rome—adopted from an Asian design. The stirrup made it possible for a mounted fighter to strike with his lance without falling off his horse, greatly increasing the force that could be put behind such a blow. It proved decisive in the Franks' efforts to turn back the marauding Saracens who invaded western Europe in the eighth century, despite the superior numbers of the invaders.

Charles Martel, leader of the Franks, understood from his victory that the stirrup hadn't simply improved the effectiveness of his forces, as a new weapon or fighting formation might have done. Rather, it changed his entire military strategy. Stirrups made possible a mounted cavalry, a new element in the battle equation, and Charles Martel immediately made them a permanent feature.

Who would have thought that stirrup and E-commerce had anything in common?

Another good definition of "killer app" comes from www.searchweb services.techtarget.com, which is "powered by" whatis.com. This website, in a section that credits contributor Reg Harbeck, says that a killer app is "jargon in the computer industry for an application program that intentionally or unintentionally gets you to make the decision to buy the system the application runs on. A classic example of a killer app was the spreadsheet program, the first of which was called VisiCalc, followed later by Lotus 1–2-3. The spreadsheet application helped introduce the personal computer into the department level of large and small businesses. A killer app can refer to a generic type of application that hasn't existed before, to a particular product that first introduces a new application type, or to any application with wide appeal."

That website goes on to say that when any sort of new computer hardware is released, the manufacturers want other companies to develop a killer app for the product, as the app will fuel sales.

Most businesses would probably relish the chance to be credited with introducing a killer app. (Particularly if they marketed it profitably.) But from the user point of view comes at least one cautionary note. Consider these thoughts, published in an article by Thomas Claburn online in Informationweek, November 13, 2006 (www.informationweek.com). (The article is entitled "Blogs and Wikis Move In as E-Mail Overload Becomes Unbearable).

E-mail, the Internet's killer app, is killing productivity. Even for workers who insulate themselves from pitches for porn and pills—up 59 percent in October from the previous month, according to e-mail management company Postini—occupational spam takes a toll: Mailing list messages, workgroup updates, e-mail alerts, and corporate communiqués demand attention, if not a reply. Dealing with e-mail easily can become a full-time job. Heavy users receive 1,000 messages and 1,500 spam messages a week, estimates Richi Jennings, lead analyst with the e-mail security practice at Ferris Research.

What are the next killer apps? Are they already in use, but not yet reaching their full potential? Consider an article that appeared on www.pda .mobileeurope.co.uk/magazine/features (Nexus Media Communications). Entitled "Out of the Maelstrom," and online on November 14, 2006, the piece was credited to Mike Dallimore, Radio Frequency Systems Vice President Broadcast, Towers and Defence Systems. It said: "There is presently a great deal of industry hype surrounding 'mobile television.' Said by some to be the next 'killer app' of the mobile sector, and dismissed by others as having no sustainable business model, mobile TV is a conjure of possibilities. It lies at the eye of a maelstrom of technologies, network models and frequency bands, waiting for many trials to end and the manifestation of a clue as to the most practical and commercially viable direction."

That's one possibility.

See also: Innovation

Further Reading

Unleashing the Killer App: Digital Strategies for Market Dominance, by Larry Downes and Chunka Mui, Harvard Business School Press, rev sub ed. (March 2000).

Knowledge Management

Knowledge management is the art (and science) of managing the "knowl-edge" that a company possesses. To manage knowledge explicitly is to treat knowledge as a part of the business that needs to be recognized in a company's strategy—and in its practices. If a company engages in knowl-edge management, for example, some employees' performances may be measured, in part, on their contributions to the acquisition of knowledge, and their skill at disseminating it to their colleagues. Knowledge is seen as an explicit contributor to the company's results. Some companies have dedicated knowledge functions—that is, departments or groups of people dedicated to gathering and managing the company's knowledge. In some firms, the people from this department might work with managers from other areas in the company to "capture" what they've been learning and write it up for all to read. In other companies, knowledge work might be spread through different divisions.

The idea of managing knowledge explicitly has taken hold as the term "knowledge worker" has gained in use and popularity. Both terms were for a time associated primarily with "information-based businesses," such as service businesses. But now, all sorts of companies are recognizing that knowledge can be a useful way to think about what it is that employees know that translates into a competitive advantage for the business.

Any size company can engage in knowledge management—and many do so without even calling it knowledge management. Say for example, the company in question is a marketing firm. The knowledge that the marketing consultants acquire as a result of working with one client may prove valuable to other consultants in future engagements. Not the knowl-edge of the clients (nor any proprietary information) but rather, the knowledge of what it is like to work on a particular sort of campaign, with certain logistical challenges, or characteristics. This firm may call what they do "knowledge management," but they may also not have a name for it, and simply do it as part of how they operate.

Managing knowledge explicitly—that is, recognizing it as an asset, and something that can be counted as part of what gives a company its com-petitive edge—is difficult, in part because knowledge is an "intangible asset." As an article in *Fast Company* magazine, noted:

The trick is to balance the "hard" with the "soft"—tapping the knowledge locked in people's experience. This "tacit knowledge" is

213

frequently overlooked or diminished by companies. In contrast, most companies have elaborate systems to capture and share their "explicit knowledge"—the stuff that shows up in manuals, databases, and employee handbooks. This kind of knowledge never translates into a winning strategy. What good is a database if it doesn't include what the employees really know? ("Strategy as if Knowledge Mattered," by Brook Manville and Nathaniel Foot, Issue 2, April 1996, page 66).

In order for a company to be able to tap into employees' knowledge successfully, the company's other policies and practices must also be supportive of knowledge development. If a company wants to "capture" what its employees know, those employees must feel that they are encouraged to speak up and share their thoughts about the company and how it operates. A company in which employees are not encouraged to speak freely is going to have a more difficult time gathering their knowledge.

It is also difficult for many companies to assess what their knowledge is worth. An essay published in the *Journal of Knowledge Management Practice*, August 1999, titled "A Viable System Model: Consideration of Knowledge Management," by Allenna Leonard, PhD, contends that individual and organizational knowledge is difficult to value and therefore difficult to manage.

You must learn to manage yourself and your formal and informal exchanges and interactions with others. This must be done in the context of your understanding of who you are: your goals, your capabilities, your knowledge of your own strengths and weaknesses; and your appreciation of your social, technical, and business environments.

A report titled, "What is the Knowledge Economy?" published by Ernst and Young, August 31, 1999, discusses the increasing importance of knowledge as an asset in business. In an age where more businesses gain competitive advantage on the information they control and provide, it is also increasingly important to manage knowledge internally.

The report states, "There is now considerable evidence that the intangible component of the value of high technology and service firms far outweighs the tangible values of its physical assets, such as buildings or equipment. The physical assets of a firm such as Microsoft, for example, are a tiny proportion of its market capitalization. The difference is its intellectual capital."

The quotation that begins the report, attributed to the *World Development Report*, 1999, sums it up as follows:

> For countries in the vanguard of the world economy, the balance between knowledge and resources has shifted so far towards the former that knowledge has become perhaps the most important factor determining the standard of living—more than land, than tools, than labour. Today's most technologically advanced economies are truly knowledge-based.

See also: Competitive Advantage; Drucker, Peter; Intellectual Capital; Knowledge Worker

Further Reading

"People, Knowledge And Technology: What Have We Learnt So Far,?" *Proceedings of the First Ikms International Conference on Knowledge Management, Singapore 13—15 December 2004*, World Scientific Publishing Company (December 31, 2004).

www.advancingknowledge.com
www.cfses.com/documents/knowledgeeconprimer.pdf
www.futureofinnovation.com
www.theworkfoundation.com

Knowledge Worker

Knowledge workers are people who are employed to use information or data in a way that enhances the performance of their company. In an age where education is becoming increasingly important in the workforce, and more companies are trying to compete in the way in which they use or disseminate information, knowledge workers are increasingly in demand.

Peter Drucker coined the term "knowledge worker," in his book, *Landmarks of Tomorrow*, first published in 1959 by Heineman. As he said (www.brainyquote.com), "Today, knowledge has power. It controls access to opportunity and advancement."

Knowledge workers are people whose jobs have to do with gathering and sharing or passing along information. When you buy a toaster, you're purchasing a product. But when you buy advice (as in consulting, for example, or legal advice) you're buying knowledge. So consultants and attorneys are "knowledge workers." But knowledge workers can also work in any other type of business (including toaster manufacturers!) If you are an employee, and your knowledge (of the market, of the organization's design, of the way in which the organization makes deals with other companies) helps your company improve its performance, then you are a knowledge worker. Today, although the term "knowledge worker" is often associated with service or "information" types of businesses, "knowledge workers" really work in all kinds of companies.

In an article titled "Managing 'Knowledge Workers'" in the October 13, 2005, issue of the *Economist* magazine, professor and author Thomas Davenport said that finding ways to improve the productivity of knowledge workers is "one of the most important economic issues of our time." In an interview with Alan Alter, "Knowledge Workers Need Better Management," published August 5, 2005, by www.cioinsight.com, Davenport said that knowledge workers are going to be the "key source of growth" in most companies going forward. "New products and services, new approaches to marketing, new business models—all these come from knowledge workers."

Davenport went on to say that most knowledge workers are not managed as well as they should be, and, as a result, most are not achieving their full potential for their companies. Most companies still treat knowledge as a separate entity from employees, but it would be better to find a way to integrate the knowledge that a company is amassing into the daily lives of employees. As Davenport explained, it's one thing to accumulate knowledge and store it somewhere. It is another thing (and far more preferable and useful) to be able to have knowledge-acquisition and sharing be a part of people's day-to-day life at work. Not only should it be accessible, but it should be routinely and regularly tapped into. As he said, "The best way to use technology is to bake the knowledge into the job."

In large part because of the increasing numbers of information-based businesses, and businesses that operate in and around the Internet, knowledge workers are often seen as those with advanced education, employed in professional service fields, technology industries, or other "new economy" arenas. Knowledge workers are not all located in these areas, though. And the term "knowledge worker" to some, in fact, encourages

Why I Do This: Reference Librarian
Beth Slater

I am a reference librarian for a public library. There are many different jobs in a library, and mine is to help people find answers to questions they have, and to show them how to get those answers. I help people face-to-face, on the telephone, and via e-mail. How you do your job depends on the size of the library where you work. In a small library, you may have to help put the books away (called shelving) and check books out to people as well as help them find information. In a large library your job may be limited to assisting people at the reference desk, and your other duties would be to recommend items for specific areas of the collection and to weed. Weeding involves removing items that are too old to keep or items that have become damaged or too worn out for people to take home. Another part of my job is to teach basic computer classes for the public to take for free, so computer experience is recommended.

How did I discover this job? I wanted to get a Master's degree where I could do research. My older sister asked about librarianship since I have always enjoyed books and learning, and I found out that librarians need (in most cases) a Master's degree. It seemed like the perfect idea—this way I would not be limited to research in one area, I could research anything for anybody. I've worked in a medical library, a research library, and two public libraries. I found out that I enjoy working with the public the best. I like to help people find answers and I also like to find new authors for people to enjoy reading, which is called Reader's Advisory. I am an avid reader, mainly in the fiction areas of mystery and fantasy, and there are people of all ages who enjoy the same kind of books.

There is an unexpected area to my job. The people you help everyday help you to understand how different everyone is, and how people communicate ideas and questions differently. You have to become adept at fishing for information, because most of the time what a person asks for is not exactly what they want, and a few careful questions can make a big difference in where to find answers. People who become librarians are usually people who could not decide on one area of interest—they like to learn a lot about everything, and they never want to stop learning.

an inaccurate or limiting perception of the knowledge that employees in other industries must bring to bear at their jobs.

Meredith Levinson wrote in "ABC: An Introduction to Knowledge Management" (www.cio.com), that

a golf caddie is a knowledge worker who provides advice to the golfer based on his or her knowledge of the course, the clubs, and the condition, or immediate context (weather, for example). A caddie also provides a good example of how knowledge management can be used to get the most out of a knowledge worker. Say, for example, the caddie provides good advice and the golfer in turn offers a bigger tip. This simple exchange could be parlayed into a knowledge benefit for the golf course, as follows: "The caddie master may decide to reward caddies for sharing their tips by offering them credits for pro shop merchandise. Once the best advice is collected, the course manager would publish the information in notebooks (or make it available on PDAs), and distribute them to all the caddies. The end result of a well-designed KM program is that everyone wins. In this case, caddies get bigger tips and deals on merchandise, golfers play better because they benefit from the collective experience of caddies, and the course owners win because better scores lead to more repeat business.

Mike Rose, a professor at the UCLA graduate school of Education and Information Studies, wrote that the term "knowledge worker" is too often associated with the "new economy," and that that context is limiting. As Rose wrote in an opinion piece entitled "Workers Must Use Their Brains as Well as Their Hands," published in the *Buffalo News* on September 11, 2007:

Take, for example, the waitress. In the busy restaurant, the waitress has to remember orders and monitor them, attend to a dynamic environment, prioritize tasks and manage the flow of work, make decisions on the fly. If we want to create an economy that optimizes the conditions for workers to use their minds, then let us do that in a broad and expansive way.

See also: Drucker, Peter; Knowledge Management; Learning Organization

Further Reading

Knowedge Management: Concepts and Best Practices, by Kai Mertins, Peter Heisig, and Jens Vorbek (eds.), Springer; 2nd ed. (August 5, 2003)
www.babsonknowledge.org
www.cio.com

L

Lean Manufacturing

Lean manufacturing is also known as the Toyota Production System, which is a philosophy organizing manufacturing logistics at Toyota. The concept was created by the founder of Toyota, Sakichi Toyoda, his son, Kiichiro Toyoda, and the engineer, Taiichi Ohno, who drew heavily on the work of W. Edwards Deming and the writings of Henry Ford.

The idea calls for factories to reduce cycle times—the time it takes to make a given product or component—by eliminating waste. This can be wasted time, due to unnecessary steps or motions. It can also be wasted "output" due to overproduction.

According to the Rockford Consulting Group, Ltd. (1999), the concept's "key thrust is to increase the value-added work by eliminating waste and reducing incidental work. The technique often decreases the time between a customer order and shipment, and it is designed to radically improve profitability, customer satisfaction, throughput time, and employee morale."

The benefits generally are lower costs, higher quality, and shorter lead times. The term "lean manufacturing" is coined to represent half the human effort in the company, half the manufacturing space, half the investment in tools, and half the engineering hours to develop a new product in half the time.

Fast Company magazine took a look at what has made Toyota so successful in its December 2006/January 2007 issue. The article says that "Lean manufacturing and continuous improvement have been around for more than a quarter-century. But the incessant, almost mindless repetition of those phrases camouflages the real power behind the ideas. Continuous improvement is tectonic. By constantly questioning how you do things, by constantly tweaking, you don't outflank your competition next quarter.

You outflank them next decade"(*Fast Company* magazine, "No Satisfaction at Toyota," by Charles Fishman, Issue 111, page 82).

See also: Made in Japan; Six Sigma; Total Quality Management

Further Reading

Lean Manufacturing that Works: Powerful Tools for Dramatically Reducing Waste and Maximizing Profits, by Bill Carreira, AMACOM/American Management Association, 1st ed. (October 30, 2004),

Learning Organization

A "learning organization" is one that isn't ever satisfied with the status quo. Learning organizations are made up of people who are fully engaged in their work, who want to see the organization continually improve its performance, and who are open to new ideas, and are flexible enough to adapt them.

The term "learning organization" is credited to Peter Senge, a senior lecturer at the Massachusetts Institute of Technology. Senge coined the term in his book *The Fifth Discipline: The Art and Practice of the Learning Organization*. Senge is the founding chair of the Society for Organizational Learning.

He talked about learning organizations in an interview with *Fast Company* magazine in April 1999:

> I have never seen a successful organizational-learning program rolled out from the top. Not a single one. Conversely, every change process that I've seen that was sustained and that spread has started small. Usually these programs start with just one team. That team can be any team, including an executive team. . . . Just as nothing in nature starts big, so the way to start creating change is with a pilot group—a growth seed. As you think about a pilot group, there are certain choices that you have to make in order to make the group work. The first choice goes back to the issue of compliance versus commitment: Will the change effort be driven by authority or by learning? ("Learning for a Change," by Alan M. Webber. Issue 24. Page 178. April 1999).

Why I Do This: Educational Support Personnel "ESP"

Nanette P. Jacob

My job is working in an elementary school K through 8th grade with the children. A few years ago I would have been called a Teacher's assistant. I find my job very interesting and never boring. Each year I have new kids to work with. My day is spent helping special education kids with everything from English, math, social studies, science to art, gym, and music—whatever the need is for the child or group of children. I may take a group out of a classroom to read. Or I may take one child to study on a particular test or problem in class. This year I am taking kids out of 1st grade to do reading groups. When I am not doing that, I am a 1-to-1 aide with an autistic child. I help that child with math.

This can be a very challenging job on certain days but it is always rewarding. I found my job ten years ago when my kids were in the school and I heard that they needed a part time assistant. I am now full time. The older kids will ask me "don't you hate being in school all day working?" They don't know it's not a bad job to get up every morning knowing I'm going to hang out with kids. It's a lot of fun.

What's unexpected about my job? I have found that working with kindergarteners and 8th graders is about the same. They need the same amount of attention and they will give you all of theirs.

This job doesn't have the best pay, but the benefits make up for it. Christmas vacation, February vacation, spring vacation and all summer off. That is not too tough to handle.

Harvard Business School professor David Garvin is also well known for his research and thinking on learning organizations. His book, *Learning in Action: A Guide to Putting the Learning Organization to Work* (Harvard Business School Press, paperback edition, May 2003), explores the contexts in which employees can create learning organizations, and also the challenges that many companies face when trying to build a learning organization.

In a discussion of that book published November 13, 2000, in the Harvard Business School *Working Knowledge* newsletter ("Managing to Learn: How Companies can Turn Knowledge into Action") author Laurie Joan Aron wrote that "Garvin's concept of a learning organization is one that is 'skilled at creating, acquiring, interpreting, transferring, and retaining knowledge, and at purposefully modifying its behavior to reflect new knowledge and insights.'" Although new ideas are essential, he advises, lots of lightbulb epiphanies alone do not a learning organization make.

The necessary complement is a mind-set of inquiry and experimentation, plus a knowledge-sharing process that enables everyone in a company to act in an informed way upon what's been learned before.

See also: Action Learning

Further Reading

The Fifth Discipline: The Art & Practice of the Learning Organization, by Peter M. Senge, Currency (2006).

Learning in Action: A Guide to Putting the Learning Organization to Work, by David L. Garvin, Harvard Business School Press (2003).

Leveraged Buyout (LBO)

A leveraged buyout (LBO) is the acquisition by one company of another using a significant amount of borrowed money to meet the cost of the acquisition, according to Investopedia (Investopedia, Inc., 2007) "Often, the assets of the company being acquired are used as collateral for the loans in addition to the assets of the acquiring company. The purpose of leveraged buyouts is to allow companies to make large acquisitions without having to commit a lot of capital."

In an LBO, in other words, the acquired company is the one responsible for the interest payments that the purchasing company created in the transaction. According to Investopedia, "In an LBO, there is usually a ratio of 90 percent debt to 10 percent equity. Because of this high debt/equity ratio, the bonds usually are not investment grade and are referred to as junk bonds."

Investopedia notes that leveraged buyouts "have had a notorious history, especially in the 1980s when several prominent buyouts led to the eventual bankruptcy of the acquired companies." What happened in those cases was that the acquired companies were simply unable to make the interest payments and continue to operate; they didn't have the cash.

Investopedia also notes that "It can be considered ironic that a company's success (in the form of assets on the balance sheet) can be used against it as collateral by a hostile company that acquires it." For this reason, some regard LBOs as an especially ruthless, predatory tactic. According to Investopedia, the largest LBO (as of 2006) was "the acquisition of

HCA Inc. in 2006 by Kohlberg Kravis Roberts & Co. (KKR), Bain & Co., and Merrill Lynch."

An article by Bloomberg News titled "KKR to Pay $837 Million in Fees for 2006 Buyouts," published Jan. 5, 2007 that appeared in the *International Herald Tribune* (http://www.iht.com/articles/2007/01/04/bloomberg/bxkkr.php) discusses leveraged buyouts in detail, particularly the acquisition of HCA Inc.

The article says leveraged buyout firms use a combination of debt secured on the companies they buy and money from their own funds to pay for the takeovers. They seek profit by increasing sales, selling assets, and cutting costs and then usually sell the business in five years.

> Private equity firms have about $409 billion in cash to invest and can raise another $1.2 trillion in non-investment grade bonds and loans, according to Morgan Stanley. KKR alone is gathering more than $15 billion for its biggest-ever buyout fund . . .
>
> New York-based Blackstone Group's takeover of Equity Office Properties Trust capped a record $326 billion of takeovers announced by private equity firms in the United States in 2006, according to data compiled by Bloomberg. The firms announced $216 billion of European purchases, including the €7.6 billion takeover of the Dutch publisher VNU by a group including Blackstone and Kohlberg Kravis Roberts in July. Financial advisors also reap handsome benefits.

According to the article: "Wall Street firms typically charge clients about 0.6 percent of the value of a deal for their takeover advice. They earn an average fee of about 6 percent of the value of an IPO in the United States and about 2.3 percent in Europe," according to Bloomberg data.

The company that acquires another company may do so in order to make a profit, but it seems that in the world of leveraged buyouts, those firms that guide the deal may have the surest returns.

For further information on leveraged buyouts: http://privateequity.dowjones.com is the source of LBO Wire, which provides daily news and analysis of the buyouts market.

See also: Sarbanes–Oxley Act of 2002

Further Reading

The Art of M&A: A Merger Acquisition Buyout Guide, by Stanley Foster Reed and Alexandra Reed Lajoux, McGraw-Hill, 3rd ed. (December 1998).

Lifetime Employment

Lifetime employment means that when a person is hired by a company, they are assured of being employed with that company until they retire.

It was the traditional approach to employment in Japan—and is still a widespread practice—and was once also the "norm" in big companies in the United States, such as IBM.

As Mike Moran wrote on webpronews.com/blogtalk on June 25, 2007, "The IBM I joined years ago was a very paternalistic (maternalistic?) culture, where excellence occurred but was not really rewarded. IBM famously promised lifetime employment—no layoffs—rarely firing anyone even for incompetence. When it came time to give out annual raises, I used to joke that they'd rather give ten people a dime than one person a dollar."

IBM's near-death experience in the early '90s caused it to modernize its approach to emphasize value to the customer rather than value to its own employees, a wrenching but needed culture change." (Moran, who is an IBM Distinguished Engineer, and the author of *Search Engine Marketing, Inc.* [IBM Press, 2006], as well as a regular blog, writes in this piece that IBM is a "better fit" for him now because the company tolerates his "idiosyncrasies in return for the value" that he brings to the organization.)

IBM, like most other big U.S. companies, has moved away from the practice of lifetime employment. And Japan is doing the same, albeit slowly. An article by Sheryl WuDunn, published in the *New York Times* on June 12, 1996, entitled "Lifetime Employment Is No Longer a Given at Japanese Companies (sourced on www.hartfordhwp.com/archives, and in the *New York Times* archives, listed as "Downsizing Comes to Japan, Fraying Old Workplace Ties"), discussed how when one fifty-three-year old executive at a Japanese firm was asked to resign, he refused, and so the company simply had him sit at a desk and continually churn out reports on the same topic: his "Second Life." The article went on to say that to unemployed workers, this man had it pretty good. But that in Japan, it is becoming more important to perform at work than to have seniority. And that increasingly, employees are leaving companies to start their own, or, simply, to spend time with family. The "backdrop" the article says, "is the harsh new reality that the guarantee of a lifelong job, declared on the way out before but still a staple of many of the country's biggest companies, is finally beginning to break down."

The article goes on to say that the lifetime employment model helped spur commitment to a company, and also helped build Japan into an economic powerhouse. But over time, that approach created a "bloated workforce, particularly in the white-collar sector, which proved to be a painful drag that prolonged [Japan's eventual] economic troubles."

That was 1996. A news analysis found on www.cnn.com called "The Changing Face of Japanese Employment" written by Marina Kamimura, CNN Tokyo Bureau Chief and posted on the web July 29, 1999, discussed how employees at Japanese companies no longer expect to be treated like family, and no longer expect the same types of benefits, or commitment from the company. Employees, the article said, are also no longer as committed to the companies as they were traditionally.

The article quoted a twenty-three-year-old named Miki Harada on the new realities of Japanese employment. Harada said, "Our parents were so-called 'company people,' who only thought of what they could do for the company, rather than what they could do for themselves," Harada said. "For me, my career is important, but so is my private life."

Subsequent news reports echo those views; employment norms in Japan continue to change. As they do all over the globe.

Thomas L. Friedman's book *The World is Flat: A Brief History of the Twenty-First Century* (Farrar, Straus and Giroux, 2005), excerpted in *Blueprint* magazine, May 31, 2005, in an article entitled "Globalization3.0" (www.dlc.org), contains the following nugget about lifetime employment, and what might take its place:

Since lifetime employment is a form of fat that a flat world simply cannot sustain any longer, compassionate flatism seeks to focus its energy on how government and business can enhance every worker's lifetime employability. Lifetime employment depends on preserving a lot of fat. *Lifetime employability* requires replacing that fat with muscle. The social contract that progressives should try to enforce between government and workers, and companies and workers, is one in which government and companies say, "We cannot guarantee you any lifetime employment. But we can guarantee you that government and companies will focus on giving you the tools to make you more lifetime employable."

Friedman, a Pulitzer Prize-winning *New York Times* columnist, writes that the Earth is now amidst "Globalization 3.0" and that today's political and technological landscapes have fueled necessary changes in the way we think about business and traditional structures in economics.

See also: War for Talent

Further Reading

"Japanese Lifetime Employment: A Century's Perspective," by Chiaki Moriguchi and Hiroshi Ono, in *Institutional Change in Japan*, by Magnus Blomstrom, and Sumner La Croix (eds.), pp. 152–176, Routledge (2006). http://ideas.repec.org/p/hhs/eijswp/0205.html. See also: http://ideas.repec .org/p/hhs/hastef/0624.html

---

Signs of Changing Culture: Workplace Loyalties Change, but the Value of Mentoring Doesn't

Published: May 16, 2007 in Knowledge@Wharton

Reproduced with permission from Knowledge@Wharton (http:// knowledge.wharton.upenn.edu), the online research and business analysis journal of the Wharton School of the University of Pennsylvania.

In Homer's great poem *The Odyssey*, Odysseus had a tough time finding his way home to his palace in Ithaca after the Trojan War, what with all those monsters, dangerous whirlpools, Sirens, and Lotus Eaters threatening to derail his journey. But Odysseus at least had the comfort of knowing that he had left a wise and trusted fellow named Mentor to be the guardian and teacher of his son, Telemachus, during his absence.

Modern employees need mentors as much as Telemachus, especially in these times of corporate upheaval. One of the most notable shifts in the workplace in recent years has been the rapid disappearance of the prototypical loyal employee who would work 30 or 40 years for the same corporation and then retire with a gold watch and a pension. Many workers today hold positions at multiple companies during their careers, and may feel no particular loyalty to remain at any organization for any great length of time. By the same token, many companies feel no special loyalty to their workers.

Despite this sea change in corporate culture—and in some instances because of it—mentoring is just as important as it ever has been for younger workers looking to learn the ropes from more experienced employees, according to experts at Wharton and other business schools. Indeed, mentoring may also be more important than ever for organizations themselves, since linking up a mature mentor with a promising protégé is an excellent way to keep valued up-and-comers from jumping ship and taking jobs elsewhere.

Increasingly, management experts view mentoring not just as a one-on-one relationship but as a component of social networking, where protégés, also known as mentees, gain valuable knowledge by interacting with many experienced people. Mentees, for example, often look to more experienced co-workers for career guidance and professional advice and use them as sounding boards for ideas and problem-solving. Mentors also help employees learn about, and become acclimated to, an organization's culture and politics.

Yet these days, frequent job changes by younger workers could actually dissuade senior managers from volunteering to be mentors, since they may not wish to spend valuable time with someone who might leave the company before long. Therefore, young workers who want guidance should be more aggressive in seeking to build relationships with mentors than they were in the past, according to these experts.

Peter Cappelli, a Wharton management professor and director of the school's Center for Human Resources, says mentoring has assumed a different guise in recent years in response to the disintegration of the traditional employer-employee contract as a result of downsizing and outsourcing.

"If you go back a generation ago, your immediate supervisor had the responsibility to develop you; the mentor was your boss," says Cappelli. "Bosses knew how to be mentors. They knew what employees needed to do and they knew how to give employees a chance to accomplish things. Mentors were assessed based on the number of subordinates who got promoted and how the subordinates moved along in their careers."

But the boss-subordinate model of mentoring shifted in the 1980s. "Companies had a surplus of white-collar managers, and reengineering waves in corporations were about getting rid of people," Cappelli notes. "Companies told mentors, 'We're trying to get rid of people, so we can't promote your mentee.'"

Although bosses continued to play an important role as mentors when they could, the supervisor-subordinate model waned and companies sought other ways to help workers navigate their way in the workplace. According to Cappelli: "Companies said, 'What do we do for these folks? Bosses aren't helping them anymore.' The idea became to find mentors who weren't necessarily someone you worked closely with or for. Instead of your supervisor, your mentor became somebody you could bounce ideas off of and get career advice from. It became more low-impact."

Safe to Let Your Guard Down

Terri A. Scandura, a management professor and dean of the graduate school at the University of Miami, says most Fortune 500 companies see mentoring as an important employee development tool, with 71 percent of them having mentoring programs.

Various academic studies since the 1980s have demonstrated the many benefits of mentoring. "Clearly, employees who have mentors earn more money, are better socialized into the organization and are more productive," Scandura says. "They experience less stress and get promoted more rapidly. Because of the positive benefits shown to mentors, companies are still very interested in this process."

Wharton management professor Katherine Klein says what mentees look for in a relationship with a mentor is "having a sounding board and a place where it's safe to be vulnerable and get career advice. It's a relationship where one can let one's guard down, a place where one can get honest feedback, and a place, ideally, where one can get psychological and social support in handling stressful situations."

For their part, effective mentors are experienced people who should possess knowledge of career paths inside, and even outside, the organization, Klein says. "Mentors also should have an understanding of the organization's values, culture, and norms so they can pass these along to mentees. The mentor should be sensitive to the mentee's needs and wishes, and enhance the mentee's career potential, while simultaneously looking for ways the mentee's potential can benefit the organization."

And what do mentors derive from the relationship? "You get the satisfaction of seeing somebody develop. And don't forget that mentees may be in a position to help the mentor at some point. Mentees may also make the mentor look good. There's no question that Tiger Woods made his father look good," says Klein, referring to Earl Woods, who taught the golf champion how to play the game at an early age and served as his coach into adulthood.

Scandura adds that mentors can obtain more than just a glow of satisfaction at having helped someone: They can actually learn a lot about their companies and discover new ideas by engaging with mentees. "Dealing with a person who is your junior improves your network," she says. "Mentors know more about what goes on in lower levels when they deal with mentees. Junior people can provide information to mentors. . . . [They] are up on the latest technology and knowledge. So it's an interactive process: Mentors and protégés become co-learners."

Mentoring also offers benefits to organizations. For one thing, firms enjoy increased employee engagement and productivity. A positive mentoring relationship can go a long way to helping a firm retain its best employees, thus improving an organization's "bench strength," according to Scandura.

If a company wants to implement a successful formal mentoring program, both the mentor and mentee must be genuinely excited about the initiative, adds Jennifer S. Mueller, a Wharton management professor. "It has to be a long-term program with frequent meetings, and the meetings have to be meaningful, not arbitrary. You can't just meet to talk about 'stuff' three times a year."

Scandura agrees. Companies can set up mentoring any number of ways, but the most effective approach "is where the human resources department—or even top management—identifies the people who have the experience and knowledge and says, 'We want them to be the most involved in the mentoring program.'"

Sun Microsystems Study: Higher Retention Rates

In October 2006, Sun Microsystems, a technology company based in Santa Clara, Calif., released the results of a study that explored the value of mentoring. The study, conducted by Gartner, a research and advisory firm, and Capital Analytics, a software and services company, used statistical analysis to examine the financial impact of mentoring and how Sun could target its spending in this area. The study concluded that "mentoring has a positive impact on mentors and mentees, producing employees that are more highly valued by the business."

The researchers looked at data from more than 1,000 Sun employees over a five-year period, broken down by job classifications, such as administrators and engineers. The study examined sixty-eight variables—including product area, base pay, previous job code, and reason for termination—to find correlations with a half-dozen metrics: employee salary grade, salary grade change, job performance rating, promotion, merit increase in salary, and salary increase due to promotion.

The study found that 25 percent of employees in a test group who took part in the company's mentoring program had a salary grade change, compared with 5 percent of employees in a control group who did not participate in the program. The research also showed that the program had positive financial benefits for mentors: 28 percent of mentors in the test group had a salary grade change as opposed to just 5 percent in the control group. In addition, the study determined that administrators benefited more from the mentoring program than engineers. "This result was somewhat counterintuitive, since Sun had expected that higher skill positions would benefit most from the program," the study reported.

The researchers also learned that Sun's mentoring program was least effective for the highest performers. This was an especially startling result since most mentoring programs focus on developing high performers with high potential, and led the researchers to conclude that "the better investment for Sun would be to spend the money on lower performers to help them raise their level of performance."

Other findings from the study include: Mentors were promoted six times more often than those not in the program; mentees were promoted five times more often than those not in the program; and retention rates were much higher for mentees (72 percent) and mentors (69 percent) than for employees who did not participate in the mentoring program (49 percent).

Men Mentoring Men

Formal mentoring programs are only one way for young workers to increase their knowledge. Informal mentoring relationships are often more typical and more beneficial to both mentor and protégé, according to Klein. "Mentoring often happens informally," she says. "It happens most commonly when somebody senior starts giving advice and starts playing the role of a sounding board. When I go to somebody and say, 'I'm considering taking that job, what do you think?'—that can be the beginning of a mentoring relationship."

Formal corporate mentoring programs are worthwhile, but they can founder if the mentor and protégé do not hit it off. "A formal mentoring program is like a blind date set up by somebody who ostensibly knows both people, but it might not be a good match," Klein notes.

"And if a formal mentoring program simply tells the mentor to initiate an hour-long conversation with the protégé about his or her career every quarter, it's not going to be terribly meaningful. But it can be meaningful if it sets a relationship in motion. I don't think there's anything necessarily wrong with formal programs. But in some cases, it might be more productive for a company to simply say to managers that it's important for them to play a development role for junior people and ask the managers to reach out to them."

It is particularly important for senior management to encourage mentors to offer help to women and minorities, according to Klein. "Companies should be mindful of the fact that it may be difficult for women and minorities to find mentors. Senior management should tell all managers to 'step out of your comfort zones and provide support and advice for a broad section of employees.' Statements like that, backed up by the most senior people, can make a big difference."

Klein says it is particularly important for protégés to be proactive in trying to establish a relationship with a senior person and be energetic in keeping the relationship going. She uses the phrase "irresistible protégé" to describe these employees.

"Research shows that protégés influence the amount of mentoring they receive," according to Klein. "You're more likely to get mentored if you're talented, have an outgoing personality and are career- and goal-oriented. Once a mentor sees that you're eager, the more likely it is the mentor will want to spend the time and social capital on you, introduce you to the right people, and so on. One unfortunate consequence of this is that sometimes people who are most in need of guidance don't have mentors, which means companies must make a special effort to reach out to the people who really need mentors."

Klein points to one study, for instance, that showed it is easier for young men to get mentored by senior men than it is for young women to get mentored by senior men. Since men continue to hold most of the senior positions in organizations, it can be difficult for young women to get mentored. There is nothing necessarily nefarious about this tendency, says Klein, adding, "Each of us tends to attract people like us." But organizations do need to tackle this issue.

Young people may also wish to be assertive in trying to establish a mentoring relationship because they may not stay with the same organization for more than a few years. Failing to find a mentor might result in the younger person missing out on career-advancement opportunities at their current firm or making bad choices by moving to another firm or changing careers, says Klein. But management scholars do not yet know a lot about how this change in the workplace is affecting the mentor-mentee relationship.

"If the employment contract is shorter and looser than before, if people do not stay in organizations for decades like they once did, what does that mean for people who need mentors?" Klein asks. "If you find a mentor in Company A and you move to Company B and the mentor moves to Company C, can you still get mentored by this person? Or are people having to rebuild mentoring relationships with greater frequency because everybody is moving around more than before? We don't know the answers to those questions yet."

But Wharton's Mueller suggests that even if a mentee leaves a corporation after four or five years, the corporation may still reap long-term benefits from having mentored that young person. "The organization can benefit when an employee leaves if the person rises in prominence," Mueller says. "That person can generate alliances. If the person moves to a company that is not in direct competition with you, he or she may stay in touch with people at your company and exchange valuable information."

In the end, some employees may find that the best mentors are their managers—whether they call them mentors or not.

"In my years of observation of people in organizations and their development, I find no method more powerful for the development of management skills than, simply, working for top-notch managers," says David Sirota, co-author of *The Enthusiastic Employee: How Companies Profit by Giving Workers What They Want*. "By 'top-notch' I mean both that they know how to manage—and are therefore good role models—and that they have a strong interest in their subordinates' development so that they take the time and provide the challenging job assignments that facilitate this development.

"This is not to say that mentoring programs, formal management development and job rotation are not important. They help. But a caring managerial role model has, in my observation, by far the biggest impact. Companies, then, in planning for the development of employees who they feel have high potential should be certain to provide them with that kind of experience."